ENVIROPOP

Studies in Environmental Rhetoric and Popular Culture

EDITED BY
Mark Meister and Phyllis M. Japp

Westport, Connecticut
London

Library of Congress Cataloging-in-Publication Data

Enviropop : studies in environmental rhetoric and popular culture / edited by Mark Meister and Phyllis M. Japp.
        p.   cm.
    Includes bibliographical references and index.
    ISBN 0–275–96928–2 (alk. paper)
    1. Mass media and the environment.   2. Popular culture.   I. Meister, Mark, 1968– .
    II. Japp, Phyllis M.
    P96.E57E584   2002
    306—dc21   2002019622

British Library Cataloguing in Publication Data is available.

Library of Congress Catalog Card Number: 2002019622
ISBN: 0–275–96928–2

First published in 2002

Praeger Publishers, 88 Post Road West, Westport, CT 06881
An imprint of Greenwood Publishing Group, Inc.
www.praeger.com

Printed in the United States of America

The paper used in this book complies with the
Permanent Paper Standard issued by the National
Information Standards Organization (Z39.48–1984).

P

In order to keep this title in print and available to the academic community, this edition
was produced using digital reprint technology in a relatively short print run. This would
not have been attainable using traditional methods. Although the cover has been changed
from its original appearance, the text remains the same and all materials and methods
used still conform to the highest book-making standards.

Contents

1

Introduction: A Rationale for Studying Environmental Rhetoric and Popular Culture

Mark Meister and Phyllis M. Japp

Can we learn about social issues through popular culture? For example, does a television commercial for a sport utility vehicle represent environmental values beyond its obvious marketing motives? What we do know is that nature is a prominent backdrop for advertising. Whether we are watching television advertisements for soda pop or shampoo or turning the pages of a nature magazine, we constantly encounter the very powerful symbol of nature. Nature, as symbolically constructed in popular culture, is a highly utilitarian construct. Popular culture (through the powerful modes of advertising, board games, newscasts, print news, cable television, greeting cards, film, and animated cartoons) teaches us to emphasize nature's "use-value." Simply, we consciously and unconsciously learn from popular culture the practice of consuming nature.

Popular culture is an incredibly powerful epistemological force. So pervasive are its messages that cultural critics from Habermas to Marx and Raymond Williams to Judith Williamson (to name only a few) have commented extensively on the power of popular culture in shaping society. As John Fiske (1989) notes, "The combination of widespread consumption with widespread critical disapproval is a fairly certain sign that a culture commodity is popular" (p. 106).

Unquestionably, popular culture is a major contributor to our understanding of many facets of life, including the environment. So what and how do we learn environmental knowledge from popular culture? This volume offers a rhetorical and critical perspective from which to assess the power of nature messages in popular culture. The chapters in this book offer a variety of examples of how popular culture has rhetorically constructed environmental issues.

In his critique of the image events of environmental justice groups, Kevin DeLuca (1999) points out that traditional rhetorical criticisms of environmental issues generally focus on reasoned discourse and verbal arguments. DeLuca charges critics to take "image events seriously [and] challenges the association of rhetoric with a notion of discourse as limited to words" (p. 17). DeLuca's challenge reminds us that rhetoric functions in highly complex ways. Reasoned discourse, or rhetoric, is not limited to words, but obviously includes such visual elements as images, computer-generated special effects, and technologically enhanced manifestations. The nature symbol is a powerful and popular visual as well as verbal construct that is consistently modified, manipulated, and redefined in popular culture. Thus, the premise driving the examples of "Enviropop" criticism contained in this volume is that when nature is defined as a commodity for consumption it becomes, in a capitalistic society, culturally significant. That is, the rhetorical function (Foss, 1996) of Enviropop discourse is its highly anthropocentric associations that, in either words or imagery, link nature and environmental issues with economics. Alexander Wilson (1992) points out that nature is symbolically transformed into a variety of cultural texts because it is used in the mass production and marketing of commodities. Consequently, nature, like the shampoo and laundry detergent bearing its "likeness," becomes a mass-produced commodity designed for cultural consumption.

Certainly Wilson's assumption is valid, particularly when one witnesses nature's prominence as a salient human symbolic and visual construct in commercial advertisements and marketing of commodities, the most obvious example being found in "green advertising." Yet, the consumption-based orientation toward nature seeps into other dimensions of popular culture, genres whose motives are not necessarily as overt or strategic as green advertising. In all, the "nature as commodity" perspective is found throughout the landscape of popular culture.

As the chapters in this book evince, nature's use-value is ubiquitous in popular culture. This introductory chapter provides a rationale for our focus on environmental rhetoric and popular culture. We examine the dimensions of popular culture, outline what is meant by a rhetorical critical approach to popular culture, and give special attention to the role of popular culture in commodification. Finally, we briefly profile the following chapters in this book.

WHY FOCUS ON ENVIROPOP?

Environmental scholars have explored historical and political arenas of meaning construction, such as electoral politics, policy, economics, history of ideas, and education. Environmental scholars have also investigated journalistic reporting on the environment for biases or inaccuracies. The advertising industry has been given its due as a force in worldwide commodification. Relatively few studies, however, have inquired how the average person constructs meanings of the environment, posits the relationship of humans to nature, imagines the environment, attributes responsibilities for environmental problems and chooses courses of action or inaction. We believe that for most citizens, popular culture is a primary site of meaning construction, probably the major arena in which most understand, reinforce, and/or modify the circumstances of their lives. As

Anderson (1997) notes, lack of attention to popular culture has "limited our understanding of the complex ways in which perceptions of the environment are produced and consumed" (p. 4).

For example, consider the average, middle-class American family. Neither parents nor children are experts on environmental issues, nor do they read scientific or other expert literature on the subject. Rather their knowledge and understandings of the environment are constructed and maintained via a constant stream of language and images derived from popular culture. On a typical day, Mother glances at the kitchen calendar with the beautiful mountain photographs as she puts on the morning coffee. While completing breakfast, she turns on the Weather Channel and, while waiting for the local forecast, views scenes of hurricanes in the South and tornado damage in the Midwest. Changing the television channel to the morning news, she half absorbs a thirty-second clip on global warming and hears a report that local environmentalists plan to oppose situating a new baseball stadium on the wetlands across town. Father comes into the kitchen for coffee in time to catch both the newscast and an ad showing an SUV being driven up impassable mountain trails and perching atop the Grand Canyon. Mother and Father head to work in separate cars, drive on crowded freeways, and park on massive cement slabs surrounding their offices. On her lunch hour, Mother shops for some greeting cards, selecting those with nature photographs that depict a serenity and beauty woefully absent from her harried life. Father grabs a sandwich at his desk and leafs through travel brochures to decide where they should spend their summer vacation; he leans toward a driving tour of several national parks but the kids want to go boating and jet-skiing on the lake. Meanwhile, Jimmy, a fourth grader, is working on a geography assignment and cutting photos out of old *National Geographic* magazines to illustrate various parts of the world. Judy, an eighth grader, is involved in a recycling project at her school. Mother stops by the grocery store on her way home and is asked if she wants paper or plastic sacking to hold her over packaged and chemically saturated food choices. After dinner, the television in the family room emits a steady stream of advertising and programming, all depicting the environment as a backdrop for human activity. Finally comes the late news, with a report that several national parks are in peril from overuse, a prediction that high gasoline prices may cause a recession, and an announcement that the President wants to open the Alaska oil reserves to increase supply.

This stream of images and ideas from popular culture is a messy domain, filled with fragments of information, bits of dramatic stories, visual images, and examples, literally a kaleidoscope of images of places, spaces, species, geographies, and landscapes. Certainly, for non experts, understandings of environmental issues and policies are constructed from such mediated news reports, literature, or entertainment. Mediated popular culture, as Anderson (1997) asserts, provides us "with the frames with which to assimilate and structure information about a whole range of social problems and issues" (p. 18). Wilson (1992) concurs:

Our experience of the natural world whether touring the Canadian Rockies, watching an animal show on TV, or working in our own gardens is always mediated. It is always shaped by rhetorical constructs like photography, industry, advertising, and aesthetics as well as by institutions like religion, tourism, and education. (p. 12)

News reporting and images of nature, from pristine beauty to polluted lakes, shape our desires or arouse our indignation (Harre, Brockmeier, & Muhlhausler, 1999). Entertainment provides us with dramas of human experience taking place against backdrops of nature or with human achievements built upon the acquisition of land and goods. Advertising constantly urges us to consume more of everything, arguing that satisfaction and happiness are achieved through purchasing goods of all sorts (Jhally, 1987). Our games, our sporting activities, our lifestyle choices are connected to the availability and utilization of nature. Thus, the languages and images of popular culture situate humans in relation to natural environments, create and maintain hierarchies of importance, reinforce extant values and beliefs, justify actions or inaction, suggest heroes and villains, create past contexts and future expectations (Cantrill & Oravec, 1996; DeLuca, 1999; Herndl & Brown, 1996; Killingsworth & Palmer, 1992, Myerson & Rydin, 1996; Neuzil & Kovarik, 1996).

WHAT IS POPULAR CULTURE?

Definitions of popular culture abound. John Storey (1993), for example, provides a definition that emphasizes mass production and products. Storey (1993) states, "Ultimately, I have argued that popular culture is what we make out of the products and practices of mass-produced culture" (p. 201). Thus, understanding popular culture involves understanding the capitalistic process of production and consumption that is assembled by what Marxist critics Theodor Adorno and Max Horkheimer (1972) label the "culture industries." Fowles (1996) provides a summative definition of popular culture, noting that popular culture "is produced by the culture industries, composed of symbolic content, mediated widely, and consumed with pleasure" (p. 11). Yet beyond its mediated capacity for pleasure and gratification, popular culture reinforces and creates discourses and ideas that solidify "common knowledge" within the cultural psyche.

Consistent with the definitions cited above, we conceptualize popular culture broadly as the materials, ideas, processes, and understandings that most people in a given culture are aware of in some degree or another. Popular culture provides many with the common knowledge of what things are and what they mean. Brummett (1994), for example, defines popular culture as "systems of meaning and/or artifacts that most people share and that most people know about," part of the "everyday knowledge and experiences of most people" (p. 21).

Certainly this includes all forms of mass media but also games, food, music, shopping, and other daily processes and activities. The definition allows for degrees of knowledge, attachment, involvement, and attitudes, of course. For example, whether one loves rap music or hates it, few are totally unaware of its existence. Likewise, there is a general awareness of many aspects of popular culture such as television news and entertainment programming, popular films, games such as *Monopoly*™, and sports competitions. Most people shop at least occasionally in shopping malls, purchase greeting cards, decorate homes on holidays, and participate in other common cultural practices. This vast domain of popular culture, then, includes what we read, watch, wear, use, play with, talk about, and argue about over time and with enough consistency to form conscious and unconscious impressions of various aspects of life.

One example of common knowledge constructed and reinforced by popular culture is that of living a so-called good life. This cultural ideology of a good life, based not on quality interpersonal and social relationships but rather on the individualistic imperatives of convenience, leisure, and recreation, is especially relevant for our understanding of how popular culture constructs knowledge, in this case that of the relationship between nature and human gratification. According to Burke (1984a), a good life emphasizes our innate interest in physical and material conditions, our imaginative and transcendent symbolism in the pursuit of these conditions, and how we maximize opportunities to symbolically express our desires for material conditions. Burke defines the "good life" as the "[m]aximum of physicality. Insofar as people outrage the necessities of the physical economic plant, they become soulful in grotesque ways" (1984a, p. 256). Burke emphasizes the human concern with physical and material conditions provided by popular culture: "[s]o completely do we now accept capitalistic standards that we test everything as a commodity for sale" (1984a, p. 259). The materialism promoted by popular culture encourages acquisition, leisure and recreation. Burke cautions us to this point: "[t]here will be no better day until or unless a society at home in comedy will have been established long enough for its citizens to lose their reverence for these exploitive playthings" (1984a, p. 256). Thus, Burke is skeptical of human nature's inclination to leisure, and cautions us against popular culture's lure of "the psychologically unemployed, and the over-sedentary leisured" (1984a, p. 256).

In Burkean thought, the good life, promotes an "over-emphasis upon 'things of the mind,' due partly to snobbism (the insignia of mental work ranking higher than the insignia of physical work)" (1984a, pp. 256-257). The good life is a human mental and symbolic construct, reinforced by popular culture that exemplifies our fixation on materialism. As Burke points out in *The Philosophy of Literary Form* (1973), "[t]his they could best accomplish by accepting a picture of the 'good life' built around the idea . . . with culture taken to mean the maximum purchases of manufactured commodities" (p. 248). Nature becomes the raw material from which one builds the commodities and experiences that comprise the cultural ideology of the good life.

WHAT IS A CRITICAL RHETORICAL PERSPECTIVE ON POPULAR CULTURE?

As noted above, much of popular culture is accessed through mediated

sources, from books and magazines to television, film, or computer. While popular culture consists of many interlocking and reinforcing genres (for example,
news, advertising, entertainment, games, and recreation), one finds across these
genres common underlying narratives, metaphors, and images that coalesce
around a variety of cultural concerns (for example, race, gender, health, and
aging) and, of course, the environment. This coalescence of ideas and images
comprises the discourse of a given concept, in this case what we call the
popular culture discourse of the environment. Benton and Short (1999) define
discourse as

a framework that includes whole sets of ideas, words, concepts, and practices. Discourses
are the general context in which ideas take on a specific meaning and inform particular
practices. A discourse is a set of widely held ideas that a society relies on to make sense
of the world, a set of general beliefs about the nature of reality. (p. 2)

Popular culture's discourse of the environment is comprised of the bits and
pieces of mediated communication and everyday behaviors experienced by us all
and typified by our imaginary American family. A critical, rhetorical perspective
suggests that this discourse be investigated for implicit equations and connections that define the relationship between humans and nature, for the assumptions
and values it supports, the behaviors it rewards. For example, stories that implicitly or explicitly explain, justify, and describe human-environment relationships
are fundamental aspects of popular culture. The critic asks what these stories
imply as acceptable actions, how they situate agents concerning the environment.
Much of the critic's work requires attention to visual discourse. Certainly visual
displays of nature provide a powerful backdrop for promoting environmental
sensitivity. The preferred reading of "greenwashing" popular culture, for example, often reminds people of nature's beauty (Wilson, 1992). Still, "green" popular culture (like "green" advertising) is exceedingly anthropocentric; it visually
biases human and cultural discourses as natural (in much the same way that sex
and pornography predicates sexual objectification and consumption over biological sexual functions) (Goldman & Papson, 1997). In all, the greenwashing of
popular culture relegates images of nature to background status while the cultural ideology (i.e. good life) messages occupy the foreground. The "foreground-
ing" of cultural ideology in green popular culture emphasizes a good life based
on the consumption of nature, conditioning us to understand nature in only its
economic and use-value; its inherent value as marketable and consumable
(O'Connor, 1994; Schnaiberg & Gould, 1994).

The use of environmental images in popular culture and advertising consti-
tutes what cultural theorist Andrew Ross (1994) calls the "ecology of images."
Ross (1994) notes that a "better understanding is required of the role currently
played by media images that are considered ecologically meaningful" (pp. 169-
170). Since the ecology movement emerged in the 1970s and 1980s, images of
the natural environment have figured quite distinctly in American culture. These
images generally include those depicting a dying planet, complete with diseased

water, air, and animal life caused by belching smokestacks, floating debris, and oil-slick waterfowl. Conversely, environmental images also display a healthy, green, and pastoral earth, "crowned," according to Ross (1994), "by the ultimate global spectacle, the fragile, vulnerable ball of spaceship earth" (p. 171). The result of these images is a spectrum in which at one end exists an activist perspective (images of ecology for ecology) and at the other an eco-content perspective (images of ecology not necessarily about ecology) (Ross, 1994, p. 172). Green popular culture generally occupies this end of the "ecology of images" spectrum (images of ecology not necessarily about ecology). Green messages in popular culture are in no way promoting activism but are, rather, exceedingly consumption oriented. In this respect, nature is both the means and the end of consumption. The challenge for the social and cultural critic, according to Ross (1994), is to consider the social and industrial organization of images and "the process by which they are produced, distributed, and used in modern electronic culture" (p. 172).

Equally important in a critical perspective is to notice what is not included in the ongoing streams of words and images, the stories *not* told, the images *not* displayed. As Burke (1984b) insists, every supposed reflection of some facet of experience is in reality a selection, or a choice from among options selected to represent the idea or issue under focus. Such selections are inevitably deflections; they hide and obscure what lies outside the selection. Over time, one forgets (if indeed one ever realized) that the selection does not reflect the whole, only a chosen aspect or part of that whole. It is then accepted un-problematically as a valid reflection. As Burke (1969) notes, this process is an inevitable aspect of symbol use, although it certainly at times may be a conscious strategy. It is difficult or impossible for people to "think outside the box" of the consistent themes, assumptions, ideas, and images that comprise the discourses surrounding a given topic. Those who do become aware of what is deflected, of elements missing from the equations, narratives, and metaphors, must not only challenge what is presented but also create new equations and narratives, broaden and refocus extant assumptions.

POPULAR CULTURE AND COMMODIFICATION

Popular culture is a world where commodification reigns, a world in which everything is a product for consumption; everything is for sale in some aspect or another. The environment is thus a product to be consumed, whether in the form of raw materials for production of goods, the source of experiences to be appropriated, or aesthetic images to enjoy or promote a product. Whereas the human by-products of capitalism and industrialization once threatened nature, in a postmodern commodified culture such by-products are seen as natural. Nature, with all its rhetorical/cultural connotations of ecology, sustainable development, sustainable agriculture, business ecology, and spirituality, becomes an intrinsic component in how we buy and sell commodities. For example, in his book *Competitive and Green*, Daniel Kinlaw (1993) describes how green business practices will profit by associating with nature. Kinlaw (1993), as eco-business priest and guru, states: "Only by managing and working green, by making the environment an explicit part of every aspect of the organization's total operation, can the leaders of an organization expect to maintain its competitive position and ensure its survival" (p. xiii). Likewise, in *Agenda 21*, the published proceedings from the 1992 Earth Summit held in Rio de Janeiro (United Nations Conference on Environment and Development [UNCED]) the United Nations makes the following prophetic challenge: "In order to promote sustainable development, more extensive knowledge is required of the Earth's carrying capacity, including the processes that could either impair or enhance its ability to support life . . . the study of the human dimensions of the causes and consequences of environmental change . . . is essential" (UNCED, 1992, p. 259). Whether in instances of business, agriculture, or international policy development, referencing nature in cultural terms is central to discussions of both economic gain and quality of life improvement.

In this cultural ideology of nature commodification, nature (such as food, trees, landscapes, geographies, and places) becomes associated with economic practices (cost/benefits, consumption, mass production, and dissemination; in Marxist terms "economic use-value" and commodity "fetishism") (Meisner, 1995). This highly anthropocentric ideology, contends Meisner (1995), is exemplified in the words and terms we use in reference to nature. This "resourcist language," according to Meisner (1995), argues that "words and phrases which reflect and in turn re-present a resourcist ideology of nature . . . [are] . . . decidedly economic in [their] outlook" (pp. 1, 3). In this view, all of nature is seen through the lens of economics and commerce, a point made by Max Oelschlaeger (1995) in his description of resourcism:

The value of wild nature is construed strictly in economic terms, either directly through operation of the market according to "laws" of supply and demand, or indirectly through cost-benefit analysis. The market makes a mountain meadow worth more as a ski development and resort, complete with condominiums and shopping centers, than as a wilderness preserve. (pp. 287-288)

Visually, nature is often juxtaposed with cultural ideologies into a seamless display. Disney, for example, demonstrates how our sense of place can reference both natural and cultural visions (Featherstone, 1991). The illusion occurs when cultural places become "naturalized" places. Stephen Fjellman (1992) argues that Walt Disney World "is the most ideologically important piece of land in the United States" (p. 10), because in it the seemingly human emphasis on consumption and commodification is naturalized and made part of a natural system. Visitors to the "Greatest Place on Earth," identify with what is illustrated as natural because it is presented as consumable. We forget, while walking down Main Street, USA, or touring Europe, Asia, and South America in the Epcot Center, that we are in a rhetorically created combination of built and modified space that is constructed to visually reflect the natural or the real. In an odd way, in contemporary capitalistic society, commodification of nature is natural (Williamson, 1978).

As Benton and Short (1999) note, the pressures of consumer society are so great and its assumptions so pervasive that even many environmental groups have found it necessary to engage attention by marketing goods for sale. To attract new members and raise money, they advertise nature in the form of calendars, coffee mugs, sweatshirts, and other consumer goods, thus conveying a mixed message that says "save the environment by buying products that you don't really need with sanitized nature images that can conspicuously be displayed in your already overly crowded cupboards and closets" (Benton & Short, 1999, p. 203). Thus, even those who oppose commodification are inevitably coopted into its fundamental assumption: "I consume, therefore I am."

THE CHAPTERS IN THIS BOOK

The essays in this volume focus on U.S. popular culture, although much of U.S. mediated popular culture has been globalized, thus disseminating its ideas and images throughout the world (Kamalipour, 1999). The chapters critically examine the implications of taken-for-granted norms of popular culture, the connection of nature to automobiles in advertising, national parks as commodities in Milton Bradley's *Monopoly*™, images of nature in greeting cards, pastoral values in Hollywood films, "tree-huggers," global warming, advertising fantasies, *The Simpson's*, and the Home and Garden Television Network. In each case, the critic has discovered that ideologically driven selections of words and images mask important issues, discourage vital challenges, and create and support ways of thinking and acting that seem natural, normal and true.

The book begins with two chapters that focus on how nature and popular culture are salient to our everyday life practices. Diana Rehling's chapter "When Hallmark Calls Upon Nature: Images of Nature in Greeting Cards," discusses the influence of nature imagery and language in greeting cards. According to Rehling, the everyday practice of shopping for and purchasing greeting cards reinforces an idealized and sanitized visual depiction of nature. Consequently, according to Rehling, these idealized images of nature complement the idealized versions of relationships and occasions depicted in greeting card sentiment. Andy Opel's "*Monopoly*™, The National Parks Edition: Reading Neo-Liberal Simulacra" critiques the board game *Monopoly: The National Parks Edition*™. Opel illustrates how the everyday practice of playing board games mythologizes "America's special places" with use-value politics that emphasize privatization and globalization.

Of course, film and television entertainment are a vital dimension of popular culture that clearly influences perceptions of nature. Three chapters explore this dimension of Enviropop. Jean Retzinger's "Cultivating the Agrarian Myth in Hollywood Films" focuses on how the Hollywood genre of "farm" or "country" films reinforces not only nature's use-value, but also the mythic values of Jeffersonian agrarianism (yeoman farmer). Yet striking in the agrarian myth is the absence of any discussion of gender; its highly masculinist discourse of agrarian values relegates both nature and women to the margins. Retzinger argues that Hollywood films help to shape our understanding of the natural environment in rural America, as they reinforce the subjectification of both nature and women.

In "Prime Time Subversion: The Environmental Rhetoric of *The Simpsons*," Anne Marie Todd critiques the popular television sitcom's comments on environmental issues. As an animated, weekly series, *The Simpsons* exhibits profound influence and, as Todd's analysis illustrates, makes a significant appeal to American environmental consciousness. The environmental themes of *The Simpsons* are enhanced, according to Todd, by the show's comic and visual appeal.

On cable television's Home and Garden Television Network (HGTV), nature is endlessly modified to create garden spaces and quiet places. In "Purification through Simplification: Nature, the Good Life, and Consumer Culture," Phyllis M. Japp and Debra K. Japp critique the ideology of living a good life, as manifested by the HGTV weekly series *The Good Life*. Accordingly, *The Good Life* reinforces, both visually and verbally, how so-called simple living is imbued with the values and practices of commodity culture, illustrating that in a commodity culture even pastoral nature is a commodity, something that can be desired, sought out, purchased, and enjoyed as essential to the quality of life.

No edited collection critiquing environment and popular culture would be complete without essays that focus on print journalism. The next two chapters address this aspect of popular culture. In "An Analysis of the 'Tree-Hugger' Label," Mark DeLoach, Michael Bruner, and John Gossett critically investigate newspaper stories related to environmental issues. In all, DeLoach, Bruner, and Gossett track the grammar and rhetoric of the "tree-hugger" label in popular newspaper accounts and argue that the term attacks and ridicules environmentalists as absurd and, most interestingly, that the label is a linguistic device that gives rhetorical advantage to business or scientific stakeholders.

Whereas DeLoach, Bruner, and Gossett's analysis focus on supposedly credible print journalism sources, Donnalynn Pompper investigates how environmental risk is communicated in another type of print journalism, that of the supermarket tabloid. Pompper's chapter, "From Loch Ness Monsters to Global Warming: Framing Environmental Risk in a Supermarket Tabloid," investigates how environmental risk is framed in tabloids. Pompper notes that the framing of environmental risk is often accomplished by the creation of villains and heroes, with nature generally constituted as heroic and humanity as tragic.

Three final chapters focus on how nature is incorporated in advertising. Julia Corbett's "A Faint Green Sell: Advertising and the Natural World" provides a critical and theoretical overview of the nature symbol in advertising. Corbett points out how the ideologies of nature promoted in green advertising are interwoven into other social institutions, namely, how corporate conglomerates benefit from the image of corporate responsibility connotated in "green advertising." Next, in "Environment as Consumer Icon in Advertising Fantasy," Diane S. Hope provides an analysis of how advertising coopts the nature symbol as a religious icon for consumer fantasies and fetishes. The concept of advertising and fantasy is also addressed in the final chapter. Richard K. Olsen's "Living Above it All: The Liminal Fantasy of Sport Utility Vehicle Advertisements" argues that the popularity of the SUV is fundamentally symbolic and not pragmatic. The popularity is based not on what SUVs actually do for their owners, but on a fantasy created by SUV advertisements as a whole.

REFERENCES

Adorno, T. & Horkheimer, M. (1972). The culture industry: Enlightenment as mass deception. In J. Cumming (Trans.), *Dialectic of enlightenment*. New York: Seabury Press.

Anderson, A. (1997). *Media, culture, and the environment*. New Brunswick, NJ: Rutgers University Press.

Benton, L. A. & Short, J. R. (1999). *Environmental discourse and practice*. Malden, MA: Blackwell Publishers.

Burke, K. (1969). *A grammar of motives*. Berkeley: University of California Press.

Burke, K. (1973). *The philosophy of literary form: Studies in symbolic action.*Berkeley: University of California Press.

Burke, K. (1984a). *Permanence and change*. Berkeley, CA: University of California Press.

Burke, K. (1984b). *Attitudes toward history*. Berkeley, CA: University of California Press.

Brummett, B. (1994). *Rhetoric and popular culture*. New York: St. Martin's Press.

Cantrill, J. G. & Oravec, C. L. (Eds.). (1996). *The symbolic earth: Discourse and our creation of the environment*. Lexington: University Press of Kentucky.

DeLuca, K. M. (1999). *Image politics: The new rhetoric of environmental activism.*New York: Guilford Press.

Featherstone, M. (1991). *Consumer culture and postmodernism*. Newbury Park, CA: Sage.

Fiske, J. (1989). *Understanding popular culture*. Boston: Unwin Hyman.

Fjellman, S. (1992). *Vinyl leaves: Walt Disney World and America*. Boulder, CO: Westview Press.

Foss, S. K. (1996). A rhetorical scheme for the evaluation of visual imagery. *Communication Studies, 45*, 213-224.

Fowles, J. (1996). *Advertising and popular culture*. Thousand Oaks, CA:Sage.

Goldman, R. & Papson, S. (1997). *Sign wars: The cluttered landscape of advertising*. New York: Guilford Press.

Habermas, J. (1970). *Toward a rhetorical society: Student protest, science, and politics*. Boston: Beacon Press.

Harre, R., Brockmeier, J., & Muhlhausler, P. (1999). *Greenspeak: A study of environmental discourse*. Thousand Oaks, CA: Sage.

Herndl, C. G. & Brown, S. C. (Eds.). (1996). *Green culture: Environmental rhetoric in contemporary America*. Madison: University of Wisconsin Press.

Jhally, S. (1987). *The codes of advertising*. New York: St. Martin's Press.

Kamalipour, Y. R. (1999). *Images of the U.S. around the world: A multicultural perspective*. Albany, State University of New York Press.

Killingsworth, J. M. & Palmer, J. S. (1992). *Ecospeak: Rhetoric and environmental politics in America*. Carbondale: Southern Illinois University Press.

Kinlaw, D. C. (1993). *Competitive and green: Sustainable performance in the environ-mental age.* San Diego, CA: Pfeiffer & Company.

Meisner, M. (1995, April). Resourcist language: The symbolic enslavement of nature. Paper presented at the Conference on Communication and Our Environment, Chattanooga, Tennessee.

Myerson, G. & Rydin, Y. (1996). *The language of environment: A new rhetoric.* London: UCC Press.

Neuzil, M. & Kovarik, W. (1996). *Mass media and environmental conflict: America's green crusade.* Thousand Oaks, CA: Sage.

O'Connor, M. (1994). *Is capitalism sustainable? Political economy and the politics of ecology.* New York: Guilford Press.

Oelschlaeger, M. (1995). *Postmodern environmental ethics.* Albany: State University of New York Press.

Ross, A. (1994). *The Chicago gangster theory of life: Nature's debt to society.* New York: Verso.

Schnaiberg, A. & Gould, K. A. (1994). *Environment and society: The enduring conflict.* New York: St. Martin's Press.

Storey, J. (1993). *An introductory guide to cultural theory and popular culture.* Athens: University of Georgia Press.

United Nations Conference on Environment and Development (UNCED), (1992). *Agenda 21: The United Nations program of action from Rio.* New York: United Nations.

Williamson, J. (1978). *Decoding advertisements: Ideology and meaning in advertise-ments.* London: Boyars.

Wilson, A. (1992). *The culture of nature: North American landscape from Disney to the Exxon Valdez.* New York: Oxford University Press.

2

When Hallmark Calls Upon Nature: Images of Nature in Greeting Cards

Diana L. Rehling

> Only by knowing wholly about our ways with symbols can we become pious-
> ly equipped to ask, not only in wonder, but in great fear, just what may be the
> inexorable laws of non-symbolic motion which our symbolizing so often
> "transcends," sometimes to our "spiritual" gains and sometimes to our great
> detriment. (Burke, 1973, p. xvi)

While meanings for the term nature have changed substantially across time
and cultures, one common understanding of it today is that of nature as the
"world as it exists without human beings or civilization" (*Random House
Webster's College Dictionary*, 1999, p. 880) or "the world apart from human
influence" (Evernden, 1992, p. 21). And while one might successfully argue
that there is no part of the earth that has not been influenced by humans and our
cultures, in the Western civilization sense taken here, nature refers to those parts
of our environment where human influence is not clearly discernible.
Mountains, wild lions, and rainbows are, from this perspective, part of nature
because they are not human-made and because societal influences on them are
not readily apparent.

In adopting such an understanding of nature, we create a dichotomy: the
natural and the human divided from each other. Culture, language, and all that
is associated with them become part of the human domain; nature becomes
the realm of the pristine or uncontaminated, the simple and unmanipulated or
"natural" order of things. And while upon reflection we may realize that the
terms, the definitions, and even the dichotomy are all human-made, in popular
understanding and usage humans and nature stand separated (Carbaugh, 1996,
p. 39).

Simultaneously, many sites in popular culture bring images of nature into
the human realm. Photographs of forests, deer, and fields of flowers decorate

the calendars in our kitchens and offices. Images of beaches and starry nights provide the backdrop for poetry and other messages of inspiration on the posters that decorate our walls. Friends and family on vacations send us post-cards with pictures of baby seals and sunsets over calm lakes.

One site within popular culture where images of the human and nature regularly mingle, with implications for both worlds, is within commercially made greeting cards. On the front covers of greeting cards, and sometimes on the inside pages as well, images of nature abound. A field of pastel flowers, through which runs a gentle-flowing river, provides the backdrop for expres-sions of sympathy. A pair of swans floating on a lily-pad-laden lake introduces a message of love and romance. Rugged mountain peaks set the scene for a sentiment of encouragement or congratulations. Such uses of nature within the ritualized communication of greeting cards are likely to feel familiar to us, common enough as to often go unnoticed and unexamined.

Greeting cards and the images associated with them are so integrated into the everyday life of nearly every American that they seem unremarkable. According to the Greeting Card Association, on average each American receives more than twenty cards each year (Greeting Card Association, 2000). Last year alone Americans spent seven billion dollars to purchase greeting cards for each other (Greeting Card Association, 2000). Mass-produced inter-personal communication has become an accepted part of our cultural landscape. Through their regular appearance and the repetition of their messages and images, greeting cards also help shape and reflect our understanding of the world and the relationships within which we live.

Few researchers have examined the images of nature within the artifacts of popular culture, such as greeting cards, nor have scholars considered the sig-nificance of such portrayals to cultural understandings of environmentally relat-ed matters. When studying rhetoric and the environment, scholars have tended to focus instead on such topics as texts particularly significant in the public debate about the environment (e.g., Killingsworth & Palmer, 1996; Ulman, 1996; Waddel, 1994), case studies of controversies about environmental issues or incidents (e.g., Farrell & Goodnight, 1981; Katz & Miller, 1996; Oravec, 1984; Weaver, 1996), the rhetorical strategies of environmental groups (e.g., Cooper, 1996; Short, 1991), or media representations of environmental issues (e.g., Sachsman, 1996; Schlechtweg, 1996). While such scholarship clearly advances our understanding of both the environment and rhetoric, it simultaneously ignores the symbolic representations of nature, such as those encoded within greeting cards, that pervade our everyday lives.

Popular culture artifacts are gaining increased attention from scholars, however, for the insights they can yield into cultural meanings and understand-ings. A small group of scholars have recognized the potential of greeting cards as a site for examining cultural attitudes, including attitudes toward aging (Demos & Jacke, 1981; Dillion & Jones, 1981), gender (Bridges, 1993; Murphy, 1994; Schrift, 1994), death (Huyck & Duchon, 1986; Woods &

Delisle, 1978), drinking (Finn, 1980), and body image (Schrift, 1994). Murphy (1994), in reviewing the research, concludes that the authors of these studies generally argue that "the words and images in these cards both reflect and reinforce widely-held social values regarding their respective topics" (p. 26).

Such findings are not surprising, given that the acceptance and publication of a greeting card is based on research that greeting card companies conduct to understand and predict consumer response (Schwartz, 1993). The greeting cards that make it to market from the large greeting card companies are designed and chosen based on product information services, as well as on research conducted through focus groups, telephone surveys and panels conducted at shopping centers (Sterns, 1988). Both greeting card industry representatives and greeting card writers, artists, and editors (Clark, 1997; Gephard, 1992; Voss, 1993) recognize that mass appeal is necessary for a greeting card to be successful.

To more meaningfully investigate the uses of nature in greeting cards, this chapter is presented from a cultural studies perspective. In cultural studies, popular culture is an important arena to examine because it is within popular culture that views secure dominance or hegemony. Examination of popular culture artifacts can foreground "the ideological role of the representation of 'common sense', the power of the 'taken-for-granted' " (Turner, 1990, p. 212).

In this chapter, the uses of nature in greeting cards are viewed from a stance Rosteck (1999) refers to as a "cultural rhetorical studies" position. A text of greeting cards was constructed to critically examine from within this perspective. Text is a metaphor borrowed from literary and rhetorical studies to designate the material the critic will "read" (Geertz, 1983). From such a perspective the text is always the construction of the researcher (one that artificially stops the circulation of meaning within the culture momentarily in order to enable analysis). With textual analysis done from a cultural studies perspective, a specific text is interpreted and interrogated for clues about modern culture. In studying the particular, the critic hopes to give insight "into the shared meanings and social practices (the distinctive ways of making sense and doing things) which are the basis of our culture" (du Gay, Hall, Janes, Mackay & Negus, 1997, p. 11).

The greeting cards included in this analysis were limited to greeting cards made commercially available by the three major greeting card companies in the United States, Hallmark, American Greetings, and Gibson (Bianchi, 1993). Together these three companies produce roughly 85 percent of the greeting cards available through brick-and-mortar outlets (Bianchi, 1993). Drawing from the commercially successful product lines of these major companies provides the basis for a text with wide circulation within the society. In order to secure greeting cards in which images of nature have clearly been brought into the human realm, the text was further limited to cards in which the visuals on the front cover are dominated by images of wilderness scenery, by some specific element of nature (such as the night sky or sunset), or by wildlife (non domesticated animals). Analysis of such a text can not only help us better understand how we use images of nature in popular culture and provide insight into the implications of such uses for our understandings of and meanings for nature, but can also enhance our understandings of the relationships, occasions, and communication of which these images have become a part.

The text was analyzed from the symbolic action perspective, particularly that of Kenneth Burke. Burke embraces a view of the symbolic that, while recognizing the central role of language, also allows for symbolic meaning in other forms, such as the visual arts, theater, and movies, making such a perspective particularly attractive for considering a text that is made up of both visual images and language (Burke, 1950, 1969).

In outlining Burke's perspective, Gusfield (1989) says, "the assertion here is that modes of symbolizing experience are a central part of human behavior. Symbolic representations constitute the ways in which experience is made possible and different forms of symbolic usage create different experiences" (p. 30). Japp (1990) states that Burke's program of criticism is "aimed at understanding how material conditions are defined and addressed attitudinally in and through the symbolic forms that determine meaning and delimits appropriate action" (p. 3). In Burke's (1973) phrase the symbolic forms provide "equipment for living."

Burke's writings on symbolic action are particularly valuable because they provide a critic with specific and tangible ways for thinking about the processes by which meaning is constructed. As suggested above, such a perspective not only emphasizes the symbolic means used to create the reality out of which we act, but also encourages us as critics to consider the omissions. Burke (1969) suggests that we "develop vocabularies that are selections of reality. And any selection of reality must, in certain circumstances, function as a deflection of reality" (p. 59). Considering the omissions in a symbolic representation helps our understanding of what is not expected (the values, characteristics, and associations that fall outside the symbolic construction). Burke (1969) also explores in his writing the role of symbolic activity in creating identifications, which calls our attention to commonalties and obscure differences. He notes that identification is often achieved not through a singular address, but instead through a "general *body of identifications* [emphasis in original] that owe their convincingness much more to trivial repetition and dull daily reinforcement than to exceptional rhetorical skill" (p. 26). Burke's work encourages a critic to not only consider a body of related symbolic representations, but to also examine the links between a given text constructed for examination and a range of cultural texts and the links between these texts and other cultural myths and ideologies (the stories we tell one another) (1984, p. 384). Finally, Burke's (1950) root metaphor of language as drama not only provides a critic with a way to think about symbolizing activity, but also grounds that way of thinking in the visual. When drama is enacted it depends on the visual as well as the verbal to produce meaning. In this sense the visual images of greeting cards not only help "set the scene" for the verbal sentiment of the greeting card, but also become part of the symbolic act itself.

IMAGES OF NATURE IN GREETING CARDS

The following analysis reveals four particular uses of the images of nature in greeting cards: nature scenes to set a mood or tone for the verbal sentiment, wilderness scenes as settings for human action or interaction, representations of some element of nature as a reference point or focus for the verbal sentiment, and images of wildlife to represent humans. Examining these uses of nature in more depth will provide the groundwork for better understanding our ways of symbolizing nature in popular culture. Such analysis can also lead us to better understand what is obscured and what is lost when nature is filtered through images selected for commercial gain and purpose.

Using Nature to Set a Mood

One way greeting cards make use of images of nature is as an introduction to the verbal sentiment (a way of setting the scene or establishing a mood). When scenes of nature are used in this way there is often not direct reference to them in the sentiments; the relationship between the scene and written message is only subtly suggested.

For example, Thanksgiving cards use images of falling leaves and the oranges and browns of an autumn treescape to establish a time of year. Cards for Easter picture rabbits among green grass or the pastel blossoms of trees against a blue sky to introduce their sentiments. Christmas cards use photos or artists' depictions of snowy landscapes or cardinals in snow-laden pine trees to help establish the season and tone for their holiday sentiment. Through such images our understanding of our holidays and our meanings for nature are linked together and simultaneously altered, our experiences of each influenced by the other.

One such card from Hallmark pictures a snow-covered mountain valley, replete with pine trees, deer, and moonlight. The verse on the inside of the card implicitly compares the quietude of the nature scene and the hectic rush of holiday preparations, concluding that the true spirit of Christmas is to be found not under the Christmas tree, but deep in our hearts. Set up by the artist's rendering of the mountain valley found on the cover, the Christmas "within our hearts" and the "peaceful hush" of the verse are associated with the world of nature (an understanding of Christmas available to us only outside the human realm). In addition, the verbal sentiments contrast such qualities with the commercial and social aspects of Christmas (the errands, the rushing and the gifts found under the Christmas tree, echoing and reinforcing the human/nature dichotomy discussed earlier). The "real," the "authentic," is associated with nature, while the human domain is equated with the commercial, the superficial, and the stressful. The sincere, peaceful and heartfelt are located within the natural world.

In a Hallmark sympathy card a green valley with blooming daffodils, butterflies, and a peaceful pond establishes the appropriate tone for the expression of comfort upon the loss of a grandmother. An American Greetings card encouraging the recipient to "Focus on tomorrow/for each day can bring a gift/Of grand new possibilities/to help your spirits lift" features a view of the ocean breaking over rock piles, a faint rainbow in the sky.

In all of the above examples nature provides the tone or inspiration for the verbal expression. This type of turning to nature happens particularly with the expression of sentiments that relate to spiritual matters, such as celebrating religious holidays, grieving a death, or seeking encouragement during difficult times (a kind of turning to nature for what cannot be found in commercialized society). And with comfortable familiarity, the irony that such communication comes in the form of manipulated images of nature commodified in the form of mass-produced greeting cards fades from view.

Using Nature as a Setting for Humans

As noted earlier, in some instances scenes of nature not only set the tone for the verbal messages in greeting cards, but also provide a setting for humans and for human interaction. A Gibson birthday card for a son shows a man silhouetted against a darkening sky wearing a backpack and carrying a walking stick, standing on an outcropping of rock which extends out over a tree-filled valley. The sentiment "Son, I can't help loving you and being very proud of you" is written in the upper left-hand corner of the photo. By placing the sentiment expressing parental pride within the photo, the son's accomplishments, which are mentioned later in the sentiment, are linked symbolically with the man's success in the difficult climb he appears to have made to reach the outcropping of rock on which he is pictured. The son's "accomplishments" are visually linked with the determination and strength required for such conquering of nature, the rugged scenery a fitting setting for such a courageous and independent individual. Simultaneously the man is visually presented testing himself within and against nature. The human (not coincidentally a male) is victorious and dominant over the challenging and rugged wilderness. Because the greeting cards must appeal to a large group of consumers to be financially successful, the man is pictured silhouetted against the sky, his age, race, and facial features not distinguishable, each recipient of the card able to project himself into the scene and the sentiment.

In contrast, the cover of a Gibson card "For my daughter" features an impressionistic rendering of a woman in a brimmed hat and soft white dress sitting amid a field of brightly colored flowers. As with the man in the photo discussed above, the particular characteristics of the woman are not distinguishable, but her appropriate place within nature and her association with flowers are vividly communicated.

The association between femininity and flowers represented here is echoed in the images of flowers on tens of thousands of other greeting cards for mothers, daughters, and sisters, as well as in many other places within the culture.

Greeting cards also provide visual depictions of the appropriate settings in nature for human interaction. The most popular of these is the beach. Two silhouetted lovers walk toward the ocean in the American Greetings card that speaks of angels who "sing to you in the wind" and sometimes "walk beside you." In a Gibson birthday card for a father, a man and child hold hands as they walk down the beach, their backs to the artist. By not clearly showing the individuals, the viewers of the cards are again invited to project themselves into the scenes and to imagine themselves within the encounter. Furthermore, deserted beaches are established as a backdrop for meaningful encounters with our loved ones. The setting aids in giving meaning to the human interaction, and the interaction gives meaning to the natural setting.

Using Nature to Give Meaning to Relationships and Occasions

Another way in which those who manufacture the cards use nature is to present a nature scene or an element of nature in the cover art and then directly reference it in the written sentiment to understand and give meaning to the relationship or occasion celebrated in the card. In an American Greetings birthday card, a father's love is described by comparing it to parts of nature. Five photographs of nature scenes illustrate the themes. In the card, a sentiment describing the strength and protection a great oak provides is placed opposite a photo of a large oak tree displayed against a setting sun, while a phrase mentioning a mountain's endurance appears next to a photo of a green valley with several large mountain peaks behind it. The depth of the ocean is illustrated by waves breaking against a pile of rocks and the mention of the expansiveness of the sky appears above a panoramic view of an orange sunset over a calm body of water, along with a statement about the strength, reassurance, and lasting nature of a father's love. A photo of large pine trees in front of mountains provides the illustration for the final phrases of the greeting, accompanied by a sentiment expressing gratitude for the father's dependability, love, support, and wisdom.

Here we see nature directly called on by the sentiment writers to illustrate and support the notions of fatherhood in the sentiment. Drawing on the images of nature in such a fashion not only gives substance and concreteness to the generalizations made about a father's love, but also locates the beliefs associated with them in the natural world. The natural world provides illustrations and proof of the descriptions and of the love. The love of a father depicted (clearly within the domain of the human) finds support in the sentiment writer's interpretation of the realm of nature.

Furthermore, the vision of fatherhood established and located within the natural world depends on a sentimentalized, sanitized version of nature, a view that conveniently ignores the animal fathers in nature who abandon, maim, or even kill their young.

In a Hallmark card, which uses a rose-tinted photograph of trees by the banks of a river for its cover image, the sender's reaction to natural phenomena frame's his or her reaction to the relationship he or she shares with the recipient of the card:

(Outside cover) I've been amazed by the *colors* of a sunset, surprised by the *design* of a single snowflake, humbled by the *grandeur* of a mountain range against the sky. But you and this love that we share . . .
(Inside) . . . this is the greatest miracle of all.

In this instance, the material properties of nature and the sentiment writer's interpretation of them provide a way for understanding and valuing the relationship. Simultaneously nature serves as a witness to the rightness of the relationship and the depiction of it in the cards — its "naturalness," its miracle.

A photo of an ocean sunrise across which is proclaimed "Brighter Days are Coming" is used in a card from American Greetings. On the inside left the biblical quotation "I am the light of the world,/whoever follows me,/will never walk in darkness,/but will have the light of life" appears and on the right a repetition of the picture of the ocean sunrise with the words "Believe in Him. Believe in the Light." Here a natural occurrence, the sunrise, serves not only as a source of encouragement, but also as a confirmation of religious beliefs in symbolic form. Reading such meanings onto the elements and scenes of nature provides support for our values and provides reassurance and comfort in the fact that such proof lies outside the human realm. Such merging of the natural and human domains also obscures the human role in giving meaning to natural phenomena.

In other greeting cards, a particular element of nature, such as a rainbow or the sun or stars, are pictured on the cover art in some form and then called forth again within the sentiment. A card from American Greetings picturing an artist's rendering of two flowers with the sun shining on them, while the sentiment claims "the sunlight is the blessing of being with you," illustrates this common form of finding meaning in nature. The naming of natural elements such as the sun, stars or snowflakes, as "miracles or blessings," with all the religious overtones, occurs regularly in greeting cards. If we further consider, however, that the cards typically go on to equate the miracle or blessing named in the natural world with the relationship between the individuals discussed in the sentiments, the result is to sanctify nature, the human relationship, and the connection the sentiment writer has drawn between them.

A card from Gibson uses a photo of a large fallen leaf displayed against a piece of weathered wood, another, lighter colored leaf perfectly centered upon the first. Printed over, but within the confines of the smaller leaf, appears a sentiment about how nature brings things together in perfect ways. Having visually established that nature is orderly and purposeful, packed with meaning waiting to be understood, the sentiment writer goes on to draw out the value of the photograph by comparing the visual relationship between the two leaves with the relationship between the card's sender and recipient. The sentiment inside the card mentions how perfectly our hands fit together. The possibility that the photographer may have placed the leaves as they appear is overlooked by the sentiment writer and, for the greeting card to be meaningful, must also be overlooked by those sending and receiving the card.

In some instances greeting card artists will manipulate a scene of nature and call attention to that manipulation in order to set up a sentiment that can then refer back to the manipulation. A Hallmark card that features an artist's drawing with the word *love* created by the stars twinkling in the evening sky and the inside sentiment that thanks a lucky star for the other illustrates this way of using nature.

In such instances viewers of the card are expected to recognize the manipulation in order to see the cleverness in the card. In the above example, to make sense of the card the viewer must be aware of the cultural notions of fate being "written in the stars" and of humans thanking "their lucky stars" for what fate has sent their way. To understand the card, the reader must call forth and bring into conscious use the merging of the realms of nature and the human that occurs throughout the culture. This example is typical in that the manipulation of nature, in this case the word *love* written in the stars, highlights or exaggerates a meaning that, through many avenues, the culture communicates resides in the elements of nature.

Using Nature to Stand in for Humans

The final way in which greeting card manufacturers use images of nature is to call upon animals, including wildlife, to stand in for humans. Because greeting card artists must avoid the use of people with clearly identifiable characteristics which might limit the sale of the product, animals are frequently used in greeting card visuals to represent humans. By such uses characteristics of the individuals for whom the card is intended can be suggested and yet tens of thousands of consumers can project themselves into the symbolic representations of the cover art. For example, a lone buck deer or maned lion may appear on the front cover of cards for uncles and fathers, while baby bears and rabbits typically represent children.

Equally popular in greeting card art is the use of pairs or groups of animals to represent romantic pairs, friendships, or parent-child relationships. Pairs of swans, doves, owls, rabbits, lions, zebras, or bears appear on wedding and anniversary cards, as well as on birthday, Christmas, or Valentine's Day cards between spouses or lovers. Pairs of large and small bears, rabbits or elephants can be found on cards between parents and children. A groups of birds, a bird and a rabbit having tea, or two embracing bears can set the scene for sentiments between friends. In most instances, the wildlife in greeting cards appears in artists' renderings rather than in photographs and the settings in which the animals appear is often an idealized natural one. For example, a Hallmark card for lovers shows two leopards sleeping curled up together under the night sky, while an American Greetings Easter card for "the one I love" carries a scene of two swans floating amid flowering lily pads on a river with weeping willows on its banks. In these perfected versions of the natural world, animals live peacefully in the wilds, removed from the more negative consequences within nature. Predators, disease, and threatened environments are absent. Animals, like the humans they are meant to represent, dominate the natural world, rhetorically framed as their comfortable and hospitable home.

Unambiguous examples of the anthropomorphizing of wildlife, in which wildlife appears in human settings, are also common in greeting cards. A cartoon version of a male and female lion from Hallmark pictures the female wearing an apron and carrying purse, while the male sits in a chair watching a television. A birthday card from Gibson intended for a grandmother pictures a rabbit wearing a hat, spectacles, and a dress with pearls and carrying a basket of flowers. The identification between animals and humans is emphasized within the sentiment by the phrase "You're the nicest kind/of grandmother/' anybunny'/could ever have!" While clearly the use of artists' cartoon-like depictions of animals in clothes, pictured in homes and cars is not intended to be seen as realistic, the images create a visual parallel between animals and the humans they represent.

The use of animals in greeting cards also includes the obvious manipulation of images of wildlife for the purpose of amusing the viewer and often for setting up the greeting card sentiment. In a Hallmark card that features a photograph of a herd of giraffes, one animal's neck is stretched to approximately ten times the length of the others'. The sentiment on the inside of the card then refers to and highlights the manipulation and calls forth an identification between the recipient of the card and the extraordinary giraffe with the sentiment "You are SO not average./ Congratulations." Similarly, a card by Gibson features a photograph of a hippopotamus wearing a tiny, red party hat with large white polka dots, a brightly colored party horn in his or her mouth. The photo provides a humorous image, establishes a celebratory occasion, and sets up the sentiment "This is huge./Happy Birthday" on the inside of the card. The image also, however, suggests the right and appropriateness of the human use and manipulation of nature for our own purposes and amusement.

IMPLICATIONS FOR NATURE AND HUMANS

Having examined the most common ways images of nature are used within greeting cards, we are in a position to consider the implications of these symbolic representations. For as Burke suggests in the quotation that opens this chapter, enhanced knowledge and greater awareness of our ways with symbols provide us an opening for examining what is lost and what is gained through our symbolizing (Burke, 1973, p. xvi). We are now positioned to consider the implications of bringing selected images of nature into greeting cards not only for our understanding of the realm of nature, but also for the human relationships, occasions, and individuals which are the subjects of greeting cards.

The regularity of the symbolic representations of nature can create among consumers an unwarranted sense of knowledge about or familiarity with nature (McKibben, 1992). Because such images of nature are a constant part of the cultural landscape (not only through the images of greeting cards, but also through the poster and calendar art, cartoons and picture postcards that are woven into our daily lives) we may come to feel we "know" about nature. Yet, the types of scenes, animals, and images of nature that are featured in greeting cards are carefully selected and designed by greeting card designers and manufacturers. And, as Burke (1969) suggests, selecting parts of reality to highlight in our symbolic representations, by necessity, results in deflecting other aspects of reality.

Greeting cards, like many popular culture artifacts, celebrate some parts of nature while ignoring other parts. Mountains, beaches, and river valleys appear regularly on the covers of greeting cards. Large expanses of desert, miles of open prairie, gullies, glades, and marshes, however, are generally missing in the greeting card depictions of our environment, not really vilified, but simply absent, deflected in this symbolic representation of our world. Absent are the gnats, weeds, and gray skies that are not only also part of the natural world but are also far more common than the version of nature presented in greeting cards, where the sun shines, the winds are calm, and wildflowers dot the landscape. This natural world is hospitable, comfortable, and welcoming, without floods, droughts, or raging forest fires. And while attractive images of bears, rabbits and birds are common, images of snakes, fish, and lizards are almost as rare in greeting cards as they are among stuffed animals.

In addition to being selective about the parts of nature to present, greeting cards display idealized versions of those parts chosen for representation—carefully selected views of the natural environment accomplished through editing and through enhancing reality. By presenting carefully framed views of pristine mountain scenery, unspoiled and unpopulated beaches rendered by the artist's brush, and river valleys adorned with blooming flowers more likely to exist in the artist's imagination than in the physical world, the damage humans have done to the environment is obscured. No litter is shown; erosion and the effects of toxic chemicals on the wildlife and vegetation are absent. The noise and car exhaust from the highway just out of view are missing. This is literally a cleaned-up version of our environment.

Artists' renderings of wild animals such as bears or lions are also often unrealistic, typically depicting them as cute or humorous, much like the stuffed animals or the animated characters they resemble. The ferocity, the power, and the "wildness," as well as the disease and parasites, of the actual animals' world are missing from these culturally created images.

The symbolic representations in greeting cards are not, however, only selective in the version of nature represented, but the symbols also suggest, as

Japp notes (1990), meanings for the symbolically represented nature. Peaceful lakes, mountain vistas, and pastoral river valleys are valorized in greeting cards as not only beautiful, but also inspirational. Oak trees are sturdy and dependable; ocean beaches are serene. Rainbows, sunshine, and flowers stand for hope, happiness, and beauty. In the vocabulary of greeting cards, these are the miracles, the gifts, and the blessings of nature and stand in direct contrast to human-created society.

With symbolic representations not only meanings but also appropriate actions toward the symbolized (as well as toward the unrepresented) are suggested. Deserted beaches at sunset and rivers flowing through flower-strewn valleys offer humans renewal and peace. Rugged terrains, particularly mountains, are conquered and serve as settings for testing human strength and persistence. Furthermore, in these representations nature is not threatened by humans nor does it bear the scars of our activities. And, ideal as nature appears in greeting cards, it does not require protection or conservation.

Through repetition, the scenes and the images of nature in greeting cards become familiar and comfortable to those of us who see them regularly. Encounters with commodified versions of nature in all their forms are likely to outnumber for many of us our encounters with actual wilderness. Tourists to national parks who approach bears, visitors to zoos who are surprised when the monkeys they feed bite them, and families who seek out wild cats or wolves as family pets may be more influenced by the cuddly images of popular culture discourse than by the actual animals they are encountering.

When we enter or encounter nature, we bring to the experience our meanings for, attitudes toward, and understandings of appropriate actions toward nature with us, shaped as they have been through the symbolic representations so familiar to us. The possible dangers present in the wilderness remain obscured. Humans' place in the hierarchy remains unchallenged, until in our actual experience some unexpected aspect of nature intrudes on our culturally created expectations. A violent storm transforms the serene beach. A sudden blizzard threatens not only the meaning of Christmas we read into a snowscape, but our lives as well.

Even in less dramatic ways, our actual experiences with nature are likely to suffer in comparison to the imagined versions offered in greeting cards. In comparison a real experience is likely to disappoint or even disgust us. Heat, cold, bugs, weeds, cloudy skies, wind, toads, and thorns are features of nature for which the greeting cards and related cultural texts do not prepare us. And when the symbolically created versions of nature appear more attractive and pleasurable to us than nature directly experienced, the environment and the actual experiencing of it (not the symbolic representations that have formed the basis for our unrealistic expectations) are likely to be found wanting. We complain about the mosquitoes, the stink of rotting fish, and the algae-coated water that mars our walk by the lakeside at sunset. Rather than question why we expect a picture postcard type of experience, we are likely to locate the fault in the environment. We may even find it reasonable to support policies or programs that eradicate or control the insects, weeds, or other parts of nature that interfere with experiencing nature as we have come to expect it.

The symbolic representations of nature within greeting cards also have implications for the parts of nature omitted. The aspects of our environment omitted from popular cultural artifacts, while they may be vital parts of our ecosystem, are devalued by these cultural representations and by their omission are deemed as less than picturesque, inspirational, or significant. And as the culturally constructed values and meanings of scenery and animals overwhelm the biological world, some kinds of wildlife and some types of geographical formations are more likely than others to seem worthy or deserving of preservation and protection. Mountains are more valuable than swamps; bears are more important than lizards.

When greeting card arts substitute images of wildlife for humans in greeting card cover art, meaning is also created. An identification is drawn between animals and humans and the similarities between us are highlighted. While Burke notes that identification does not negate the distinctiveness of entities, he also states that "to identify A with B is to make A consubstantial with B" (1969, 21). While such is not likely the purpose in a greeting card artist's use of a pair of swans or an adult and infant bear, we are in these presentations reminded that we share much in common with animals. Like humans, animals mate, have offspring, care for their young, travel in groups, and so forth. When in the visuals of greeting cards wildlife are further personified by being depicted as smiling, celebrating, dancing, or cuddling, the distinctive ways and substance of wild animals are even further obscured. And through their alignment with humans, animals, particularly those most familiar through popular culture discourse such as bears and bunnies, are elevated above other parts of nature, more valuable, more important than weeds or bugs.

The greeting card images of nature suggest, sometimes blatantly but most often more subtly, that nature is for the use and pleasure of human beings. An artist's depiction of a message written by the stars in the night sky or the manipulation of a photograph to elongate a giraffe's neck or the dressing up of a hippopotamus in a party hat and horn helps create a clever greeting card, while also blatantly altering nature to human purpose. The place and lives of giraffes or hippopotami in the nonhuman realm are overshadowed by the comical uses we can make of them.

More subtly, the artists' renderings of river valleys and rainbows are, as we are likely to realize at a subconscious level, being used to establish a tone or feeling, as needed by the greeting card manufacturers. The photographic images of nature, perhaps staged, airbrushed, or digitally created, most certainly cropped and selective in their framing, are used to provide moods or settings for human communication. Greeting card artists and photographers use nature as a backdrop (a kind of theatrical scenery) putting nature to work for humans' purposes and pleasure, reinforcing humans' dominance.

Involving nature in the symbolic representations of greeting cards has implications not only for our understandings of and meanings for nature, but also for the relationships, celebrations, and communication of which they are now a part. In one sense, by drawing upon scenes of wilderness and on wildlife, the depictions of our relationships and feelings in greeting cards are "naturalized" through their association with nature (the role of culture obscured). As Neil Evernden (1992) suggests, "to be associated with nature is to be placed beyond human caprice or preference, beyond choice or debate. When something is 'natural' it is 'the norm,' 'the way,' 'the given' " (p. 22).

Describing a father's love by references to oceans, oak trees, and mountains locates the foundation of the characterization not in the society that has developed the belief system that underlies it, but in the natural world. When women are pictured amid fields of wildflowers and men are depicted climbing mountains not only is nature gendered, but gender is also naturalized. When animals are shown as pairing off into couples, the cultural value reflected passes as established by the natural order.

Still further, when the sentiments of the greeting cards draw a link between the relationships celebrated in the card and the "miracles" or "blessings" of nature, the relationship and its character appear beyond dispute, now not only "natural," but also the handiwork of the maker of the entire universe. The values and roles embedded in the relationship are now ordained by a higher being. The role of humans and human society in creating the relationship ideal is obscured. No longer open to question or revision, any flaws or contradictions must be ignored given the relationship's miraculous and blessed nature. The further irony that we domesticate nature and then use it to naturalize our cultural notions of relationships and gender roles remains out of view.

In many ways the idealized and sanitized visual depiction of nature in greeting cards perfectly complements the idealized versions of relationships and occasions depicted in the greeting card sentiments (Rehling, 1998). Just as the images of nature and wildlife chosen for the greeting card covers do not include young animals starving because they were abandoned by their parents or the bloodied carcasses of older animals who have fallen victim to younger and stronger wildlife, the verbal sentiments tend to allow for no problems or troubles in the relationships or occasions they celebrate. Hurricanes, tornadoes, and floods don't wreak havoc on these beaches or peaceful valleys. Avalanches and earthquakes don't disrupt these quiet mountain scenes. The visuals chosen support, reinforce, and give substance to the sunny and flower-filled characterizations of the relationships and holidays celebrated in the sentiments. No long stretches of rainy days, no toxic pollution or annoying mosquitoes. The idealized nature of the cover art introduces the perfect relationships and celebrations of the sentiments. By involving the sentiments with images of nature, however, the impossibly perfect and positive depictions of the sentiments appear to derive support from nature and the world beyond human caprice. And just as actual encounters with nature and wildlife are not likely to live up to the visual representations of scenic nature, real relationships and holidays with all their messiness and contradictions are likely to suffer in comparison to the greeting card versions. Where, however, do we locate our dissatisfactions? Within the idealized greeting card versions of relationships and holidays or within our more complicated reality?

As noted earlier, the use of particular types of nature settings and wilderness scenes in the visuals of greeting cards, along with the movie sets and poster art with which they connect in cultural discourse, suggest the meanings or appropriate uses we humans should make of nature. We should look for the real meaning of Christmas in quiet mountain scenes covered with snow. Ocean beaches provide us with the appropriate setting for romantic walks and conversations. Peaceful rivers and lakes can offer us solace in grief. Such symbolic representations encourage us to look for particular kinds of inspiration in specific parts of our environment, or to seek particular natural settings for our relationship encounters. They also discourage us from looking for other possibilities in and out of nature. A walk along the beach has become culturally coded as romance. It stands as a symbol not just in movies and greeting cards; it infiltrates the everyday lives of members of the culture. Thanks in part to greeting cards, poster art, and movie sets, the meanings and uses of nature come ready made for us.

CONCLUSION

When humans created the term nature to refer to the world apart from human society, a dichotomy between humans and nature was created. By bringing selective, idealized images of nature and references to nature into our communication and into our cultural artifacts, we are shaping our understandings and meanings of both nature and the human world, with consequences for both. When we use the commodified versions of nature in greeting cards to help construct and support the commodified versions of human relationships in greeting cards, commodification becomes the concept that ironically transcends and unites the nature-culture dichotomy.

Burke suggests and McKerrow (1989) also argues that if, however, we reveal the manner in which we are constrained by social discourse, we open up the possibilities for reconsideration, reform, or revolt. Rajchman (1985) contends that "to question the self-evidence of a form of experience . . . is to free it for our purposes, to open new possibilities for thought and action" (p. 4). Considering the use of images of nature in greeting cards is a step toward understanding what our use of symbols might be hiding from our view and how our symbols might be using us. We are poised to ask if either humans or nature is well served by the highly selective, unrealistic images of our environment that dominate the commodified communication of popular culture greeting cards.

REFERENCES

Bianchi, A. (1994, January). Contemporary greetings. *Inc., 16,* 9.

Bridges, J. S. (1993). Gender-stereotypic perceptions of infants as conveyed by birth congratulations cards. *Psychology of Women Quarterly, 17,* 19 -205.

Burke, K. (1950). *A rhetoric of motives.* New York: Prentice-Hall.

Burke, K. (1969). *A grammar of motives.* Los Angeles: University of California Press.

Burke, K. (1973). *Philosophy of literary forms.* Los Angeles: University of California Press.

Burke, K. (1984). *Attitudes toward history.* Los Angeles: University of California Press.

Carbaugh, D. (1996). Naturalizing communication and culture. In J. G. Cantrill & C. L. Oravec, (Eds.), *The symbolic earth: Discourse and our creation of the environment* (pp. 38-57). Lexington: University Press of Kentucky.

Clark, C. (1997). *Misery and company: Sympathy in everyday life.* Chicago: University of Chicago Press.

Cooper, M. M. (1996). Environmental rhetoric in the age of hegemonic politics: Earth First! and the Nature Conservancy. In C. G. Herndl & S. C. Brown (Eds.) *Green culture: Environmental rhetoric in contemporary America* (pp. 236-260). Madison: University of Wisconsin Press.

Demos, V. & Jacke, A. (1981). When you care enough: An analysis of attitudes toward aging in humorous birthday cards. *The Gerontologist, 21,* 209-215.

Dillion, K. M. & Jones, B. S. (1981). Attitudes toward aging portrayed by birthday cards. *International Journal of Aging and Human Development, 13,* 79-84

du Gay, P., Hall, S., Janes, L., Mackay, H., & Negus, K. (1997). *Doing cultural studies: The story of the Sony Walkman.* London: Sage/The Open University.

Evernden, N. (1992). *The social creation of nature.* Baltimore, MD: John Hopkins University Press.

Farrell, T. B. & Goodnight, G. T. (1981). Accidental rhetoric: The root metaphor of Three Mile Island. *Communication Monographs, 48,* 272-300.

Finn, P. (1980). Attitudes toward drinking conveyed in studio greeting cards. *American Journal of Public Health, 70,* 826-829.

Geertz, C. (1983). *Local knowledge: Further essays in interpretive anthropology.* New York: Basic Books.

Gephart, D. (1992, May). Writing and selling greeting cards. *The Writer, 105,* 25-26.

Greeting Card Association. (February 22, 2000). GCA industry fact sheet. In Greeting card association (On-line). WWW.greetingcards.org/gca/facts.htm.

Gusfield, J. R. (1989). The bridge over separated lands: Kenneth Burke's significance for the study of social action. In H. W. Simons & T. Melia (Eds.), *The legacy of Kenneth Burke.* Madison: University of Wisconsin Press.

Huyck, M. H. & Duchon, J. (1986). Over the miles: Coping, communicating and commiserating through age-theme greeting cards. In L. Nahemow, K. A. McCluskey-Fawcett, & P. F. McGhee (Eds.) *Humor and aging.* Orlando, FL: Academic Press.

Japp, P. (1990). "A spoonful of sugar makes the medicine go down": Dr. Cromwell's "feel good" cultural tonic. *Speaker and Gavel,* 2-10.

Katz, S. B. & Miller, C. R. (1996). The low-level radioactive waste siting controversy in North Carolina: Toward a rhetorical model of risk communication. In C. G. Herndl & S. C. Brown (Eds.), *Green culture: Environmental rhetoric in contemporary*

America (pp. 111-140). Madison: University of Wisconsin Press.

Killingsworth, M. J. & Palmer, J. S. (1996). Millenail ecology: The apocalyptic narrative from *Silent Spring to Global Warning.* In C. G. Herndl & S. C. Brown (Eds.), *Green culture: Environmental rhetoric in contemporary America* (pp. 21-45). Madison: University of Wisconsin Press.

McKerrow, R. E. (1989). Critical rhetoric: Theory and praxis. *Communication Monographs, 56,* 91-111.

McKibben, B. (1992). *The age of missing information.* New York: Plume.

Murphy, B. O. (1994, Spring). Greeting cards and gender messages. *Women and Language, 17,* 25-30.

Oravec, C. (1984). Conservation vs. preservation: The public interest in the Hetch-Hetchy controversy. *Quarterly Journal of Speech, 70,* 444-458.

Rajchman, J. (1985). *Michael Foucault: The Freedom of philosophy.* New York: Columbia University Press.

Random House Webster's College Dictionary (1999). New York: Random House.

Rehling, D. (1998). Commodified family: A textual analysis of greeting card sentiments. (Doctoral dissertation, University of Nebraska, Lincoln, 1998). *Dissertation Abstracts International.*

Rosteck, T. (1999). *At the intersection: Cultural studies and rhetorical studies.* New York: Guilford Press.

Sachsman, D. B. (1996). The mass media "discover" the environment: Influences on environmental reporting in the first twenty years. In J. G. Cantrill & C. L. Oravec, (Eds.), *The symbolic earth: Discourse and our creation of the environment* (pp. 241-256). Lexington: University Press of Kentucky.

Schlectweg, H. P. (1996). Media frames and environmental discourse: The case of "Focus: Logjam." In J. G. Cantrill & C. L. Oravec, (Eds.), *The symbolic Earth: Discourse and our creation of the environment* (pp. 257-277). Lexington, Kentucky: University Press of Kentucky.

Schrift, M. (1994, Summer). Icons of femininity in studio cards: women, communication and identity. *Journal of Popular Culture, 28,* 111-122.

Schwartz, J. (1993, June 14). What is family today? For Hallmark, a challenge. *Brandweek, 34,* 22-23.

Short, B. (1991). Earth First! and the rhetoric of moral confrontation. *Communication Studies, 42,* 172-188.

Sterns, E. (1988). *The very best from Hallmark: Greeting cards through the years.* New York: Harry N. Abrams.

Turner, G. (1990). *British cultural studies: An introduction.* New York: Routledge.

Ulman, H. L. (1996). "Thinking like a mountain": Persona, ethos and judgment in American nature writing. In C. G. Herndl & S. C. Brown (Eds.), *Green culture: Environmental rhetoric in contemporary America* (pp. 46-81). Madison: University of Wisconsin Press.

Voss, B. (1993, March). Selling with sentiment. *Sales & marketing management, 145,* 60-65.

Waddel, C. (1994). Perils of a modern Cassandra: Rhetorical Aspects of public indifference to the population explosion. *Social Epistemology, 8,* 221-237.

Weaver, B. J. (1996). "What to do with the mountain people?": The darker side of the successful campaign to establish the Great Smoky Mountains National Park. In J. G. Cantrill & C. L. Oravec, (Eds.), *The symbolic earth: Discourse and our creation of the environment* (pp. 151-175). Lexington: University Press of Kentucky.

Woods, A. S. & Delisle, R. G. (1978). The treatment of death in sympathy cards. In
    C. Winick (Ed.), *Deviance and mass media*. Beverly Hills, CA: Sage.

3

Monopoly™ the National Parks Edition: Reading Neo-Liberal Simulacra

Andy Opel

In 1998, Parker Brothers, in cooperation with the National Parks Service, released *Monopoly: The National Parks Edition*. This game uses the traditional *Monopoly* layout, replacing the usual properties with familiar names of national parks. Like many variations on the *Monopoly* format released by USAopoly, a licensee of Hasbro, Inc., this version retains the rules and objectives of the original game while substituting national park names and outdoor/environmental imagery throughout the game. This cultural artifact is attractive as a research topic for its immediately apparent contradictions. While the goal of the original game is to accumulate and develop properties faster than your opponents do, in hopes of bankrupting them, this new edition leaves these motivations intact while replacing the private spaces of Marvin's Gardens and Park Place with the public spaces of Acadia and Yosemite National Parks. Instead of improvements of houses and hotels, players build tents and ranger stations as devices for increasing the "rent" when other players land on the newly privatized "national park." The game embodies the capitalist narrative of the original *Monopoly* game while invoking the natural/environmental images of our national parks. The symbolic privatization of national treasures reflects current post-fordist, neo-liberal social attitudes while creating a simulacrum of both the original game and the natural world.

Popular culture has become a common site of research for media scholars. Critical analysis of the production and consumption of popular texts is a dominant trend in American cultural studies. While popular culture texts from rock music to comic books have drawn critical attention, board games have received relatively little critical attention. This chapter draws on the cultural studies tradition and focuses on the world's most popular, best-selling copyrighted board game: *Monopoly*™. The popularity of this board game points to the game's significance as a cultural artifact that warrants critical inquiry. The *National Parks Edition* in particular is unique in the combination of a popular capitalist narrative with a popular public system of land conservation. How these two themes become confused and conflated is the critical basis of this chapter.

Two theoretical tools will be used to help unpack this popular board game: neo-liberalism and simulacra. Neo-liberal and post-fordist are terms used to describe the current model of global capitalism dominant in the post war West today. Some of the features of neo-liberal economics include: reduced influence of nation states and the welfare states within them, declining power of trade unions, increasing economic inequality, decreasing influence of political parties and the rise of special interest groups, increased international monetary mobility, political support for markets, and entrepreneurship over the regulation of business and corporate consolidation. Simulacra is a concept that helps to reveal the power and function of images and simulations. In drawing attention to the images used in this game, the simulacra concept helps to explain why these images are attractive and how they relate to a capitalist, consumer society.

This chapter "reads" *Monopoly, the National Parks Edition*. This reading focuses on the history of the production of the game, the form of the game, and a theoretical reading of the game. Because of the limits of this study, audience uses of the game are reserved for another research project. These four components (production, form, readings, and audience uses) make up the "circuit of the production, circulation and consumption of cultural products" (Johnson, 1996, p. 83). This cultural studies model points to four distinct areas that warrant attention in the analysis of a cultural text. These four points represent distinct but interrelated processes in the creation of cultural texts. Though connected, each point requires attention because how a text is produced is not transparent from the text itself nor is any one reading of the text determined by the form of the text. This chapter reads this game through three of the four points on the circuit of production. This reading can then be expanded through an analysis of audience uses and the social relations involved in game play. Before we look at this game in particular, let us review the previous work on the connections between games and culture and explore the concept of simulacra.

GAMES AND CULTURE

The background literature for this chapter falls into a number of distinct categories: the role of play and games in our society, the "reading" of popular culture texts, and the relationship between commodity culture and representations of nature. In addition, Baudrillard's concept of simulacra will be used as a theoretical tool for exploring the images and implications of this game.

In his oft-cited work on the relation between play and culture, Huizinga (1950) argues that play is the fertile ground where cultural practices are tested before they are made manifest in society. In *Homo Ludens: A Study of the Play Element in Culture*, Huizinga (1950) describes play as,

a temporary activity satisfying in itself and ending there . . . It adorns life, amplifies it and is to that extent a necessity both for the individual – as a life function – and for society by reason of the meaning it contains, its significance, its expressive value, its spiritual and social associations, in short, as a cultural function (Huizinga, 1950, p. 9).

Play and games are described as outside the biological processes of life, and intricately connected to the culture of the civilization. Huizinga (1950) asks, "To what extent does the civilization we live in still develop in play-forms?" (Huizinga, 1950, p. 195). His answer is based on the idea that professionalism and formalism have moved sports and other games out of "play" and into a more structured realm of interaction. This change is seen as transforming "play into business," and in the process limiting the potential for social learning through play.

Roger Caillois's (1961) response to Huizinga, *Man, Play and Games,* challenges the idea of play as a site of social experimentation and poses the possibility that "the spirit of play is essential to culture, but games and toys are historically the residue of culture" (Caillois, 1961, p. 58). Games are said to be remnants of a past era, "deprived of their original meaning" and "stripped of their political and religious significance" (Caillois, 1961, p. 59). Nevertheless, games are seen as cultural artifacts and indicators of a society's values.

It is not absurd to try diagnosing a civilization in terms of the games that are especially popular there. In fact, if games are cultural factors and images, it follows that to a certain degree a civilization and its content may be characterized by its games. They necessarily reflect its culture pattern and provide useful indications as to its preferences, weakness, and strength of a given society at a particular stage of its evolution. (Caillois, 1961, p. 83)

Caillois argues for what he calls a "sociology derived *from* games," where certain types of games reflect institutional forms in society and are prone to certain "corruptions." An example of this is competitive games (which *Monopoly* would be categorized as) such as sports. When institutionalized, sports correspond to economic competition and competitive examination or testing. The corruption of sports is equated with violence in society. For Caillois, games act as social indicators, marking cultural predispositions and areas of potential corruption.

Over the past thirty years, media scholars have increasingly turned their attention to popular culture as a site of research. Rock music, MTV, shopping malls and sitcoms have all become legitimate texts for cultural scholars to critically evaluate. John Fiske (1989), a leading proponent of research into popular culture, sees popular culture as a site of resistance to the dominant capitalist order. While he acknowledges the production of culture by industry, Fiske emphasizes the selection of those commodities by people as a central component to the creation and reproduction of popular culture. "The people make popular culture at the interface between everyday life and the consumption of the products of the cultural industries" (Fiske, 1989, p. 6). The relationship between the power of the dominant and the resistance of the subordinate becomes the site of popular culture practice. Struggle over the meaning and uses of cultural "texts" are embodied within popular culture artifacts. "Semiotic resistance results from the desire of the subordinate to exert control over the meaning of their lives" (Fiske, 1989, p. 10). For Fiske and many other researchers, popular culture embodies the struggles of the larger society, the power relations between producers and consumers, and the political and economic realities of commodity capitalism.

The intersection of consumerism, commodity culture and the environment has been the recent focus of some scholarly attention. Rob Shields (1992a, 1992b) has explored the spaces of consumption, and describes "lifestyle shopping" where "new modes of subjectivity, interpersonal relationships and models of social totality are thus being experimented with, 'browsed through' and 'tried on' in much the same way that one might shop for clothes" (Shields, 1992a, p. 15). The intersection of lifestyle with consumer culture is described as the "emergence of new identifications" where individuals are not passive consumers but rather active agents in the appropriation of codes and fashions (Shields, 1992a, p. 2). Shields goes on to acknowledge the importance of symbolic value in the commodity exchange, noting, "commodities become valued for their 'aura' of symbolic meanings and values rather than their use or exchange value" (Shields, 1992b, p. 99). The importance of the symbolic has been picked up by scholars concerned about the environment and the function of re-presentation in public perceptions of the natural world. In *The Abstract Wild,* Jack Turner (1996) acknowledges the power of language and image to shape our world. Instead of the usual environmental villains of mining or logging companies, Turner writes, "my enemies are abstractions, abstractions that are rendering even the wild abstract" (Turner, 1996, p. xvi). These abstractions are said to "diminish our personal experience of nature" and encourage a "preference for artifice, copy, simulation and surrogate, for the engineered and the managed instead of the natural" (Turner, 1996, p. xvi). Turner goes on to critique national parks as "created for and by tourism" and he asserts the parks are "managed with two ends in mind, entertainment and the preservation of the resource base for that entertainment" (p. 27). The parks and images of the natural world "become in large part a 'created environment' consisting of humanly structured systems whose motive power and dynamics derive from socially organized knowledge claims" (Turner, 1996, p. 109). This is seen as part of a process where wild nature and the earth are increasingly "museal – in the process of becoming a relic; a once autonomous order transformed by a single species for its own use, a species that out of a combination of mourning and respect preserves bits and pieces for worship, study and entertainment" (Turner, 1996, p. 109). Representations and images of nature then become part of a larger process of the objectification of nature, used to sell "symbolic auras" that embody nostalgia, mourning, and entertainment. These simulations serve to further our distance from the real while feeding a growing desire for the hyperreal.

In his essay "Panic Ecology: Nature in the Age of Superconductivity," Nigel Clark (1997) connects the attraction to mediated visions of the natural world to a larger narrative of "technological mastery and economic utility." Clark writes, "it needs to be emphasized that today's simulacra respond to and build on those of the past: that nature, as a cultural construct is 'always-already' undergoing revitalization" (Clark, 1997, p. 83). The simulations of nature we find so attractive are attractive because they recall a past upon which our technological present is based. Nature then becomes "re-enchanted" as a historical source of our current wealth, a source that is now viewed through the lens of modernity. Industrial society then "manufactures" nature as a product to be consumed. This commodification is described as "cosmetic surgery applied to green spaces . . . The landscaping of the American national parks and the construction of scenic routes, the surface of the natural environment was reworked into a more pristine and more visible version of itself" (Clark, 1997, p. 84). Industrial, technological society then is said to shape both the nature we romanticize and the images of that nature we view though the mediations of our culture production industries.

THEORY: BAUDRILLARD AND SIMULACRA

The concept of *simulacra* is central to the theoretical orientation of this chapter and warrants a brief exploration. Although this term has biblical roots, Jean Baudrillard (1983), who has most recently promoted the concept, describes simulacra as "copies of things that no longer have originals" (Baudrillard, 1983, p. 4). Simulacrum are said to be hyperreal, or more real than the original. Places like Disneyland and wax museums are common examples of simulacra, where Main Street, USA is referring to a place that never existed. Umberto Eco is another scholar who has used the concepts of simulacra and the hyperreal to describe aspects of American culture. In *Travels in Hyperreality*, Eco (1983) writes, "The American imagination demands the real thing, and to attain it, must fabricate the absolute fake; where the boundaries between game and illusion are blurred, the art museum is contaminated by the freak show, and falsehood is enjoyed in a situation of fullness, of *horror vacui*" (Eco, 1983, p. 8). The process and function of simulation/simulacra are central to this reading of *Monopoly* and form the theoretical backbone of this chapter.

Taking a few steps back, Baudrillard uses earlier definitions of commodities to explain the significance of symbols and simulations. Marx defined a commodity as having two values: a use value and an exchange value. For example, a shoe has a use, to protect your feet. It also has a value in relation to other things (i.e., shirts, food, hats) with which it might be exchanged. Baudrillard updates this concept by saying a third element has been added, and that element is sign exchange value. An example of sign exchange value would be the Nike swoosh on a product, making a shoe or a sweatshirt symbolically more valuable (and literally more expensive) without significantly altering the item itself. The values embedded in these symbols are said to determine the value of the commodity. Baudrillard argues that the primacy of the sign has altered the traditional configuration of capitalism. "Traditionally, 'capital' only had to produce goods; consumption ran by itself. Today it is necessary to produce consumers, to produce demand, and this production is infinitely more costly than that of the goods" (Luke, 1991, p. 348). Nike shoes are a good example. With the rise of globalization and third world production of goods, the cost to produce a shoe is small compared to the promotion fees paid to Michael Jordan and the ad campaigns designed to connect the swoosh with Jordan's talent.

So what does this have to do with simulacra? Simulacra are said to be one of the ways values are embedded into the signs attached to commodities. Baudrillard describes much of the "mediascape" as simulacra, a hyperreal world with no basis in reality. From The Practice to ER, imaginary worlds are created by distant multinational corporations and brought to our living rooms. These simulations of real life (simulacra) are said to reinforce the sign values established within commodity culture while hiding or masking opportunities for resistance. Simulacra then reinforce the dominant values attached to commodity signs. "Power in hyperreality, derives from controlling the means of simulation, dominating the codes of representation, and managing the signs of meaning that constitute what hyperreality is taken as being at any particular time" (Luke, 1991, p. 362). Simulacra are the manifestations of those who control the means of simulation, and these simulations play a major role in the production and maintenance of consumer culture. With the concept of simulacra, Baudrillard provides a concept that helps to reveal the connections between images (signs) and consumer culture. The *Monopoly*™ game models a (private) capitalist narrative while this version in particular attracts customers because of the images of the (public) national parks. The erosion of the boundaries between the public and the private is indicative of neo-liberalism and is often accomplished through the use of simulations (simulacra) that reinforce this new economic and cultural arrangement. Through a close reading of this "environmental" edition of *Monopoly*, this chapter looks for insight into the following questions. What is the history of *Monopoly* and what cultural conditions influenced its development? What is the relationship between the original game and this new edition? How are the National Parks re-presented? How can the concept of simulacra help us understand this game? How does the simulacrum embodied in this game reflect current social/political attitudes toward commodity capitalism and the environment? These questions will shape the reading of this cultural text and the messages embedded both overtly and subtly in this re-creation device.

THE CIRCUIT OF PRODUCTION: PRODUCING THE GAME

The game *Monopoly*™ is the "world's most popular board game and the best selling copyrighted game in history. . . . The game is marketed in 75 countries and translated into 26 languages, including a Russian edition . . . . 160 million units have been sold worldwide . . . Primary target audience is children 8-14 and adults 18-54, usage is 50/50 male/female" (www.usaopoly.com). This is the corporate overview of the original *Monopoly*™ game. From this original success story, USAopoly, including The *National Parks Edition*, has created fifty spin-off games.

Monopoly, the National Parks Edition was released on July 9, 1998. Developed by USAopoly (a licensee of Hasbro) in cooperation with the National Parks Foundation and the National Parks Service, this game represents a public/private partnership emblematic of neo-liberalism. Fifty cents from every game goes to the Parks Foundation, an organization "created by the U.S. Congress in 1967 as the official nonprofit partner of the National Park Service" (http://www.nationalparks.org). If the game is sold through a Parks Service store or catalogue, the Foundation receives "significantly more." The game was designed to have "broad national appeal" and reflect popular "Americana" (Maggie at USAopoly, personal communication, April 5, 1999). The target market for the game is women, ages 25-54, who usually buy the game as a gift purchase for an "enthusiast of the topic." The parks were selected by the Parks Foundation on the basis of geographical distribution and a sample of natural, historical, and cultural representations. In a telephone interview, the company noted three unique aspects to the game: educational components, historical perspective, and a charitable contribution as a part of the purchase. The game has been selling "up to expectations" and response has been "positive." The target market, women 25 to 54, is significant in light of Ellen Seiter's (1993) work on the connections between toys, mothers, and consumerism. In *Sold Separately,* Seiter details the long-standing tradition of marketing children's toys to mothers. This work acknowledges the complexities of toy marketing as it affects women and Seiter critiques the "condemnation of commercial television and cheap, mass produced toys" as having "placed an unreasonable and somewhat unnecessary burden on mothers" (Seiter, 1993, p. 229). Her analysis reveals the gains and losses involved in children's exposure to mass-produced toys and recommends adults "recognize their complexity and the ways they offer a hybrid of messages about consumer culture, violence, environmentalism, and technology" (Seiter, 1993, p. 229). In the case of the *Parks Edition* of *Monopoly*, the producers followed a predictable pattern of marketing to the mothers. Like the many toys Seiter critiques, this game offers a complex series of messages about money, success, and the environment. These messages are not monolithic and offer a variety of readings, both positive and negative.

THE CIRCUIT OF PRODUCTION: THE GAME ITSELF

"National parks are America's special places – the soul of this country" (www.usaopoly.com). Thus begins the USAopoly web site description of this game. The website goes on to invite customers to play this new version of a classic American tradition: "So join Mr. Monopoly on a hike through America's national treasures from Yosemite to Yellowstone, Valley Forge to Mt. Rushmore. Outdoor enthusiasts will enjoy the country's most cherished natural and cultural resources year-round in an attempt to own it all – in classic Monopoly style" (www.usaopoly.com). The game is packaged as an "encounter" with "American experience." Gameplayers are said to "gain a deeper understanding of the ecological, historical and cultural values which are part of that experience" (www.usaopoly.com). All this learning is supposed to come from playing the game by the traditional *Monopoly* rules. The properties have been renamed, though game play remains exactly the same. The board is colorful, with pictures of each park added to the property spaces, though the property deeds players gain upon purchase differ from the originals only by name. The "rents," color coding, and property values remain the same as the original deeds. No information about the parks is included on the game deeds or other playing cards. Within the instruction booklet, a brief paragraph describes each park and a general theme is assigned to the color groups, such as "Spirit of America" for the first two properties on the board after the "GO" square. In the original game, these are called Baltic and Mediterranean Avenue. In this new game, they are renamed "National Mall" and "Mt. Rushmore." Interestingly enough, the parks dedicated to our government's history are placed so as to receive the lowest value on the gameboard. The new game retains many features of the original. All four corner squares (Go, Jail, Free Parking, and Go To Jail) are the same, as are the "Chance" and "Community Chest" squares. The cards for these squares have been given outdoor themes and the railroads have been replaced by hiking trails. Aside from the colorful pictures identifying each park and a large photo of Grand Teton filling the center of the board, the game retains much of the look of the original design. The original tokens have been replaced by

"8 pewter collectable tokens." The originals were a dog, racecar, top hat, iron, battleship, canon, shoe, thimble, wheelbarrow, and horse and rider. This new game has a hiking boot, bear, tent, canoe, ranger's hat, covered wagon, different canon, and hiker. Wooden "tents" and "ranger stations" have replaced the plastic "houses" and "hotels." Their cost, rent and mortgage values remain the same as the original values. The money has been changed to show a picture of "Rich Uncle Pennybags" holding binoculars and a fishing pole. The game is still titled "Monopoly" with the phrases, "Property Trading Game from Parker Brothers" and "2 to 8 Players Ages 8 to Adult" appearing a number of times on the box.

CIRCUIT OF PRODUCTION: READING THE GAME

Having established an overview of the process of production and a description of the game itself, we can now look at some of the possible readings of the game with the theoretical help of Baudrillard. A first look at the game reveals a close similarity to the original *Monopoly*™ game. If this game is viewed as simulacrum, a copy of something that has no original, the original must be contested. In *The Billion Dollar Monopoly Swindle,* Ralph Anspach (1998) chronicles the history of this board game and discovers a discrepancy between the history as told by Parker Brothers and the history that he discovered. Anspach describes Parker Brothers' attempt to rewrite history as a way to obscure the anti-capitalist roots of this game.

Parker Brothers cites Charles Darrow as the creator of the game and places the date of origin as 1934 (www.usaopoly.com). After changing "52 fundamental playing errors," the company is said to have published the game in 1935. This popular history links the game to the depression era. The popularity of the game is said to have been originally based on people's desire to pretend to get rich after the devastating years of the Depression (Costello, 1991, p. 59). What this popular history leaves out is the existence of *The Landlord Game,* patented in 1904 by a woman named Elizabeth (Lizzie) J. Magie (Anspach, 1998; Costello, 1991). Like *Monopoly*™, this game contained forty spaces, four railroads, two utilities, and twenty-two rental properties whose value increased as players moved around the board. "There are spaces for Jail, Go To Jail, Luxury Tax and Parking. But there's no Go; in this game, the first space is called Mother Earth" (Costello, 1991, p. 59). This game predated the Depression by twenty-five years and is said to be based on "the single-tax theory of Henry George, which held that only land should be taxed.... She (Magie) presented The Landlord Game to the then-reigning King of Games, George Parker. He pronounced it 'too political' " (Costello, 1991, p. 59). After years of success and fine tuning, Magie renewed the patent in 1924. Ten years later, when Parker Brothers patented their *Monopoly*™ game, they also bought the patents to *The Landlord Game* as well as *Finance*, another similar game from this era.

This summary of the controversial history behind *Monopoly*™ calls into question the nature of an "original" *Monopoly*™ game, and makes the *National Parks Edition* a copy of a game whose history has been revised. Parker Brothers' manipulation of the history of this game is an example of simulacra's ability to "mask historical tensions between labor and capital." While *The Landlord Game* had an explicit political message, which George Parker deemed "too political," *Monopoly* has an implicit political message acceptable to Parker and wider audiences. *The Landlord Game* appears to have arisen at the height of the first wave of industrialism and the robber barons. Players of the game could mimic the actions of Vanderbilt and Rockefeller by literally putting other players out of the game by bankrupting them. The 1890 Sherman Antitrust Act was enforced in 1911 against Rockefeller and resulted in the breakup of Standard Oil. Players of *Monopoly*™ could be seen as modeling the illegal behavior of one of America's most ruthless industrialists. In our present era of neo-liberal, global capitalism, a new wave of consolidations across a wide variety of industries has produced what some theorists describe as "new wave monopoly capitalism." The popularity of this game throughout the twentieth century and now spreading around the world appears connected to the attractiveness of the idea of owning entire industries and putting everyone else out of business. While 160 million games have been sold to people trying to simulate this action through game play, an increasingly smaller group of people is winning the "real" monopoly game, bankrupting third-world countries through global currency manipulations and increasing the debt load of "players" in first world countries.

The images of the national parks connect the monopolistic practice to "America's special places – the soul of this country." Although the game is marketed for its educational component, the only information about the parks is printed in the back of the instruction manual. When asked why the property cards did not include text about the parks on the back of the cards, the response from USAopoly was, "Parker Brothers did not want anything to interfere with game play" (Interview with USAopoly). This is significant because of the implicit message that information about the natural world should not interfere with the game play of *Monopoly*™ (capitalism). The objectified images, one from each park, are all that players are allowed to know as they embark on a process of acquisition of public spaces. The simulation of the privatization of public spaces, without any information beyond a pictorial image, can be seen as representing the symbolic attempt of monopoly capital to purchase "the soul of America." Simulacra such as this are said to function in such a way as to "sustain the political, economic and cultural reproduction of a society" (Luke, 1991, p. 348). The historical tension between capital and labor and the public and private ownership of land is effaced by the simulacra of this game. The parks themselves were established as a protection against the ravages of privatization and the potential for pristine natural and cultural places to be owned, altered, and marketed by the driving engines of capitalism. In the game, there is no government mitigating the private acquisition of these "national treasures" and players have only symbolic knowledge of the items they seek to acquire. As with the original game, players "improve" the parks (properties) by developing them. These developments consist of tents and ranger stations. Unlike the real world, where public money is used to "improve" the parks, the game player's private money is used to build tents and ranger stations that then allow the player to increase the "rent" other players must pay to "use" the national parks. This simulation of the privatization of a public resource is parallel to the real world case of the broadcast spectrum. In the broadcast spectrum case, a limited public resource was auctioned off to the highest bidder (television and radio station conglomerates) and the public is forced to "pay" up to 14 minutes of every hour by being subjected to advertising. This situation has evolved over time to the point where it is taken as a given by many and calls for renewed public access to what was a public resource have fallen on deaf ears within the government and the broadcast industry. Modeling this practice through a game, targeting our National Parks, presents young people with a distorted picture of the national parks system and the policies that have allowed for the creation, preservation, and maintenance of over 375 natural and cultural treasures.

This message of privatization of our national parks is not limited to a board game. Over the past decade, proposals to increase concession franchises and corporate sponsorships within the parks have appeared in Congress. These proposals, though defeated as of now, have been coupled with reduced funding of the parks system, creating infrastructure problems and constructing a need for private money to keep the system going. The Associated Press cited the top ten most endangered parks and quoted a $6 billion figure in backlogged repairs within the system of parks, monuments, and historical sites (Herbert, 1999). The problems range from leaking sewage systems to vandalism and looting to a push for wider use of motor vehicles within the parks. Critics have charged that the policy of inadequate funding has been a deliberate strategy to create such a financial burden that private money (and influence) will have to be sought. With young people accustomed to the idea of people buying parks through exposure to games such as this *Monopoly*™ edition, such a program may be more publicly acceptable as these children come into voting age.

CONCLUSION

The history of the *Monopoly*™ game is a contested subject. The time frame offered by the company and contested by Costello and Anspach allows for two very different interpretations of the historical and cultural conditions during the development of this game. The very nature of this contested history provides an interesting background for explorations of the game, placing the game itself in a monopolistic historical context. Looking at the connections between the original game and the *National Parks Edition*, we see a strict adherence to game play over education, in spite of marketing statements emphasizing educational components. With the only information about the parks appearing in the instruction booklet, opportunities for information beyond the photographic image are limited to the inquisitive and those able to retain instructions within a game over the life of the game. Many of the heavily used board games, in many households, become tattered boxes barely able to retain game pieces, much less instructions. By omitting specific environmental information from the game itself (endangered species lists, cultural histories, etc.) the educational opportunities are limited and learning is steered back into the game of monopoly, the game of capitalist acquisition, development, and the goal of the elimination of your fellow players. In describing games such as this, Ellen Seiter (1993) notes how toys often allow for "the consideration of problems typically limited to those for which capitalism itself offers remedies – through consumption" (Seiter, 1993, p. 11). The problem of the parks becomes a problem to be solved by buying them, developing them, and charging people more and more to use them.

The concept of simulacra works with this game on a number of levels. The game itself is a copy of a contested original whose history has been altered from an era of critique of capital (1900) to a celebration of capital (1930s) while the images of the national parks are themselves simulations and objectifications of natural and cultural landmarks. The game can be seen as functioning in much the same way as simulacra; masking the historical tensions between labor and capital, the public and the private. This game actually models an action that contradicts the ideas underlying the creation of the National Park system, yet does so in such as way as to eliminate the overt appearance of contradiction or conflict. This is the classic function of simulacra: taking an interest in the national parks and the environment and steering that interest back into a capitalist, consumer impulse. If the parks can be seen as places protected from the exploits of monopoly capital, then this game provides a way to subvert that idea under the guise of education and celebration of the parks. This game is also connected to the trends of neo-liberalism. Public treasures are symbolically purchased by private individuals who then "improve" them only to increase the cost of access to the point where game players are bankrupted for their continued use of the national parks. Thus, natural wonders preserved for generations for the specific purpose of continued enjoyment by a diverse public are symbolically closed off to all but the most wealthy, creating a narrative that connects access to the wonders of nature to class status. Only the rich end up with access to these public spaces in this neo-liberal game where everything public is now subjected to the forces of the private monopoly capital marketplace.

Finally, this complex inversion of the environmental impulse is intimately connected to a growing environmental discourse in our society. This discourse is potentially threatening to commodity culture and contains themes contrary to capitalist ideals. The proliferation of environmental consciousness contains a powerful threat to the captains of industry. Industry has responded to the environmental impulse by attempting to appropriate green images and repackaging a consumer lifestyle as an environmental position. This can be seen in the proliferation of advertisements that place SUVs (sport utility vehicles) in rugged wilderness settings, connecting four-wheel drive with access to nature.

The reality of these vehicles can be seen in their poor emissions, low gas mileage, and price for debt creation. This piece of green marketing is indicative of corporate attempts to appropriate the potentially resistant environmental impulse and redirect it back into a consumer impulse. The *National Parks Edition* of *Monopoly*™ can be read as serving a similar function, aimed at young people, encouraging the desire to one day "own it all – in classic *Monopoly*™ style!"

REFERENCES

Anspach, R. (1998). *The billion dollar monopoly swindle*. Palo Alto, CA: American Publishing.
Baudrillard, J. (1983). *Simulations*. Paul Foss (trans.). New York: Routledge.
Caillois, R. (1961). *Man, play and games*. New York, NY: The Free Press.
Clark, N. (1997). Panic ecology: Nature in the age of superconductivity. *Theory, Culture and Society, 14*, 77-96.
Costello, M. J. (1991). *The greatest games of all time*. New York: John Wiley & Sons.
Eco, U. (1983). *Travels in hyperreality*. New York, NY: Harcourt Brace & Co.
Fiske, J. (1989). *Reading the popular*. London: Unwin Hyman Ltd.
Herbert, H. J. (1999, December). Environmentalists sound alarm about national parks. *News and Observer*, p. 11a.
Huizinga, J. (1950). *Homo ludens: A study of the play element in culture*. Boston, MA: Beacon Press.
Johnson, R. (1996). What is cultural studies anyway? J. Storey (ed.), *What is cultural studies? A reader*. London: Arnold.
Luke, T. W. (1991). Power and politics in hyperreality. *The Social Science Journal, 28*, 3-14.
National Park Foundation (accessed 5/99). Charter and Mission. [On-line]. Available: http://www.nationalparks.org/about-mission.htm
Seiter, E. (1993). *Sold separately: Children and parents in consumer culture*. New Brunswick: Rutgers University Press.
Shields, R. (1992a). The individual, consumption cultures and the fate of community. In R. Shields (Ed), *Lifestyle shopping: The subject of consumption*. London: Routledge.
Shields, R. (1992b). Spaces for the subject of consumption. In R. Shields (ed), *Lifestyle shopping: The subject of consumption*. London: Routledge.

USAopoly Collector's Corner (accessed 5/99). Monopoly game facts. [On-line].
    Available: http://www.usaopoly.com/collectors/collectorsfacts1.html

4

Cultivating the Agrarian Myth in Hollywood Films

Jean P. Retzinger

> Those who labour in the earth are the chosen people of God, if ever he had a chosen people, whose breasts he has made his peculiar deposit for substantial and genuine virtue. . . . Corruption of morals . . . is the mark set on those, who not looking up to heaven, to their own soil and industry, as does the husbandman, for their subsistence, depend for it on the casualties and caprice of customers. Dependence begets subservience and venality, suffocates the germ of virtue, and prepares fit tools for the designs of ambition. . . . [G]enerally speaking, the proportion which the aggregate of the other classes of citizens bears in any state to that of its husbandmen, is the proportion of its unsound to its healthy parts, and is a good-enough barometer whereby to measure its degree of corruption.
>
> (Jefferson, 1787/1982, pp. 164-165)

The agrarian society of Thomas Jefferson's America has disappeared. Jefferson described a nation whose farmers constituted fully 90 percent of its citizenry; currently about 1.5 percent of the U.S. population engages in farm labor. Though 954 million acres remain in agricultural production, this number too has been shrinking (*Statistical Abstract*, 1999, pp. 426, 678). The remaining pastures, fields, and feedlots (which constitute 40% of all U.S. land) garner relatively little attention among either environmentalists or the public at large though ample reason for concern exists. As agricultural lands are lost to urban spread and development, fewer acres are continuously asked to produce more. The results may be found in an ever-increasing dependence on chemical pesticides, herbicides, fertilizers, and antibiotics in food production; in rates of soil erosion exceeding those of the 1930s "dustbowls"; in a loss of genetic diversity in both crops and livestock; and in the contamination and depletion of the nation's groundwater.[1]

Yet such problems are not readily visible. For the casual observer, the view from a car window of pastures dotted with cattle, fields ribboned with corn, or hills blanketed with wheat evokes tranquillity (or boredom) more than alarm. Rural landscapes often look more beautiful than threatened, and increasingly looking seems to encompass the whole of our relationship to those lands.

Changing demographics alone (the fact that most of us have not lived or worked on a farm) cannot account for an ever-widening gap between the country and the city. Nor can that gap be attributed to distinctive urban and rural psyches or a separate producer and consumer class. For farming practices increasingly emulate those of corporate America and farm families purchase the same consumer goods, including their groceries, as do their urban and suburban counterparts. Instead, intermediate and largely hidden stages of food production (from slaughterhouses to processing plants) have severed most direct links between farm fields and family tables. Global rather than regional markets further twist and stretch those links. In place of information about farm economies or the agricultural practices which feed us, our recognized links to rural lands and rural lives are primarily visual, framed by car windows or television and film screens.

Of these views, the ways in which Hollywood films help shape our understanding of the (not-so-) natural environment in rural America deserves closer attention. Mediated and fictional versions of farm life shimmer larger than life on a cinema screen or slip into urban living rooms as videos played out on television sets, temporarily bridging the gap between the city and the country. Farmers and farming have provided story lines for films for more than seven decades, from the era of silent films to the present. Such films cannot be classified as a genre; there is no "Midwestern" equivalent of the western. Though the majority of these films use farms as a setting rather than as a subject, in several instances films made during the most visible periods of crises in American agriculture have attempted to depict and address specific economic, political, or environmental problems affecting farmers. More often than not, rather than making either the roots or consequences of such agricultural problems more understandable, Hollywood films leave confused and contradictory messages in their wake.

This chapter includes examples drawn primarily from three films made in the 1930s and 1940s (*Our Daily Bread* [1934], *The Grapes of Wrath* [1940], and *The Southerner* [1945]), three films all released in 1984 (*Country, Places in the Heart,* and *The River*), and, more recently, *A Thousand Acres* (1997). Additionally, *Summer Stock*, a 1950 musical starring Judy Garland and a precursor to the 1984 films that focus on farm women, is also included.[2] These films (with the exception of *Summer Stock*) are somewhat unique in focusing directly on farmers and farming and the (largely economic) problems they faced. Of particular interest is the starring role that the agrarian myth plays in each, but in an abridged version which concentrates on character—while ignoring the specific farming practices Jefferson believed engendered those character traits. Gender, too, plays an increasingly important role in these films, one which updates the agrarian myth, placing the films squarely within their respective historical moments, while leaving the myth itself largely intact.

Films offer their viewers far more than a straightforward mirror of social reality; they serve as well as expressions and storehouses of public dreams or myths. While films may be fruitfully explored from the concerns of industry/production or audience reception, this chapter engages critical analysis as a means of investigating "the pragmatic concerns of cultural identity" (Collins, Radner, & Collins, 1993, p. 5). In James Carey's (1989) simple but elegant definition, communication—including, of course, the material artifacts of popular culture—"is a symbolic process whereby reality is produced, maintained, repaired, and transformed" (p. 23). Cinema, as Desser and Jowett (2000) note, can serve as an especially important resource for exploring that symbolic process and thereby examining historical changes in twentieth century society and culture. Films permit scholars to trace and visualize societal changes, and in doing so to explore the role that film itself plays in bringing about those transformations (pp. xi-xii). The centrality of myth and archetypal characters in film are crucial in this process.

SETTING THE STAGE: THE AGRARIAN MYTH

In conversation with Bill Moyers, Joseph Campbell (1988) seems to suggest that films, because of their "magical" qualities and the fact they are viewed in a "special temple like the movie theatre" (pp. 15-16), are particularly well suited to the dissemination of myth in modern society. A myth, according to Mircea Eliade (1963), offers "models for human behavior and, by that very fact, gives meaning and value to life" (p. 2). For Campbell (1988), myths perform four functions: mystical, cosmological, sociological, and pedagogical. Of these, the third and fourth seem particularly significant for an analysis of film, for the sociological function serves to support and validate a particular social order, while the pedagogical function teaches an individual "how to live a human lifetime under any circumstance" (p. 31). Myths are adept at bridging the universal and specific, linking timeless precepts and guidelines for human behavior with the particular space and time-bound contingencies of a given society. As Campbell (1988) notes, "myths are so intimately bound to the culture, time, and place that unless the symbols, the metaphors, are kept alive by constant recreation through the arts, the life just slips away from them" (p. 59). Film, then, provides one channel by which myths are both perpetuated and reinvigorated within a culture, even myths as seemingly outdated as those associated with an agricultural way of life.

Though the agrarian myth is centuries old, it persists, continuing to shape our perception of these rural landscapes and the individuals who inhabit them. America's agricultural roots remain deeply embedded in the cultural psyche. The yeoman-farmer according to Jefferson (1787/1982) was both the ideal person and the ideal citizen. The farmer's list of traits was long: virtue, independence, self-sufficiency, self-reliance, honesty, health, happiness, wholesomeness, simplicity, and morality. Many of these traits persist in modern conceptions of the farmer, though honesty and simplicity at times dwarf the other characteristics, resulting in the creation of film characters rendered as benign bumpkins. By contrast, non-farming rural residents often fare far worse. As Carol Clover (1992) argues convincingly in *Men, Women, and Chain Saws*, horror films in particular often demonize the country, making "rednecks" a contemporary replacement for the Westerns' "redskins," and paving the way for a modern annihilation of the offending "other" (pp. 134-135).

In describing those who "labour in the earth" as "the chosen people of God," Jefferson uses the land as the vital link between humans and God. Looking to the earth and to individual industry as much as to heaven constituted a farmer's virtue; cultivating the soil is synonymous with cultivating good works. Yet it was not the labor alone that mattered. For Jefferson the virtues exemplified by farm families depended on direct links between production and consumption. Family farms and subsistence farming practices meant economic security, and thus, in Jefferson's view, a freedom from the "casualties and caprice of customers" (p. 165). The belief in agriculture was a "belief in individual freedom and in private property as its means" (Griswold, 1948, p. 45) for clearly it mattered to Jefferson that farm labor was performed on one's *own* land. Only small landowners whose fields and farmyards directly supplied their needs could be independent, freed from subservience, from want, and from volatile markets.

Gender plays a role in this myth also, though it is mostly present in its absence, in being relegated to the margins. While the landowner/farmer was always a "he," women served to complete and reproduce the family farm across the American frontier. Perhaps, though, the most important role for the feminine was metaphorical — as even the titles of some of the seminal works on this topic make clear: Henry Nash Smith's *Virgin Land* and Annette Kolodny's *The Lay of the Land: Metaphor as Experience and History in American Life and Letters*. For if the farmer embodied virility and masculinity, the environment in which he labored was feminine. Within the agrarian myth the earth is both a virgin and a mother. Beyond the pastoral refuge, men and women alike are debased; the city is a seductress and trade a whore. Thus the pastoral middle ground (neither wilderness nor city) serves an important function as the setting for this myth. The farm and ranch lands of the American prairies and Great Plains have offered a stage that authors from Walter Prescott Webb to Annette Kolodny to Jane Tompkins have claimed as particularly well-suited to acting out the drama of gender construction.[3]

For more than two decades, ecofeminist theory has explored discursive connections between nature and woman and in doing so has offered an alternative analysis of environmental degradation. D'Eaubonne, who coined the term ecofeminism in 1974, explicitly linked the consequences of male domination of both the land and women. Arguing that the "male system" (neither specifically capitalist nor socialist) has "seized control of the soil, thus of fertility (later, industry), and of woman's womb (thus fecundity)," the result has been a "double peril, menacing and parallel: overpopulation (a glut of births) and destruction of the environment (a glut of products)" (quoted in Bullis, 1996, p. 124). It is important to note, as does Connie Bullis, that examining these long-standing discursive links between nature and woman is not to claim that such a connection is either "natural" or "essential" (p. 125). Instead, such analysis "functions as a material, historical grounding to encourage a better understanding of how current discourse evolved and how it oppresses" (p. 125). Within these films, the links between gender and nature are more fluid than fixed, further supporting the ways in which films both reveal and shape cultural change.

The agrarian myth has been tempered somewhat with the passage of time. Of interest are not only its surviving features but the details which have changed, and the ways in which both constrain these films. Examining the agrarian myth as the machine begins to enter the garden brings these adaptations into sharp focus, for the reliance on tractors rather than horses facilitated important changes in farming practices and farm economics. The wide-scale introduction of these technologies roughly corresponds to the time frame covered by these films, and the resulting Hollywood revisions to the agrarian myth alter our view of the garden and its residents, both male and female.[4]

HOLLYWOOD'S GARDEN

The farm settings depicted in King Vidor's *Our Daily Bread* (1934) and Jean Renoir's *The Southerner* (1945) represent an Eden in the midst of economic hardship. These films may, in fact, borrow as much from Genesis as from the agrarian myth. Though the first is conceived as a collectivist farm (pooling together the skills and labor of families displaced by the Depression) and the second a tribute to the independence and self-sufficiency of the nuclear family, both films advocate renewal distinctly outside the confines of the city.

Yet, in contrast with both the agrarian myth and later films, the land serves as a proving ground, not property. While these farms offer a setting in which to demonstrate character, in both films it is a borrowed stage. Neither family owns the land they farm; they are temporary tenants only. Their presence results from someone else's generosity, a gift that once given is never mentioned again.

Farming offers the male protagonists an opportunity to prove themselves as men, testing their ideas and their skills alike. As Sam Tucker of *The Southerner* explains, "I can do it all in my own way, and don't have to answer to nobody." Farming offers the female protagonists an opportunity to prove themselves as wives and mothers, standing staunchly beside their husbands, holding the family (or a collectivist community) together. More interesting than the simple fact of their heroism is its texture. The virtues extolled in these films are depicted as inversely proportional to the technologies employed. No tractors are ever shown in either *Our Daily Bread* or *The Southerner* — though an early scene in the former establishes that a tractor (of some sort) exists.[5] In *The Southerner* the one character who mentions the possibility of Sam and Nona Tucker eventually getting a tractor has been clearly positioned throughout the film as the representative and defender of the city. While his ideas are treated with respect, the Tuckers clearly occupy the moral high ground.

Though the new Eden of Vidor's *Our Daily Bread* admits some sin (including temptation in the form of Pepper, a "slovenly, slatternly city girl," who briefly lures John Sims away from both his wife and the farm [Nash, 1985, p. 2295]), it is heroism and the work ethic in the form of hard physical labor that the film celebrates.

A scene to meant to illustrate the promise of communal effort gathers men and plows together at the edge of the field to begin the farming cycle. A single horse pulls the first plow out into the field as John pronounces, "We start here." Next, six men in harness drag a second plow and the camera lingers on the image. A motorcycle pulls a third plow; two cars line up to tow the next two plows. Finally, men armed only with shovels and axes march out across the field.

In the film's climactic ending, men wielding shovels and pickaxes labor together in "some of the most dramatic and dynamic scenes ever put on celluloid" (Nash, 1985, p. 2295) to dig an irrigation ditch. For nine full minutes the audience watches bare-chested men with sweat glistening on their shoulders swinging pickaxes and shovels, felling shrubs and trees with machetes, axes, and saws, hefting boulders by brute force (and with the help of the horse). Day turns to night and back to day again before the trench is completed, the signal given, and the water allowed to rush downstream toward the parched cornfield. For three more minutes the camera follows the water's path as men shore up the channel with boulders and boards and their own bodies. The message throughout is clear: sheer will and muscle have harnessed nature to battle nature. Brawn and brain have saved the crop. This is the work of men.

Women and children cheer on the men and some few grab a shovel to help dig the irrigation ditch's final feet. But their true role throughout has been to offer comfort and encouragement to the men, and to model purity and fidelity to the dream. If men are measured by their actions, women's value lies in their spiritual and metaphorical relationship to the land.

In *Our Daily Bread*, Mary Sims sits alone at the field's edge, gazing at the newly sprouted corn. Her husband John, the transplanted city dweller, joins her and remarks in awe,

John: It really works, doesn't it?

Mary: Of course, didn't you think it would?

John: It makes you feel safe, confident. Well, like somebody was kinda watching over you. . . . There's nothing for people to worry about. Not when they've got the earth. It's like, like a mother. It's wonderful.

To make this point even more explicit, the other members of the commune gather behind John and Mary. One man leads the rest in prayer; another announces the birth of a child.

In Jean Renoir's 1945 film *The Southerner*, the earth is gendered both masculine and feminine in instructive analogies. When the Tucker family first arrives on the farm, Sam assures Nona that the land which has lain fallow for years is good. "With dirt like this a fellow could raise the best crop in the country. . . .

The earth's kinda like men, you know. It needs a rest every once in a while. Maybe that's the reason the Lord invented Sundays." It's safe to presume that "men" is not used generically (for humans) in this scene. The work week described is one reserved for paid laborers, not those performing childcare or housework (double) duties.

In a later scene in *The Southerner*, Sam offers a second personified description of the land (now planted in cotton but flooded by a violent storm). Though he first draws a parallel between himself and the land, he then genders it feminine: "For a while I didn't seem to believe in nothing no more. But now my clothes are starting to dry. I'm beginning to believe again. I guess that's the way the earth feels when she's wet. But the sun will start drying her out and she'll start calling to me again, just the way Nona does sometimes." The earth here is neither a virgin nor a whore, but a loving wife (and presumably, by extension, a mother).

Finally, it is worth noting that this film ends with a flood. No technological "solution" is offered. Instead viewers are left to believe that this family will simply persevere, plant a new crop, hope for a better year. For the director Jean Renoir (1974), "What I saw was a story in which all the characters were heroic, in which every element would brilliantly play its part, in which things and men, animals and Nature, all would come together in an immense act of homage to the divinity" (p. 234). Nash (1985) elaborates, "In *The Southerner*, man is just another part which makes up the whole of this land, he is not in control of the divine elements but subject to their wrath" (p. 3053). *The Southerner*'s garden remains distinctly anti-technological. Though death and temptation have entered Eden, the machine has not yet slipped through its gates.

While these films convey the agrarian myth in its most pristine form, they leave a rather significant hole at its center: agriculture itself. A physician in *The Southerner* encourages the Tuckers to raise vegetables for their child. They plant the fields in cotton. No garden at all is shown in *Our Daily Bread*, though dozens of families needing to eat populate the collectivist farm. Their fields are planted in corn, a crop grown not for (direct) human consumption, but to feed cattle. (It is doubtful they could grow and sell enough corn to buy enough beef to feed them all.)

TECHNOLOGY'S HARVEST

When the machine enters the garden, it redefines both the garden and its inhabitants. John Ford's *The Grapes of Wrath* (1940) serves as a pivotal film in this transformation, greeting the entrance of the machine with profound distrust, yet foreshadowing the myth's later re-workings. A decade later, as the 1950 musical *Summer Stock* illustrates, Hollywood's revised version of the agrarian myth was firmly established. Its formula reappears in the 1980s farm films (no matter the decade they depict). Virtually every relationship explored by these later farm films changes: the characters' connection to the land, to each other, to technology. Throughout, the agrarian myth is stretched and pulled, but not relinquished.

The land is no longer a gift, a temporary refuge and opportunity to start anew, but an inheritance fraught with economic and emotional weight. The films repeatedly emphasize the significance of deep-rooted family ties to a particular tract of land. Muley, the Joads' Oklahoma neighbor in *The Grapes of Wrath*, confronts the government agent serving his eviction notice with the words,

Well, I'm right here to tell you, Mister. There ain't nobody going to push me off my land. My grandpa took up this land 70 years ago. My Pa was born here. We was all born on it. And some of us was killed on it. And some of us died on it. That's what makes it our'n. Being born on it. And working on it. And dying. Dying on it. And not no piece of paper with writing on it.

Muley stays, forced to hide out and to draw sustenance from his gun rather than his plow. The Joads and the rest of their neighbors are forcibly evicted from the garden, however. The film makes clear that pieces of paper, representative of private property, carry considerable weight and, however suspect they may be, they do triumph. Borrowed stages no longer provide a viable setting on which to play out a pastoral dream.

The later films fail to question private property at all, but rather celebrate it. Jewell Ivy in *Country* states emphatically, "We're not going to sell this land. This land's been in my family for over 100 years." When a banker tells Tom Garvey in *The River* that he owes the bank "more than your place is worth," Tom's response is "I'm not looking to sell; I'm looking to stay." Later he reminds his wife, "This is our home place, Mae. My people are buried here." And, finally, in *A Thousand Acres*, the viewer is reminded repeatedly that the Cook family has lived on their Iowa farm for four generations. The eldest daughter, Ginny, states in the voiceover narration which opens the film, "Rose and I had lived on this land all of our lives. We never imagined living anywhere else." Severing these long-established ties is tantamount to severing family bonds. Dissolving family farms means destroying the families who reside on them.

Yet once the land is cast as property, agriculture itself is reduced to an economic enterprise. Ownership provides crucial motivation to fight the good fight. And that fight becomes two fold: against nature cast in the form of violent storms (dusters, floods, tornadoes) and against a vague (unnamed) enemy who would pull these families from their farms. At times the two enemies are joined, as when a natural disaster leaves a family vulnerable to an economic challenge and the threatened loss of the family farm.

Farms represent a landscape in which nature is contained and ordered. When nature escapes from that constrained role, it is depicted as a violent and direct threat to the family's well-being. Floods, droughts, winds/dustbowl, an invasion of grasshoppers all function literally and metaphorically in these films to alter both the physical and psychic landscape. Crops (and other property) are jeopardized or destroyed altogether; humans are endangered or injured. Nature represents a formidable, but usually only temporary, opponent. These storms function to release a crucial tension that Kolodny (1975) sees as central to the American psyche: "the sense of guilt aroused by the conflict between the impulse to see nature as bountiful and the desire to dominate it and make it bountiful" (p. 88). Both human frailty and courage can be demonstrated in the face of natural disasters, while human triumph is assured in the end. Nature is subdued and farming practices resume unchallenged.

The second enemy, usually an economic threat, in most cases becomes the central focus of these films, and two distinct strategies are deployed to depict this enemy. In *The Grapes of Wrath*, Muley's attempts to discover those responsible for his eviction result in a nearly infinite regression of denial extending from the officials to federal agencies; no one assumes responsibility. The final message of the film suggests the blame lies solely in the tenant system, not the capitalist practices that support it.[6] In the later films, villainy repeatedly is reduced to an individual level in the form of heartless local bankers and loan officers, seed company officials, and government agents. Confronted with mounting debts, Tom Garvey in *The River* reminds the unsympathetic banker, "Ten years ago you people was tripping over yourselves trying to get me to borrow the money." Similarly, Gil Ivy, the struggling farmer in *Country*, confronts the FHA loan officer in a local bar.

Gil: What are you trying to do to us, McMillen?

McMillen: Listen, you owe the money. Nobody forced you to borrow it.

Gil: Yeah, that's right. That's right. Wasn't it you who was giving all those great speeches here a few years back about 'We're going to feed the world; we're going to expand. Plant fence post to fence post.' Wasn't that you?

Farmers may be virtuous, but that doesn't necessarily prevent them from being victimized.

Regardless of the "enemy" a farmer confronts, the battles themselves become tests of character to be faced largely alone. Self-sufficiency is celebrated, though it is colored also by slight nods to community. Even so, dependence extends only to a small circle of like-minded individuals. If a farm family can't save their farm alone (from bankers or from nature), they may look temporarily to an intimate community of neighbors for assistance. Asking for such help is viewed as a difficult and significant break from tradition, albeit a necessary one. Seeking help from others, significantly, is nearly always initiated by the female lead. Again and again, these films explore the question of dependency only within a narrowly circumscribed realm and only at moments of crisis. While the underlying causes responsible for the problems faced by farm families remain cryptic, the solutions offered within the films are primarily individual. Rather than questioning or critiquing current agricultural policies and practices, the films are content to offer sympathetic portraits of individual courage in the face of personal hardship.

Hollywood farm families prove their mettle not so much by their actions (as stewards) but by their perseverance. Faced with adversity, their task is to shore up their claims of rightful ownership. Technology enters in multiple ways, yet the machine's presence in the garden is surprisingly consistent in its redefinitions of gender.

Tractors and bulldozers entered the garden of John Ford's *The Grapes of Wrath* with dire effects. There is no mistaking the sinister qualities attributed to machinery here. In an early flashback scene, Muley tells Tom what has transpired in his absence. While he speaks, the screen fills with low-angle shots of a solid phalanx of tractors rolling across a field.

Muley: They come. They come and pushed me off. They come with the cats.
Tom: What?
Muley: The cats. The Caterpillar tractors. And for every one of them, there was 10 to 15 families throwed right out of their homes. A hundred folks. And no place to live but on the road. Lots of folks you and me know. Throwed right out on the road.

In case viewers are left with any doubt about the ominous consequences of mechanization for these farm families, we are made witness (again in flashback) to the destruction of Muley's home. One of the "cats," driven by a neighbor desperate for money to support his own family, crashes through the house and continues on its way as the family stands helplessly outside. Muley cannot bring himself to fire his rifle at a man he knows, and is left impotent in the face of technological change and the destruction of a way of life. For all its phallic symbolism, the gun is clearly out-sized by a Caterpillar tractor, a far more powerful phallus.[7]

In later films the tractor continues to play an important role in constructing both masculinity and femininity. By 1984, as machines replaced muscles in performing the bulk of farm labor, depicting men's virtue required a strategy other than simply equating character with sweat and toil. At the same time, the resulting de-emphasis on physical strength offered women more prominent roles. The revised agrarian myth found a means of incorporating technology (with tractors representing a deep entrenchment in a capitalist economy) while still emphasizing independence and self-sufficiency. While the strategy employed wears on its face a feminist message, ultimately both the films' strivings for realism along with the film's purported feminism are severely undermined.

Both *The River* and *Country* (1984) contain long and detailed scenes of farmers repairing their old and well-worn farming equipment. This combination of thrift and skill becomes part of a larger lesson in manhood as a father instructs his teenaged son in the art of welding or auto mechanics. Yet the stripped down and older model farm implements and vehicles shown jar with the information we receive that these same families have somehow amassed (in the case of the Garveys in *The River*) a $214,000 debt in farm equipment alone. The Garveys sell the one new piece of farming equipment they own —a planter with a retail value of $6,000 (for which they receive $1,100). We are left to our own devices to complete the calculations required to make the remaining battered equipment add up to $208,000 even when it was new. Offered only scenes of their fiscal conservatism, we are hard pressed to understand how they could have fallen so deeply into debt. The scripts ask us to believe this is the fault of others.

The implication that these farm men have somehow failed allows the female characters in these latter films a newly expanded presence. Farm women move increasingly from the shadows (as partners and hidden wells of strength) to the foreground. This shift at times demands an absence (sometimes only temporarily) of "equal" male counterparts (*Summer Stock, Places in the Heart, The River*) or the outright emasculation of those men who remain present (*The Grapes of Wrath, Country, A Thousand Acres*). While women still assume their heroic mantle specifically as mothers with their own fecundity paralleling that found in the land, they are also empowered (and masculinized) by their adoption of technology. Tractors provide a specifically gendered solution that women seize as a means of engaging in farm labor and saving their family/farm.

The 1950 musical *Summer Stock* provides the first and most explicit instance of this shift. Judy Garland, playing the part of Jane Falbury, is faced with a debt-ridden family farm and hired hands who have abandoned her to look for work in the city. Her housekeeper is certain the women will lose the farm, unable to perform the requisite labor. "How about the field work, heavy work?" she asks. "Women can't do that." But Jane has spotted a photograph of a tractor on the wall calendar. "Yes, they can," she answers. "We could do the heavy work if we had a tractor." Jane goes to town, is given a tractor by her (presumed) future father-in-law (as a means of saving her farm from outstanding debts!), and drives it back home past men with horses and wagons. As she waves cheerily to her neighbors, she sings a particularly upbeat song whose chorus reminds us that "If you work for Mother Nature, you get paid by Father Time." The father in this case, however, is less likely to be time than the patriarchal system of market capitalism.

After successfully harvesting her first cotton crop, Sally Field as Edna Spaulding in *Places in the Heart* (1984) begins to get grandiose dreams of expansion and economic prosperity, despite the film's 1930s setting. With her first check safely pocketed, she tells Mose, her black laborer,

Edna: All we need is one good crop of cotton.
Mose: Miz Spaulding —
Edna: Just one good crop and we could afford to buy us a tractor.
Mose: A tractor. Always wanted to have me a tractor. Always felt that if I had me a tractor ain't no telling what I could do.

Mose is also swept up in this dream of (phallic) empowerment, for the tractor represents if not manhood itself, then the next best thing, the ability to compete with (white) men on their terms. (Mose, however, soon afterward is attacked by KKK members, reduced to tears, and chased off the farm. Black men would have to wait a bit longer than white women in the South for the tools of empowerment.)

In a less obvious, but equally significant way, *The River* makes it clear that the ability of Mae Garvey (played by Sissy Spacek) to run the family farm in her husband's absence depends on her mastery of farming technologies. Much of the film emphasizes the pastoral (with machinery making only occasional forays into the "garden") through scenes of children fishing, running among free-range chickens, and milking cows by hand. When Tom Garvey leaves, to work in a distant factory, Mae moves outside of the kitchen (where she has been baking bread, making pies, and teaching these same skills to her daughter) and outside of the barn (where she tended a sick cow) to the cornfield (where she assumes all of the mechanized farming chores). (The fact that she is pinned and injured by a tractor may be intended to serve, if not as a mixed message on machinery per se, then as a warning to women who stray too far into the male province. The family farm, this film implies, does need a father to keep it functioning properly.)

Technology, presumably, empowers women to farm with the same self-sufficiency deemed a virtue for men. Yet placing women in the role of field laborers neither challenges nor changes the relationship of humans to the land. In the only scene depicting pesticide application in any of these films, in fact, a woman drives the tractor (The River).[8] Thus a form of feminism is invoked (more or less explicitly), appropriated as a justification for farmers to further exploit the land — and to become even more deeply entangled within a capitalist (patriarchal) economic system. But it is clearly a pseudo-feminism that encourages only the adoption of masculine models for dominating and exploiting the land. Again, agricultural practices themselves are left unexamined. Instead we are asked to marvel at feminine spunk, while ignoring that it is yoked to the machinery of environmental degradation.

But even when a Hollywood film does begin to explore the environmental consequences of current agricultural practices, any feminist message it may offer is even further confused. A Thousand Acres (1997) poses explicit links between women and the land, treating them as equivalents in a clearly post-Edenic state. Ginny (played by Jessica Lange) and Rose (played by Michelle Pfeiffer), who have spent their entire lives on the thousand-acre family farm in central Iowa, are physically marked by that close association. Rose suffers from breast cancer (the same disease that killed her mother); Ginny has suffered five miscarriages. The implication (made explicit in Ginny's case) is that the practices associated with intensive agriculture, specifically the use of chemical fertilizers, pesticides, and herbicides, may be directly linked to these health problems. The incest theme that underscores this film offers yet one other means of equating women and the land. Just as their father Larry has subdued those thousand acres, so has he controlled his daughters. The land, formerly under water, has been transformed through a (largely invisible) system of tiles and drainage ditches. Similarly, his uncontrolled sexuality has left deep psychic scars on both Ginny and Rose.

When Rose inherits the land, however, she is unable to alter past patterns of destruction. On her deathbed, she tells Ginny: "I don't have any accomplishments. . . . I didn't work the farm successfully. . . . All the people around town talk about how I wrecked it all. Three generations on the same land. Great land.

Daddy a marvelous farmer and a saint to boot." The land is slated to be sold off to a giant agricultural corporation. The family has been fractured and largely destroyed, all in seeming accordance with Larry Cook's prediction, "By God, they'll starve. The land won't produce for the likes of them." Land and woman are equated, but only to remind us that both are vulnerable and damaged. The feminine model ultimately is powerless to effect change.

CONCLUSION

The agrarian myth plays an essential role in these Hollywood films, but in a way that obscures rather than clarifies our view. For Jefferson the virtues exemplified by farm families depended on direct links between production and consumption. In Hollywood films employing only a partial version of the myth, those virtues still exist, but independent of any larger context, making them (at once and ironically) individual, universal, and inscrutable. The myth's presence in its partial form excludes from even the widest cinema screen a great deal of agriculture. These films set us down on the farm, introduce us to a family (and perhaps a few of their neighbors), allow us occasional (and always frustrating) forays into town, and gesture only vaguely at a still larger world. We learn (in sometimes intimate detail) all about the family, but little about the farm. Audiences watching these films may leave the theater feeling sympathy for the struggles faced by individual farmers and supportive of the concept of the family farm. But they would be hard pressed to carry the "lessons" learned from these films very far. Within these films, the agrarian myth reaffirms the familiar (individual virtue), but ultimately clouds and confuses the relationship of agriculture to the environment or to capitalism.[9]

Rather than bridging the gap between urban and rural citizens, then, again and again these films construct a different gap, one that lies between an agrarian and pastoral myth and the commercialized, corporate forms of agriculture practiced in the United States (and exported abroad). What these films never ask, perhaps what they cannot ask, is why these farmers are growing only corn or only cotton. Why are they tied to producing a cash crop, reproducing a capitalist manufacturing and market system? Even in embracing a seemingly feminist sensibility, these films serve only to reproduce rather than question the status quo of contemporary American agriculture. The prominence given to the female characters in these films serves to promote and further justify capitalist practices. Men are emasculated and women are granted independence, but only through the
temporary beneficence of patriarchy. Rather than offering an alternative vision, the pseudo-feminism employed by these films serves to further oppress and subordinate women and the land.

The purpose of this chapter's examination of the agrarian myth and its presence in Hollywood films is not to abolish it once and for all in order to further pave the way in agriculture for the "inevitable results of the industrial revolution" (Griswold, 1948, p. 8). Instead, the intent lies in whether the myth, by illustrating the direction and distance of our drift, might perform the opposite task, leading us toward an agriculture both local and sustainable. Myths, as Robert Reich (1988) has noted, "are no more 'truth' than an architect's sketches are buildings. Their function is to explain events and to guide decisions" (p. 40). The agrarian myth as currently played serves neither function, but the fact that it still speaks at all suggests we would be wise to listen. Myths can serve as useful cultural tools, but only to the extent that they bridge gaps rather than further erode them. And film may represent the most effective medium with which to cross a cultural divide, drawing audiences willing both to look and to learn. The agrarian myth (examined in full, updated, and made responsive to local contexts) along with a genuine eco-feminist critique might yet serve as a blueprint for refashioning a healthier agriculture, a guide for reconnecting urban and rural lives, farm fields and family tables. Only with those connections in place will our vision match the myths we cherish.

NOTES

1. This represents only a very partial listing of ecological problems confronting agriculture. For further information see Lester Brown, ed. (1989), *State of the World, 1989*; Wes Jackson (1980), *New Roots for Agriculture*; Ronald Poincelot (1986), *Toward a More Sustainable Agriculture*; and Judith D. Soule (1992), *Farming in Nature's Image: An Ecological Approach to Agriculture*.

2. While the films discussed in this chapter (and the additional films listed in the bibliography) do not represent an exhaustive list of all farm films, they represent my best efforts to include those major studio (and a handful of independent) American films that directly concern farming or farmers' lives or in which a farm setting plays a significant role. The full list ranges in date from D. W. Griffith's 1920 *Way Down East* to the 1998 documentary *The Farmer's Wife*. Two recent documentaries—*Troublesome Creek: A Midwestern* and *The Farmer's Wife* — are highly recommended as offering views that clarify many of many of the issues discussed in this essay.

3. For further discussion of these points, see Thomas Jefferson (1787/1982), *Notes on the State of Virginia*; Richard Hofstadter (1969), *The Age of Reform*; A. Whitney Griswold (1948), *Farming and Democracy*; Walter Prescott Webb (1931), *The Great Plains*; Henry Nash Smith (1978), *Virgin Land: The American West as Symbol and Myth*; Leo Marx (1964), *The Machine in the Garden: Technology and the Pastoral Ideal in America*; Annette Kolodny (1975 and 1984), *The Lay of the Land: Metaphor as Experience and History in American Life and Letters*, and *The Land Before Her: Fantasy and Experience of the American Frontiers, 1630-1860*; and Jane Tompkins (1992), *West of Everything: The Inner Life of Westerns*.

4. Gasoline-powered tractors were first available about 1910. Ownership grew fairly steadily, though with distinct spurts corresponding to World War I and following World War II. According to the *Historical Statistics of the United States: Colonel Times to 1970* (1975), even following the World War I spurt, under 1 million gasoline tractors were in use in 1930 and their numbers had increased to only 1.5 million in 1940. Tractor ownership almost doubled in the first decade following World War II, from 2.3 million in 1945 to 4.3 million in 1955. The figures have remained fairly constant since then, indicating that by the mid- to late 1950s nearly all US farms had converted from using horses to tractors (469).

5. John questions a prospective member of the collective whose responses cast him as both sinister and aloof.

John: What can you do?

Louie: What's to be done?

John: Didn't you see the signs? We need men skilled in basic trades like farmers, carpenters, mechanics.

Louie: Have you got a tractor?

John: Well, you could call it that.

Louie: I'll drive the tractor.

John: Do you know anything about farming?

Louie: I said I'd drive the tractor.

While the stranger stays on, neither he nor anyone else ever drives a tractor across farm fields or cinema screen.

6. Ultimately, even Muley seems to conclude that nature is responsible for what befalls the Okies. "Listen. That's the one that done it," he tells Tom. "Dusters, they started it anyways. Blowing like this year after year. Blowing the land away. Blowing the crops away. Blowing us away now." His words echo the government agent's view, "The fact of the matter, Muley, after what them dusters done to the land, the tenant system don't work no more."

7. It is not only Muley whose masculinity is challenged in this film. The Joad men relinquish their male prerogative one by one. Grandpa dies, Tom is forced to leave. In Ma's farewell speech to Tom, she makes this point explicit. "Noah, he's a hankering to be off on his own. Uncle John's just dragging around. And Pa's lost his place; he ain't the head no more." Even the youngest son, Winfield, is growing up wild, "just like [an] animal."

8. The fair-skinned Sissy Spacek, dressed in a sleeveless shirt in this scene, wears no protection against either the sun or the agricultural chemicals she is applying, conveying a message that these known carcinogens pose little danger. The films seem insistent in their depiction of the pastoral landscape as a safe and healthy refuge.

9. Ironically in Senate hearings concerning the plight of the family farm during the mid-1980s, Jessica Lange, Sissy Spacek, and Sally Field were invited (presumably as expert witnesses) to testify. The confusion between the mythic farm (especially one of Hollywood proportions) and the lived experience of farm families may be even more pronounced than this chapter can begin to explain.

FILM SUMMARIES

Our Daily Bread (1934): John and Mary Sims flee unemployment in the city and start a collective farm on her uncle's land. The corn crop is threatened by drought, but the farm's residents dig an irrigation ditch and divert water from a nearby stream.

The Grapes of Wrath (1940): Based on John Steinbeck's novel, the film follows the Joad family's migration from Oklahoma to California and their experiences in farm labor camps.

The Southerner (1945): The Tucker family battles poverty, illness, a hostile neighbor, and a flood in their first year of farming, but persevere and prepare for a second year.

Summer Stock (1950): A summer theater company takes over the barn on the Wingate farm for their musical production—and helps out with the farm chores. Judy Garland stars as farm woman turned leading lady.

Country (1984): The Ivy family of Iowa faces the 1980s farm crisis. When the bank threatens to foreclose on their loan, both the family and the farm are threatened. Gil seeks solace in alcohol; his wife, Jewell, tries to organize neighbors to stop their farm sale.

Places in the Heart (1984): Set in Texas in the 1930s, the film follows Edna Spaulding's struggle to keep her family together following her husband's murder. With the help of Mose (a black farmhand) and Mr. Will (a blind boarder), she raises, harvests, and sells a cotton crop.

The River (1984): Tom and Mae Garvey battle floods and an attempt by the owner of a local seed company to acquire their property as part of his plan to build a dam and reservoir. Tom is forced to take temporary scab factory work for extra income while Mae keeps the farm operating.

A Thousand Acres (1997): When Larry Cook decides to turn the farm into a corporation, a struggle reminiscent of King Lear ensues. The family is divided and broken (amid sibling rivalries, marital difficulties, and recovered memories of incest), and the farm is lost.

FILM BIBLIOGRAPHY

Blessing (1994, USA). Director: Paul Zehrer.
Country (1984, Touchstone). Director: Richard Pearce.
Days of Heaven (1980, Paramount). Director: Terrence Malick.
The Farmer's Daughter (1947, David O. Selznick). Director: H. C. Potter.
The Farmer's Wife (1998, David Sutherland Productions/Independent Television
      Service ITVS). Director: David Sutherland.
The Grapes of Wrath (1940, Fox). Director: John Ford.
Heartland (1980, Wilderness Women Productions). Director: Richard Pearce.
The Man in the Moon (1991, MGM/United Artists). Director: Robert Mulligan.
The Milagro Beanfield War (1988, MCA). Director: Robert Redford.
Northern Lights (1978, Cine Manifest). Directors: John Hanson and Rob
      Nilsson.
Our Daily Bread (1934, Viking). Director: King Vidor.
Places in the Heart (1984, Tri-Star). Director: Robert Benton.
Rebecca of Sunnybrook Farm (1921, Fox). Director: Alfred Santell.
The River (1984, Universal). Director: Mark Rydell.
Sarah, Plain and Tall (1991, Hallmark Hall of Fame). Director: Glenn Jordan.
The Southerner (1945, United Artists). Director: Jean Renoir.
Summer Heat (1987, Paramount). Director: Michie Gleason.
Summer Stock (1950, MGM). Director: Charles Walters.

A Thousand Acres (1997, Touchstone). Director: Jocelyn Moorhouse.
Tomorrow (1971, Filmgroup). Director: Joseph Anthony.
Troublesome Creek (1995, West City Films, Inc.). Directors: Steven Ascher and
Jeanne Jordan.
Way Down East (1920, D. W. Griffith). Director: D. W. Griffith.
Witness (1985, Paramount). Director: Peter Weir.

REFERENCES

Brown, L. (Ed.). (1989). *State of the world, 1989*. New York: Norton.
Bullis, C. (1996). Retalking environmental discourses from a feminist perspective: The
radical potential of ecofeminism. *The symbolic earth: Discourse and our creation of
the environment*. In J. G. Cantrill and C. L. Oravec, (Eds.). Lexington: University of
Kentucky Press.
Campbell, J. (1988). *The power of myth*. (B. S. Flowers, Ed.). New York: Doubleday.
Carey, J. (1989). *Communication as culture: Essays on media and society*. Boston: Unwin
Hyman.
Clover, C. (1992). *Men, women, and chain saws*. Princeton, NJ: Princeton University
Press.
Collins, J., Radner, H, & Collins, A. P., (Eds.). (1993). *Film theory goes to the movies*.
New York: Routledge.
Desser, D. & Joweet, G. S. (Eds.). (2000). *Hollywood goes shopping*. Minneapolis:
University of Minnesota Press.
Eliade, M. (1963). *Myth and reality*. (W. R. Trask, Trans.). New York: Harper & Row.
Griswold, A. W. (1948). *Farming and democracy*. New Haven, CT: Yale University Press.
Historical statistics of the United States: Colonial times to 1970. (1975). Washington, DC:
U.S. Department. of Commerce, Bureau of the Census.
Hofstadter, R. (1969). *The age of reform*. New York: Knopf.
Jackson, W. (1980). *New roots for agriculture*. Lincoln: University of Nebraska Press.
Jefferson, T. (1787/1982). *Notes on the state of Virginia*. (W. Peden, Ed.). New York:
Norton.
Kolodny, A. (1975). *The lay of the land: Metaphor as experience and history in American
letters*. Chapel Hill: University of North Carolina Press.
Kolodny, A. (1984). *The land before her: Fantasy and experience of the American fron-
tiers, 1630 - 1860*. Chapel Hill: University of North Carolina Press.
Marx, L. (1964). *The machine in the garden: Technology and the pastoral ideal in
America*. New York: Oxford University Press.
Nash, J. R. (1985). *The motion picture guide*. Chicago: Cinebooks.
Poincelot, R. P. (1986). *Toward a more sustainable agriculture*. Westport, CT: AVI.
Reich, R. (1988). *Tales of a new America: The anxious liberal's guide to the future*. New
York: Random House.
Renoir, J. (1974). *My life and my films*. London: Collins.
Smith, H. N. (1978). *Virgin land: The American west as symbol and myth*. Cambridge,
MA: Harvard University Press.
Soule, J. D. & Piper, J. K. (1992). *Farming in nature's image: An ecological approach to
agriculture*. Washington, DC: Island Press.
Statistical abstract of the United States: 1999. 119th ed. Washington, DC: U.S.
Department of Commerce, Bureau of the Census.
Tompkins, J. (1992). *West of everything: The inner life of westerns*. New York: Oxford

University Press.
Webb, W. P. (1931). *The great plains*. New York: Grosset & Dunlap.

5

Prime-Time Subversion: The Environmental Rhetoric of *The Simpsons*

Anne Marie Todd

On April 19, 1987, America was introduced to the Simpsons, the title family of the first animated prime-time television series since the 1960s. Described by its creator and executive producer Matt Groening as "a celebration of the American family at its wildest" (Steiger, 1999, p. 1), *The Simpsons* offered a critical view of mainstream social and cultural norms. In a television world dominated by upper-middle-class storybook families like the Huxtables of *The Cosby Show*, *The Simpsons* presented a satirical documentary of a more complex family whose characters and plots related more directly to the familial experience of America's television audience. In fact, *The Simpsons* first aired on prime-time television opposite *The Cosby Show*, assuming a revolutionary position toward mainstream television and the network establishment. The series exhibited a realism that appealed to a widely diverse audience and established *The Simpsons* as a fixture of American prime-time. When the show debuted, it quickly became the FOX Network's highest rated program (Korte, 1997, p. 1). The success of *The Simpsons* is evident in the show's impressive popularity with a heterogeneous audience that spans generations. The program has also won critical acclaim, and has received numerous awards, including the Peabody Award (1997), the People's Choice Award (1990-1991) and several Emmies (Steiger, 1999, p. 2). As Steiger argued, *The Simpsons'* "vicious social satire" and subtly profound "pop-culture allusions" had a "considerable impact on the television landscape of the nation" (p. 2).

Multiple layers of profound social and cultural commentary distinguish *The Simpsons* from conventional television programs. "The critical humor, self-reflexiveness, intertextuality and form" of *The Simpsons* solidify the literary significance of the series' postmodern commentary (Korte, 1997, p. 3). Such rhetorical elements help establish the Simpson family as an icon of American popular culture. In 1998, *Time* magazine listed Bart Simpson on behalf of the entire series as one of the key cultural and most influential figures of the twentieth century (Steiger, 1999, p. 2). The realism of the characters and plot lines of *The Simpsons* give the series a dramatic quality; the Simpsons' family adventures expose the nuances of American family life while simultaneously informing the social and cultural experience of the television audience.

Critical and popular acclaim for *The Simpsons* distinguishes the series as a rich multi dimensional text for rhetorical analysis. In countless interviews, Matt Groening has described *The Simpsons* as a show that rewards its audience for paying attention (1997, p. 9). As the most counter cultural cartoon to hit prime-time, the series is ripe for rhetorical inquiry into its potential as a vehicle for critical political and social commentary. *The Simpsons* contributes significantly to critical analysis of popular culture, particularly in the study of television media because the show is more literary and complex than regular television programming (Korte, 1997, p. 7). In a decade, *The Simpsons* has secured immense popularity, and its established prime-time slot confirms the magnitude of the show's viewing audience. With its copious literary and cinematic references and interminable political commentary, *The Simpsons* is indisputably embedded in American culture, and thus offers a lens into the rhetorical dimensions of human experience. Rhetorical analysis of popular culture is indispensable in the exposition of the social, cultural, and political motivations of human action. Our understanding of meaning and our comprehension of rhetorical symbols are best achieved through the explication of human motives. Rhetorical analysis of popular culture discloses how communication of symbols in the interpretation of personal experience promotes a persuasive rhetoric that engenders critical commentary regarding the social and cultural dimensions of human experience.

This chapter explicates the meaning and significance of *The Simpsons'* social commentary through two mediums of rhetorical criticism. The first method of analysis utilizes Kenneth Burke's (1959) comic frame to determine the meaning of the show's multi textual rhetoric. Analysis of televisual communication requires an enhanced application of the comic form through a second mode of inquiry, the explication of the symbolism of *The Simpsons'* visual argument. The show presents a unique rhetorical form that exhibits profound pop-cultural influence, and in particular makes a significant impression on American environmental consciousness. This analysis begins with an explication of the utility of the comic frame and visual argument as prolific tools of rhetorical criticism. The synthesis of these two approaches engenders an enriched analysis, which articulates *The Simpsons'* intertextual environmental rhetoric. Next, the convergence of comic and visual critical practices is examined, which illuminates the symbolic elements of the show's environmental rhetoric. The abundance of episodic material, teeming with rich dialogue and resplendent visuals, rendered focusing this analysis an enigmatic task. As a directive for this criticism, two predominant metaphors are explored:

Springfield's nuclear power plant as an icon of irresponsible energy use and the figurative role of nonhuman characters in the series. This project's conclusion articulates the coherent ecological message in *The Simpsons'* rhetoric, and thus renders a conclusive evaluation of the show's televisual environmental commentary. Specifically, I propose that the show's rhetoric presents a strong environmental message regarding the relationship between humans and the rest of nature.

This message is most clearly articulated in the show's rhetorical strategies, which reveal a pervasive ecological criticism of human activity, produced through comedy and visual argument—rhetorical tools that successfully engage the audience in *The Simpsons'* critical environmental commentary. This rhetorical criticism examines the first ten seasons of the series in recognition of the rhetorical force with which these animated social texts exhibit the interface of environmental communication and popular culture. The analysis was conducted by viewing various collected videotapes of the series' first ten seasons (4/9/87–5/16/99)—approximately 80 percent of the episodes—and supplemented with data from Matt Groening's two-volume guide to the show. The ten years of episodes in the sample provide hundreds of rhetorical propositions of ecological tone. Conducting a satisfactory analysis of all such references in the confines of this chapter is impossible. Thus, I focused primarily (almost exclusively) on the show's principal environmental symbols and themes. As a result, the discussion focuses on only a few entire episodes, significant plot lines, familiar environmental themes, and explicit recurring rhetorical symbols. Focusing on the dominant characteristics of *The Simpsons'* environmental limited the scope of criticism and thus fostered a more informed evaluation of the show's overall environmental message. These televised visual and linguistic images disclose that the show itself is an expression of environmental activism and expose the salience of *The Simpsons'* environmental rhetoric.

THE COMIC FRAME: TRANSCENDING THE SOCIAL
ORDER THROUGH SYMBOLIC ACTION

In *A Rhetoric of Motives* (1950), Kenneth Burke describes the study of rhetoric as the understanding of human motives, and his theory of symbolic action provides the basis for innumerable conceptions of the study of rhetoric. Contextualizing the comic frame within a theory of rhetoric as symbolic action, Arne Madsen cites Burke's definition of humans as symbol-using creatures that construct responses to everyday experience's. That is, human action involves using and manipulating symbols to respond to interpretations of experience (Madsen, 1993, p. 166). In this way, rhetorical criticism relies on the explication of symbols to understand human responses to experience. The rhetorical critic must analyze such behavior in order to understand human motives and to comprehend how the manipulation of symbols influences human behavior. Burke expounds on this concept of symbolic rhetoric as an explanation for human motivation in *Language as*

Symbolic Action (1966). He argues that human communication involves the expression of symbolic meaning in order to directly influence the behavior and conduct of one's audience (Burke, 1966, p. 28). That is, we use symbols to construct arguments, and conceptually plan courses of action based on our interpretation of our experience.

This discussion of the symbolic expression of motives provides a context for Burke's presentation of the comic frame in *Attitudes toward History* (1959). He introduces the comic frame as a means to enhance scholars' understanding of human motivations and foster better evaluation of the social and cultural meaning of symbolic action. The comic frame enables individuals to "be observers of themselves, while acting [to create] maximum consciousness. One would transcend himself by noting his own foibles" (Burke, 1959, p. 171). Burke envisioned that applying the comic frame would create social consciousness to exposed the impotence of the status quo— the existing social order—and create public awareness to address the failings of the social system. The comic frame fosters more than an ironic self-aware-ness, but also constructs a position of semi-detachment, where one is able to reflect and comment on human foibles without guilt, shame, or other nega-tive emotion, or without undue involvement in the human comedy. Toward this end, Burke established the utility of frames as tools for rhetorical criticism; he described frames as the perspectives that direct all interpretations of human experience. That is, frames provide symbolic structure that enables human beings to impose order upon their personal and social experiences. Rhetorical criticism involves the dual-purposed application of frames to episodes of human experience—frames function as blueprints for actions that fix social attitudes according to a particular perspective. Frames also embody attitudes and motives, empowering scholars to determine various social and cultural forms of symbolic action (Burke, 1959, p. 20). In this way, the comic frame enriches rhetorical criticism by revealing the flaws of the present system, enabling alternative discourse to gain public recogni-tion.

Comedy provides the means to criticize one's own complicity in the dominant social order. By acknowledging the failings of the bureaucratic system, humans create discursive space for self-analysis. Such personal criti-cism invokes a discourse that promotes historically marginalized opinions within the public sphere. Thus, the comic frame is rhetorically powerful on two levels: through recognition of human error as the cause of social ills, and through the spiritual and moral identification with humanity. By creating social distance between reformers and the clown as a scapegoat, the comic frame also conveys a preference for a social upbraiding, rather than malicious immolation, to promote the rapprochement engendered by comic consciousness. *The Simpsons* utilizes the comic frame to identify the incongruity of human action and the symbolic interpretation of the ecological context of our experience.

POPULAR CULTURE IMAGERY AS SOCIAL COMMENTARY: THE RHETORIC OF VISUAL ARGUMENT

The coherence of the environmental message of *The Simpsons* is enriched by the show's televisual rhetorical form. The series' animated realism informs traditional methods of rhetorical criticism by illuminating tactics of visual argument. Contemporary rhetorical theory, guided by Susanne Langer, Kenneth Burke, Ernest Bormann and others, emphasizes the symbolic form of rhetorical discourse (Klumpp & Hollihan, 1989, p. 88). Accordingly, the persuasive force of rhetoric is rooted in the motivational power of symbol, located in the relationship between rhetoric and the reality of the social order. The rhetorical critic's objective is to illuminate and evaluate persuasive messages (Andrews, 1990, p. 14) and thus determine the ways in which rhetorical discourse functions as symbolic action in response to different rhetorical situations. Rhetorical criticism is concerned with the persuasiveness of discourse through the "creation of social forms in human symbolic behavior" (Klumpp & Hollihan, 1989, p. 88). That is, the salience of rhetorical propositions is largely based on the correspondence of the symbolic value of a discourse with the established meaning of the existing social order. Stating the case for visual communication, Blair (1996) argues that "the concept of visual argument is an extension of rhetoric's paradigm into a new domain...[R]hetoric in a broader sense is the use of symbols to communicate...[A]ny form of persuasion, including visual persuasion, belongs within rhetoric's province" (p. 37). With the emergence of visual communication as an acknowledged persuasive force, rhetorical critics must identify ways to evaluate the meaning of visual arguments.

Contemporary analysis of the social and cultural context of human communication must account for the increased mediation of rhetorical messages. Analysis of televised communication acts requires amplified discursive frames to evaluate the complex argumentation strategies fostered by expanded media formats. Television media enjoy a substantially larger audience than traditional rhetorical settings, and thus must account for the diverse experiences of television viewers. In addition, televised messages are informed by the broader context of rhetorical symbols and are thus enabled to offer critical commentary on the social, cultural, and political experience of the American viewing public. Gronbeck (1995) offers a defense of visual argument, and argues that rhetorical meaning requires interpretation to decode the symbols of a message. He posits that symbolic meaning is not exclusively linguistic, and visual, aural, and other symbolic systems can offer propositions that affirm or deny social and cultural experience (p. 539).

Visual media are capable of symbolic expression because they are rooted in a particularly rich context of social, cultural and political influences. The complexities of the existing social order are manifest in the stream of televised visual images—elemental, socio-cultural interpretations of human experience. Effective visual communication exhibits rich and visual symbolism that incorporates signs and symbols of conventionalized images (Blair, 1996, p. 25). The symbolic form of visual argument is deeply rooted in the context of pop culture, a rubric for the innumerable vernacular of consumer cultural images. For this reason, visual arguments enjoy an appeal that eludes verbal communication: ocular recognition of pictorial images evokes meaning that is rooted in the memory of personal experience. Visual messages persuade because they provoke "unconscious identifications," which are not possible with the linguistic basis of verbal images (Blair, 1996, p. 34). Thus, visual images persuade because they give meaning to personal experience by connecting thematic elements of shared social experience (whether televised experience or actual, real experience) to individual perception. Audience members incorporate the symbolic meaning of the visual image(s) into their personal value system, affecting their individual and social worldviews (Blair, 1996, p. 34). The symbolism of visual images remains ambiguous without a stabilizing linguistic text. Thus, the rhetorical force of one visual image appeals to a heterogeneous audience because pictorial symbols adapt to individualized experience, and encompass many meanings.

Visual argument is gaining particular ascendance as a rhetorical device with the technological improvement of visual communication, notably the advent of digital technology and the remarkable realism of computer animation. A rhetoric of visual discourse employs aesthetic symbols to inform social action. Visual tactics of communication rely on personal allegiances and affinities, which evoke dramatic reactions based on the rhetorical force of the visual image. Individual interpretation entails the personal association of familiar visual images within a normalizing social context. Such personal interpretation makes individual actions meaningful because the actions are grounded in a social context, and the social context in turn guides individual behavior according to established social and cultural norms. Visual argument facilitates social change by compelling individuals to modify their behavior to accommodate the symbolic norms of visual discourse. Visual images resonate with personal experience, facilitating the production of social meaning. Furthermore, visual argument enjoys an element of realism that makes its interpretation of human experience uniquely persuasive to individuals who can understand the context of the rhetorical message.

The Simpsons is an animated cartoon rather than a show filmed with real actors in an actual physical setting. The animation creates an air of detachment from real life, in addition to the detachment created by the comic frame. Animation is a particularly salient medium to television viewers who can suspend belief for plot development (which they would not be able to do with real characters). At the same time, the show establishes a personal connection with viewers because the characters are believable.

Television programming is provocative because it engages the audience through the mediation of social situations, which imparts socially constructed norms under the guise of actual experiential knowledge. Television, particularly animation, misrepresents reality, masquerading as lived experience, in order to manipulate social contexts that provide meaning for personal experience, and guide individual action.

THE ENVIRONMENTAL POLITICS OF THE SPRINGFIELD NUCLEAR POWER PLANT

"Both overshadowing and enlightening" (Steiger, 1999, p. 4), Springfield's nuclear power plant is owned and operated by the miserly Montgomery Burns, the town's wealthiest citizen. Homer is an employee of the plant, and holds the title of safety inspector despite his egregious lack of training. A Springfield institution, the plant is prominently featured in the show as a visual scenic element or as a comedic factor in plot development. The plant's prominence as a visual symbol of the show's environmental message is exhibited in the longer version of the show's opening sequence. The camera moves in over a hillside for a view of the picturesque town, marred only by the centrally positioned image of the plant's twin smokestacks, which billow thick clouds of dark gray smoke. The rampant pollution billowing from the smokestacks juxtaposed to the unsullied town landscape is a disturbing image. This disturbing introduction exemplifies the show's dark humor, and the potent combination of visual argument and comic frame. The negative symbolic image of the plant's egregious emissions, the dark gray billowing smoke, is reinforced by its contrast with the depiction of the town, which is animated in unrealistically bright colors. The plant symbolizes the show's environmental commentary by exhibiting a wide range of ecological implications of nuclear power, in general, and of specific conditions in the building itself.

The power plant's interior affords a setting for further visual commentary regarding the pervasive negligence that characterizes company standards for disposing of nuclear waste. A recurring joke in interior scenes is the visual image of open barrels leaking bright green radioactive waste. The plant's inner recesses are overrun with barrels strewn about the halls and open areas of the plant. Painfully bright green waste, a caricature of radioactive refuse, leaks out of the barrels and even out of the trash can in the plant's coffee room (Gewirtz, 1991). The confluence of visual argument with the comic frame establishes the symbolic meaning of the leaking waste as an animated eyesore. The pervasive images of waste enhance the visual argument symbolized in the barrels. The images position the environmental rhetoric within a burlesque comic frame, which reveals the absurdity of the publicly ignored biohazard. That is, the conspicuous barrels reveal the neglect exhibited by their inadequate disposal of the barrels, and the obvious environmental hazard that they pose. The entire scene indicates the derelict administration of safety concerns.

The plant's employees remain oblivious to the adverse situation. Their blasé attitudes enhance the situation's comedic appeal. The more egregious methods of waste disposal demonstrate the comedic effect of the employees' general apathy. Lenny and Karl, Homer's coworkers, push wheelbarrows of nuclear waste down the hallways. As Lenny and Karl discuss proper locations and methods for disposal, one of the wheelbarrows crashes into a cement column and overturns. Lenny and Karl look at each other, shrug their shoulders, and continue down the hall. The waste from the overturned container spreads ominously through the passage, while the workers resume their labor apparently unaware of the toxic spill. That the employees rarely notice the plant's production of waste adds humorous appeal to this visual image, and contributes to the show's rhetorical condemnation of unsound disposal practices. *The Simpsons* mocks the nuclear safety precautions typified in the overwhelming lack of concern for the hazards of radioactive waste. Leaking radioactive waste is a visual symbol intended to evoke criticism of the pervasive human disregard for the environment.

This social criticism is made more explicit within a burlesque comedic frame, in a parody of safety videos on nuclear energy. *The Simpsons* relies on the burlesque comic frame to render its explicit criticism of current standard practices of nuclear waste disposal. In Springfield's caricature of pro-nukes propaganda, Smilin' Joe Fission describes the preferred method of disposal for nuclear waste: "I'll just put it where nobody'll find it for a million years" (Kogen & Wolodarsky, 1990). This parody represents the typical "out of sight, out of mind" strategy for waste disposal, and attacks the general disregard for the environmental consequences of nuclear waste disposal. The show uses humor to reveal the ridiculousness of such careless disposal strategies—clarifying the obvious problems with improper disposal, and subsequent disregard for the possible environmental consequences. *The Simpsons* employs a comic frame to expose the failings of the social order, and to criticize the audiences' complicity in the normalization of such environmentally unsafe methods. By making light of the impact of nuclear accidents and contamination of the environment, the show forces the audience to adopt a critical eye regarding real social practices that mirror the environmental negligence of the citizens of Springfield. In this way, the show's writers comment on the general human view of the environment and the anthropocentric methods that govern the power plant's safety code.

Through the comic frame, *The Simpsons* carefully balances harsh criticism of American bureaucratic institutions and sardonic commentary of individual consumptive habits. "The comic frame inherently bypasses the extremes of the bureaucratic mindset.... Further, the comic frame allows observation of oneself, recognizing one's own failures and limitations" (Madsen, 1993, p. 171). Members of the audience recognize themselves in the show's characters, gaining perspective on the limits and failures of their own actions. Through this self-observation, the comic frame engenders enlightened criticism of the symbolic relationships that ground social action. The comic frame enables *The Simpsons* to rhetorically connect the economic motivations for environmental exploitation with the normalizing power of profit-driven bureaucratic social institutions that foster individual anthropocentric practices.

The nuclear plant symbolizes tension between economic and environmental concerns. The plant represents the exploitation of environmental resources for wealth and power. Mr. Burns' priorities, exhibited in his operation of the plant, exemplify the attitude of economic elites and resource barons toward environmental concerns. Burns' methods of operation reveal the assumptions of characters represented by his prototype that environmental concerns are irreconcilable with economic interests. Furthermore, Burns uses his money and power to manipulate the image of his plant in order to make the environmental pollution more salient to the public.

At times *The Simpsons* abandons this charitable attitude in favor of a rhetoric well beyond the boundaries of Burke's comic frame, adopting a satiric or even burlesque style. *The Simpsons'* successful use of the burlesque comic frame is nowhere more evident than in the second season when Bart and Lisa catch a three-eyed fish while fishing near the Springfield Nuclear Reactor (Simon & Swartzwelder, 1990). When the event becomes public, a federal safety inspection team investigates the plant's emissions. In proper burlesque form, the episode chronicles the ludicrous findings of the inspection team: gum used to seal a crack in the coolant tower, a plutonium rod used as a paperweight, monitoring stations unattended, and nuclear waste shin-deep in the hallways. The Feds threaten to shut down the power plant unless Burns makes significant improvements. Rather than bring his plant up to standard, Burns runs for governor, intending to use his elected power to keep the plant open. Inevitably confronted with Blinky, the three-eyed fish—a travesty of the ecological impacts of nuclear pollution, Burns hires spin doctors to boost his public image. In a brilliant burlesque dialogue, Burns exacerbates Blinky's parodic symbolism with his dramatic interpretation of the fish's mutation as an evolutionary advance, based on the outlandish premise that three eyes are better than two.

Mr. Burns: I'm here to talk to you about my little friend, here. Blinky. Many of you consider him to be a hideous genetic mutation. Well, nothing could be further from the truth. But don't take my word for it, let's ask an actor portraying Charles Darwin what he thinks.

Darwin: Hello, Mr. Burns.

Burns: Oh, hello Charles. Be a good fellow and tell our viewers about your theory of natural selection.

Darwin: Glad to, Mr. Burns. You see, every so often Mother Nature changes her animals, giving them bigger teeth, sharper claws, longer legs, or in this case, a third eye. And if these variations turn out to be an improvement, the new animals thrive and multiply and spread across the face of the earth.

Burns: So you're saying this fish might have an advantage over other fish, that it may in fact be a kind of super-fish.

Darwin: I wouldn't mind having a third eye, would you? (Simon & Swartzwelder, 1990, in Groening, 1997, p. 38)

Mr. Burns' narrative continues the farcical tone of this episode, and performs a lampoon of evolutionary theory. Appealing to the authority of (an actor playing) Charles Darwin, Burns dismisses Blinky's (the so-called super-fish) state as a "hideous" blunder by Mother Nature. He characterizes Blinky's extra eye as an improvement on Mother Nature's original creation, and explains the mutation as the result of the evolutionary process of natural selection that begets superfish like Blinky. This imparts an explicit visual argument in the image of the fish, and articulates a profound contradiction to the verbal text uttered by Mr. Burns. The triply endowed animated fish visually "voices" opposition to Mr. Burns' claims, and through its own vivid image conveys the heinous maltreatment suffered by innumerable other animals in the same predicament in another location. The burlesque frame of this episode exposes the outlandish excuses for the plant's pollution, and offers insightful ecological commentary on several levels. Human pollution is characterized as an improvement on nature, and human progress is viewed as an integral part of human evolution. These references articulate specific criticism of current environmental regulations, specifically the lax enforcement of the regulations concerning the dumping, safe storage, and disposal of nuclear waste. Furthermore, this episode condemns the manipulation of political and economic power to disguise ecological accountability and to shift blame for environmental problems. The show comments on the lack of adherence to safety standards for the plant, and criticizes the apathetic acceptance of unforced environmental inspections. Finally, this episode explicitly criticizes media spin-doctors who distort the impacts of ecological degradation caused by wealthy corporations such as the nuclear power plant. *The Simpsons* artfully employs a burlesque comic frame to condemn the established social order that promotes media distortion of public knowledge, while encouraging self-criticism for viewers to recognize their own fallibility in the show's parody of the disingenuous politics of the resource elites.

As an icon of televised popular culture, *The Simpsons* offers critical social commentary on human experience. The show remarks on the cultural, social, and political ramifications of human activity, in recognizing the limitations of exploitative human existence. "*The Simpsons* works to encourage critique, demanding that viewers be active in their consumption" (Korte, 1997, p. 3). *The Simpsons* characterizes human activity in an incriminating light, questioning established social institutions and normalized behaviors of the dominant societal frames. The show fosters social change by providing the audience the opportunity to recognize the shortcomings of their own living practices and alter their behavior accordingly. This self-critical observation fosters a charitable attitude toward the motivations of others. The comic frame thus promotes cooperative discussion, rather than tragic blame assignment that offers no possibility for social transcendence. Certainly comic framing exposes the bureaucratic power in everyday life and creates an ironic awareness of hierarchical absurdities, but the comic frame remains charitable rather than tragic, always assuming that negotiation of environmental issues is possible. Some environmental issues, however, inevitably have tragic consequences and may be impossible to reconcile. The comic frame endows us with a sense of social awareness, but it does not necessarily promote social activism. Toward this end, *The Simpsons* offers a critical view of the dominant attitude toward nature and exposes the dangers of human-centered practices. The show's rhetorical message fosters social transformation through comedy—revealing the negative social value of anti-environmentalism in a humorous light, which conveys the potential for positive social change. The comic frame offers a dynamic vision of humanity, and thus precludes the defeatism promoted by a static view of human activity that forecloses the possibility of cooperative action. As a televised communication medium, *The Simpsons* encourages the audience to engage in such dramatistic analysis to infer the implications of the show's humorous message.

SPRINGFIELD'S OTHER CREATURES: THE ROLE AND FATE OF ANIMALS IN *THE SIMPSONS*

Through the comic frame, *The Simpsons* exposes the ecological implications of numerous types of human-animal relationships, and comments on socially accepted practices of animal exploitation. The series offers countless opportunities for rhetorical criticism, but to maintain the close focus of this project, this sections analyzes two episodes which provide the richest comedic visual text for an informed rhetorical analysis: the show's portrayal of eating and wearing animals.

In perhaps its most vivid expression of ecological commentary, *The Simpsons* chronicles Lisa's social transformation to a vegetarian lifestyle after she correlates the cute baby lamb she met at the petting zoo with the lamb chop on her dinner plate (Cohen, 1995). When her new lifestyle becomes public, Lisa is constantly under attack, most notably at school, where she is shown an outdated film encouraging the consumption of meat. A production of the beef industry, the film presents a comical depiction of the production of meat that scorns children who do not abide by the dominant social norms that compel consumption of animals. While the film offers a humorous view of dietary norms, it has a dark humor appeal because the film parody exhibits strident similarities with the meat industry's propaganda in the real world. Lisa is further ridiculed at Homer's barbecue where she is scorned for serving gazpacho, a vegetarian soup. The barbecue scene should resonate with vegetarian viewers as a depiction of the ubiquitous resistance to the provision of a vegetarian-friendly menu that offers meatless options in widely diverse social situations. At the barbecue, Lisa endures ridicule from her family as well as the guests, and she retaliates by attempting to vandalize the pig roasting on the rotisserie grill. Lisa's efforts to plunder the barbecue are themselves botched, propelling the entire barbecue—pig, pit, and all—on an airborne trajectory, ruining the year's most momentous social event in Homer's estimation. The slapstick humor of the barbecue scene employs Burke's comedic frame, and facilitates the self-observation of the audience, questioning socially constructed dietary norms. Through humor, the cookout scene reveals the calamity of intolerance of diverse lifestyles; both Lisa and Homer—representing opposite extremes of the dietary conflict—exhibited a remarkable lack of tolerance for the eating preferences of their counterparts. This egotistic clash destroyed the carnivorous and vegetarian options, demonstrating the need for socially accommodating conditions to facilitate mutual satisfaction.

As the episode continues, Lisa endures an inner conflict about whether she should pursue her individual preferences or admit defeat in a culture inundated with propaganda pushing consumption of meat. Succumbing to this social pressure to eat flesh, Lisa eats a hot dog at the Kwik-E-Mart, but is informed it is a tofu hot dog, so she has not yet compromised her personal environmental code. She then meets Paul and Linda McCartney, who school Lisa in the etiquette of good vegetarianism, respecting others' choices, yet remaining vigilant in one's protest of animal consumption. Lisa's earlier inner conflict is resolved as she reconciles her personal convictions with tolerance for the personal decisions of others. Through Lisa's struggle to resist dominant social norms, this episode sheds light on the inherent incongruity between individual experience and socially constructed normative practices. This is an essential use of the comic frame: to divest one's own fallibility and attain an enriched perspective of the established order and its incumbent social and cultural values.

The concurrence of visual argument and the application of the comic frame in *The Simpsons* establish the potency of this program's environmental message. The episodic commentary on Lisa's vegetarianism exemplifies the rich text of the show as a productive multi dimensional environmental commentary. At a base level, the show critiques social and cultural norms that vigorously condone the rampant consumption of animals. Through the narration of Lisa's struggle for a dietary choice, this episode reveals the marginalized perspective of vegetarians, which is relegated to the periphery of public discourse by the hegemonic culture of consumption. At another level, this narrative employs the comedic frame to humorously interpret the discrimination suffered by vegetarians and other dissidents against animal cruelty, for instance. The show offers a comedic interpretation of the marginalization of individuals who publicly hold counter cultural ideals and are ridiculed and ostracized for their lifestyle. This episode reveals the personal suffering of marginalized individuals to promote a culture of social tolerance, and also articulates a formative experience that facilitates the social identification of dissident individuals through common experience who persevere in the knowledge that they are not alone. Through this comedic frame, *The Simpsons* presents a critical view of human exploitation of animals, enabling the audience to perceive the excessiveness of common practices. The program enjoys such significant persuasive influence because fundamentally the show is self-critical, exerting subtle rhetorical messages to promote positive social change.

Another preeminent episode critically comments on the subordinate position of nonhuman animals perpetuated by the extermination of animals expressly for the sartorial value of their coats. Mr. Burns represents the socially established and extremely affluent upper class. He demonstrates an unbridled consumptive appetite, and his social practices are marked by exploitative tactics of manipulation that establish his disregard for persons of inferior social status (all of Springfield). Mr. Burns enjoys the privileged position of a resource elite and exhibits his privilege through excessively wasteful habits that neglect ecological conservation. Aside from his customary exploitative disposition, Mr. Burns displays a unique perspective for rhetorical analysis in his flagrant desire to destroy animals for their fur (Scully, 1995). To realize his special penchant for a fur tuxedo, Burns steals the Simpsons' litter of twenty-five puppies. This episode's literary allusion to *101 Dalmatians* is testament to *The Simpsons'* profound pop-cultural allegory, and points to the significance of the synthesis of visual argument and the comic frame in this pop-cultural, televisual text.

The episode's predominant feature is a musical number performed by Mr. Burns extolling the virtue of wearing fur. Lisa and Bart observe Burns' performance from a window where they learn of his plans for their puppies. As external witnesses to Burns' theatrics, Lisa and Bart are a cruelty-conscious counterpoint to Burns' exploitative extravagance. The children possess a contrapuntal function to Burns' gleeful display—that is, they represent a socially conscious stance in disapproval of Burns' plans to exorcise the puppies. Bart and Lisa, who remain mostly silent spectators precluded from occupying space inside Mr. Burns' room, offer a critical perspective to the television audience through visual argument. Viewers identify with the spatial positioning of Bart and Lisa's visual images because Bart and Lisa's positioning as critical observers parallels the audience's relation to the animated reality of Springfield as critical observers. Bart and Lisa, as critical observers of Burns' flaunted excessive consumerism, serve as intermediaries to the contested practice of fur consumption. Through their mediating role and the spatial position of their visual images, the Simpson children perform an argumentative function. Bart and Lisa are positioned in physical opposition to Mr. Burns' stage (his closet), in a visual representation of social criticism against fur. The symbolic force of the children's visual images comes from the rhetorical power of their counterpoint to Burns. In addition, their discursive space on the second stage of the television itself, their spatial position, empowers the television audience to adopt similar roles as critical observers. These rhetorical tactics of visual argument this scene should ideally foster critical commentary regarding the ecological implications of killing animals for their pelts, and thus induce environmentally conscious change.

Mr. Burns provides a verbal text to add meaning to the pictorial, spatial arguments of the scene. He offers the perspective of guiltless consumption that is associated with the implications of environmental degradation. Unconcerned with socially responsible behavior, Mr. Burns sings a song that offers a riotous commentary on the fur trade. "See My Vest" is a hysterical musical number in which Mr. Burns models his wardrobe, making the argument for human wearing of animals. The song is a litany of animal skins and appendages including the title item, a vest "made from real gorilla chest." Mr. Burns describes the softness of his sweater made from "authentic Irish Setter," the elegance of his vampire bat evening-wear, and the warmth of his "grizzly bear underwear." He sings of his "albino African endangered rhino" slippers, his poodle beret, his loafers made of gophers, and the hat that was his cat, and his plethora of turtle-necks (literally). Mr. Burns ends the song celebrating the magnificence of "greyhound fur tuxedo," adding two dogs should be saved for "matching clogs" (Scully, 1995, in Groening, 1997, p. 172).

Burns celebrates his successful acquisition of his impressive collection of clothing exclusively tailored from genuine animal pelts. He sings a lyrical commentary on the pleasure of owning such luxurious garments, and emphasizes the authenticity of these literally "wild" fabrics. The application of the comic frame is evident in the witty rhyming scheme coupled with the lyrical revelry of such outlandish social practices. The comic effect of Burns' eccentric performance is enhanced by the conflation of his morbid subject matter and his jubilant attitude. Burns plays the clown in this episode, performing a comic ritual that highlights social discrepancies, which warrant conscious action. The incongruity of the song's textual and musical elements articulates comedy's usefulness to identify the absurdity of normative social practice. Burns' whimsical inflection belies the literal meaning of his words, and exposes the absurdity of his message. In this way, Burns presents a farcical rendition of human consumption that fosters meaningful critical commentary through the composition of Burns' comedic message and the visual argument of Bart and Lisa's spatial position.

The Simpsons' environmental rhetoric demonstrates the power of the comic frame in pop-culture analysis, enabling the audience to see through "the obfuscation of the bureaucratic, while opening space for discourse by the minority and marginalized voices in society" (Madsen, 1993, p. 171). The comic frame exhibits a two-pronged approach for effective rhetorical commentary: exposing social ills while creating a new discursive space to incorporate marginalized opinions into the public sphere. Through comedic expression, *The Simpsons* presents a complicated environmental message. That message presents enlightened criticism of the hegemonic assumptions of the existing social order, while simultaneously maintaining a self-critical attitude that facilitates a re-conceptualization of social and cultural relationships that grounds social action.

NATURE AS IDEOLOGY: *THE SIMPSONS'* PRIME-TIME ECO-CRITIQUE

This detailed investigation into the meaning of *The Simpsons* seeks to identify the show's environmental message. Granted, most viewers might not impart such significance from thirty minutes of their prime-time experience. Determining the audience's understanding of the environmental message is admittedly difficult. Such critical analysis is crucial, however, to increasing public awareness of mediated discourse. Madsen describes the critic's ultimate task to alter social frames, which increases the chance for constructive social change (p. 170). Such endeavors help foster more informed television audience members who recognize their situation as passive subjects to the manipulation of media messages to influence and direct their behavior as consumers. *The Simpsons'* antics "mirror even our culture's most unrecognized aspects in all its tiny facets. So even if the viewer does not manage to grasp all the messages transmitted by the series' characters, he or she is always very likely to at least decode some of them" (Steiger, 1999, p. 13). *The Simpsons'* success results from a combination of rhetorical elements, which projects more than mere entertainment into America's living rooms (Steiger, 1999, p. 3). In this way, the show educates its audience while maintaining popular appeal through its humorous, animated form. The series has transferred the expression of political opinion from traditional sources such as radio, and newspapers, to television (Steiger, 1999, p. 13).

The powerful symbolic influence of *The Simpsons* is enhanced through its unique synthesis of comedic and visual rhetorical elements. Televisual media enables a critical look at the complexities of human experience through the manipulation of verbal, acoustic and visual dramatic elements. The combination of these different sense experiences creates a powerfully realistic portrayal of familiar human situations. "By animating *The Simpsons*, Groening managed to reach a higher degree of realism, while he is still entertaining and thus appealing to his audience" (Steiger, 1999, p. 4). The complex symbolism of comic and visual media presents a multidimensional perspective of reality that enjoys powerful rhetorical appeal. Televised reality enjoys an attractiveness that enables persuasive arguments against dominant social and cultural norms. The realism of televisual media is particularly persuasive when offering critical commentary against institutions and practices familiar to America's television audience. *The Simpsons* presents an alternative epistemology that critiques the environmental practices sanctioned by dominant social norms. Through the complex manipulation of multidimensional rhetorical elements, the series reveals the ecological impacts of human activity. The subversive symbolism of *The Simpsons'* environmental rhetoric functions as enlightened criticism of cultural norms of consumption, which exonerate society's ecocidal practices.

The Simpsons presents a strong ideological message about nature as a symbol—as an object for human exploitation. The characters of *The Simpsons* display an overall disregard for the environment, are separated from nature, and often oppose nature. The show portrays the mainstream culture in which the environment has a solely utilitarian value and exists exclusively for human purposes. Through humorous exaggeration, *The Simpsons* offers critical commentary on humanity and points out the danger of destroying the environment. The series' message is revolutionary because it portrays the counterculture of environmental activism as an alternative to anthropocentrism. *The Simpsons'* activism is communicated effectively through the juxtaposition of characters that represent the extremes on an ecological spectrum. Homer represents anthropocentrism, the quintessential exploitative human. Homer's character has a powerful dramatic function: increasing viewers' awareness by evoking reactions to his naivete to media influence of popular culture (Steiger, 1999, p. 5).

Lisa counters Homer's egregious anthropocentrism and symbolizes an environmental ethic of caring for nonhuman creatures. Lisa represents a moral center to the show, which enables her to reveal the irony of her father's anthropocentric actions. When Lisa bemoans the crashing of an oil tanker on Baby Seal Beach, Homer comforts her and reveals his anthropocentric perspective: "It'll be okay, honey. There's lots more oil where that came from" (Appel, 1996). Homer, not considering the ecological implications of the oil spill, instead thinks of the effects on human access to resources.

Through humor, each character's commentary functions differently, Lisa presents a moral force that opposes Homer's flagrant anthropocentrism and effectively points out the absurdity of human action. In this way, the show offers the chance for positive social change. The comic frame permits observation of ourselves, while maintaining the possibility for action by increasing societal consciousness (Carlson, 1986, p. 447). *The Simpsons* is a subversive look at the state of human existence, but is effective because of its chosen methods of rhetorical commentary. The visual communication of the show makes its criticism palatable. The show's writers are well aware that the "pastel colors of animation often blind the censors to their biting critiques of the world" (Korte, 1997, p. 7). "Combining entertainment and subversion, *The Simpsons* angers some people as much as it amuses others…Joe Rhodes of *Entertainment Weekly* noted that 'The Simpsons at its heart … is guerrilla TV, a wicked satire masquerading as a prime-time cartoon' " (Korte, 1997, p. 9). Through its unique rhetorical methods, *The Simpsons* describes the environmental harms of social ills. Through the humorous interpretations of Springfield's environmental hazards and the moral force of Lisa's portrayal of environmental activism, the show offers an alternative solution to exploitative human practices.

The Simpsons functions as a form of environmental activism and thus reveals popular culture's effectiveness as a medium for ecological commentary. The show increases public awareness of environmental issues, and educates the television audience while entertaining them. "Unlike many shows on TV, *The Simpsons* works to encourage critique, demanding that viewers be active in their consumption" (Korte, 1997, p. 3). Through humor, the show reveals the anthropocentrism of human activity in such a way that otherwise harsh criticism is palatable and potentially effects social change. By pointing out the humorous fallacies in human action, the series offers a significant look at the life of the typical American family, and in this way profoundly impacts the attitudes and beliefs of the television audience. The crude animation of *The Simpsons* transcends conventional boundaries of environmental rhetoric. The series embodies a powerful social force by presenting a multidimensional message that critically comments on institutions and practices of the normative social and cultural context, and engages the audience through rhetorical appeals to viewers' personal experiences.

REFERENCES

Andrews, J. R. (1990). *The practice of rhetorical criticism*. White Plains, NY: Longman.

Appel, R. (1996, November 24). Bart after dark (D. Polcino, Director). In J. L. Brooks, M. Groening, & S. Simon (Executive Producers), *The Simpsons*. New York: Twentieth Century Fox Film Corporation.

Blair, J. A. (1996). The possibility and actuality of visual arguments. *Argumentation and Advocacy, 33*, 23-39.

Burke, K. (1950). *A rhetoric of motives*. Berkeley: University of California Press.

Burke, K. (1959). *Attitudes toward history*. Boston: Beacon Press.

Burke, K. (1966). *Language as symbolic action: Essays on life, literature, and method*. Berkeley: University of California Press.

Carlson, A. C. (1986). Gandhi and the comic frame: "Ad bellum purificandum". *Quarterly Journal of Speech, 72*, 446-445.

Cohen, D. S. (1995, October 15). Lisa the vegetarian (M. Kirkland, Director). In J. L. Brooks, M. Groening, & S. Simon (Executive Producers), *The Simpsons*. New York: Twentieth Century Fox Film Corporation.

Gewirtz, H. (1991, October 17). Homer defined (M. Kirkland, Director). In J.L. Brooks, M. Groening, S. Simon (Executive Producers), *The Simpsons*. New York: Twentieth Century Fox Film Corporation.

Groening, M. (1997). *The Simpsons: A complete guide to our favorite family*. R. Richmond & A. Coffman (Eds.), Harper Perennial: New York.

Groening, M. (1999). *The Simpsons forever: A complete guide to our favorite family ...continued*. S. M. Gimple (Ed.), Harper Perennial: New York..

Gronbeck, B. E. (1995). Unstated propositions: Relationships among verbal, visual and acoustic languages. In S. Jackson (Ed.), *Argumentation and values* (pp. 539-542). Annandale, VA: Speech Communication Association.

Klumpp, J. F. & Hollihan, T. (1989). Rhetorical criticism as moral action. *Quarterly Journal of Speech, 75*, 84-97.

Kogen, J. & Wolodarsky, W. (1990, January 21). Homer's odyssey (W. Archer, Director). In J. L. Brooks, M. Groening, & S. Simon (Executive Producers), *The Simpsons*. New York: Twentieth Century Fox Film Corporation.

Korte, D. (1997). The Simpsons as quality television. *The Simpsons archive* [On-line]. Available: http://www.snpp.com/other/papers/dk.paper.html

Madsen, A. (1993). The comic frame as a corrective to bureaucratization: A dramatistic perspective on argumentation. *Argumentation and advocacy, 29*, 64-177.

Scully, M. (1995, April 9). Two dozen and one greyhounds (B. Anderson, Director). In J. L. Brooks, M. Groening, & S. Simon (Executive Producers), *The Simpsons*. New

York: Twentieth Century Fox Film Corporation.

Simon, S. & Swartzwelder, J. (1990, November 1). Two cars in every garage and three eyes on every fish (W. Archer, Director). In J. L. Brooks, M. Groening, & S. Simon (Executive Producers), *The Simpsons*. New York: Twentieth Century Fox Film Corporation.

Steiger, G. (1999). The Simpsons - just funny or more? *The Simpsons archive* [On-line]. Available: http://www.snpp.com/other/papers/gs.paper.html

6

Purification Through Simplification: Nature, the Good Life, and Consumer Culture

Phyllis M. Japp and Debra K. Japp

The search for the good life is a major theme in human societies, from Aristotle to the present. In its current incarnation in late twentieth century America, the term represents dual and contradictory visions. Since the beginning of the nation, two major myths of the good life have developed simultaneously. The first is the belief in happiness and fulfillment through technology, the availability and acquisition of wealth and possessions, upward social mobility, and political influence. Existing alongside and countering this mythos has been the belief that happiness and fulfillment are found in a life of simplicity, one with the minimum of possessions, a life that does not seek wealth or influence but finds joy in connection to nature and service to others. As Shi (1985) notes, "From colonial days, the image of America as a spiritual commonwealth and a republic of virtue has survived alongside the more tantalizing vision of America as a cornucopia of economic opportunities and consumer delights" (p. 277). If these are the two poles in the definition of the good life, there have been many variations over the years, as each era has engaged the tension between having less and having more.

In times of prosperity and unchecked consumption, when it seems as if the "more is better" mentality has gained complete control, a growing sense of unease and guilt seems to draw the "less is more" rhetoric into focus and odes to a simpler mode of life appear.

In popular culture, the opposing visions of the good life are integrated into advertising, entertainment, and popular literature. For example, a Sears advertising campaign informs consumers that Sears stands ready to supply the "good life at a great price, guaranteed" as we view clothing, appliances, and other commodities supposedly essential to the quality of life. Alternately, the state of Nebraska's advertising slogan is "Nebraska—The Good Life," invoking visions of endless sky and bountiful prairies, a place where life is simple and nature revered. Note that however contradictory these visions are in many respects, nature in some form is necessary to their fulfillment. In the first version, nature must provide the resources utilized to manufacture the endless list of commodities now necessary to living the good life, the SUVs and fuel to run them, the lumber for bigger and bigger homes, the land that can be converted to golf courses and resorts where one can vacation in style. In the second version, nature is a spiritual and psychological resource, a retreat from the frantic pace of urban life, a reassurance in the healing powers of the earth.

This chapter examines the conflation of these opposing visions of the good life in late twentieth century U.S. popular culture, using Kenneth Burke's theoretical perspective to identify the role of Nature in rhetoric of the good life. The major goal of this chapter is to document how nature is no less a commodity in current rhetoric of the simple life than it is in the life of excess. A television series entitled *The Good Life* provides a rich visual and verbal text for exploring how the language and images of simple living are imbued with the values and practices of commodity culture, illustrating that in a commodity culture even pastoral nature is a commodity, something that can be desired, sought out, purchased, and enjoyed as essential to the quality of life.

If the "more is better" mythos uses nature as raw material to develop and maintain the commodities necessary for the good life, the "less is more" mythos finds the real meaning of life in the human connection to natural environments. Nature plays a central role in this vision of life. Shi (1985) observes: "Contact with nature, whether the virgin wilderness, the plowed field, or the Arcadian retreat, meant turning away from the artificiality of modern civilization to more abiding realities. God and goodness always seemed more accessible in the woods than in the city. Moreover, the countryside offered fresh air and a stimulus to strenuous activity" (p. 195). And Kenneth Burke (1984b) concurs: "The most basic support of all, the Earth, is perhaps the deepest source of reestablishment for bewildered sophisticates who, having lost all sense of a moral fountainhead, would restore themselves by contact with the 'telluric' " (1984b, p. 205).

While simple living has been a consistent theme since the beginning of the republic, it remains an abstraction that can be shaped to fit a variety of conditions and purposes. As Shi (1985) notes, "the precise meaning of the simple life has never been fixed;" rather, it has always been represented by "a shifting cluster of ideas, sentiments, and activities" (p. 3). Staple ingredients in the traditional recipe have included "a hostility toward luxury and a suspicion of riches, a reverence for nature and a preference for rural over urban ways of life and work, a desire for personal self-reliance through frugality and diligence, a nostalgia for the past and a skepticism toward the claims of modernity, conscientious rather than conspicuous consumption, and an aesthetic taste for the plain and functional" (Shi, 1985, p. 3). Thus the concept survives as both an "enduring myth" and as "an actual way of living" for at least a few citizens in each era (Shi, 1985, p. 279). In a technologically oriented commodity culture, we argue, this long-standing tradition of frugal living is transformed by an inescapable dependence on, and embrace of, products and services that have come to be defined as necessities of life. The reverence for nature is transformed into consumption as well, as the natural environment becomes yet another commodity, to be owned or appropriated as part of the simple lifestyle. Thus the rhetoric of simple living is inescapably infiltrated with the attitudes and orientations of consumption.

BURKE AND ENVIRONMENTAL RHETORIC

Kenneth Burke looms as an important figure in many works on environmental rhetoric. He is well suited to be the patron theorist of environmental criticism for several reasons. First, Burke lived the life of an environmentalist, rejecting a life revolving around commodities for one closely in touch with the earth, the seasons, the rhythms of nature. Burks (1991) notes that Burke "seems to have despised consumerism and capitalism's promotion of it throughout his adult life" (p. 224). His lifestyle (Burke called himself an "agro-bohemian" with "Garden of Eden plumbing") testified to his rejection of consumer values and his need for engagement with nature (Burks, 1991, p. 224). Second, the environment is a theme that runs through his writings. Examples of the barnyard, the wren, the hapless fish with a faulty orientation, references to walking down the road, gardening and the weather not only permeate his work but provided him inspiration to develop his critical perspective. Third, Burke's theory of symbolic action, his "tools" for deconstructing rhetoric, is ideal for discovering nuances in cultural artifacts. These tools are especially useful for the investigation of popular culture, for it is clear that what we desire, buy, eat, and wear, and where and how we choose to live are symbolic responses that articulate, support, and/or challenge the power structures of cultural institutions.

While Burke makes a number of specific references to the good life, the concept implicitly pervades his thought and energizes much of his terminology. Indeed, one could argue that a subtext of Burke's corpus could be the search for the good life, with attendant warnings about those motivational patterns that placed such in peril. Writing in the 1930s, Burke was traumatized by the Depression, by economic threats to the quality of life. By the 1960s he feared that nuclear war, the technology of destruction, could destroy all that we valued in life. He increasingly believed that environmental pollution, exacerbated and excused by consumer culture, stood poised to destroy any hope of a good life lived in tune with nature. Although he personally chose a life of simplicity, he was aware that the accumulation of possessions was the definition that most citizens embraced. Thus what is examined in the rest of this chapter, the cultural tension between the simple life of "less" and the commodified life of "more," is a tension also evident in Burke from *Counterstatement* (1968) to his last essays.

"VOLUNTARY SIMPLICITY:" A 1900s VARIATION ON *THE GOOD LIFE*

A recent trend in contemporary popular culture is often termed "voluntary simplicity." This current variation on the theme of simple living is described in how-to books, films, television programming, and magazines. A recent bibliography of over 160 recent books, posted on a simple living web site, includes such titles as *Circle of Simplicity: Return to the Good Life, 101 Ways to Simplify Your Life, Six Weeks to a Simpler Life Style,* and *Skills for Simple Living.* Two simple living magazines have been recently launched, *Real Simple* and *Simplycity.* As *USA Today* observes in reviewing the magazines, "The simple life now comes with instructions" (Horovitz, 2000, p. 1A). Certainly there is much variation evident within this theme. Some advocate a complete lifestyle change and rejection of consumer values; others seek to downsize and de-stress within present circumstances. For still others, simplicity is a stylistic trend that determines which new home décor to purchase and what sort of vacation to take.

The vast amount of self-help literature surrounding this movement calls to mind Burke's (1973b) assertion that the people who consume such literature often have no intention of actually doing what is advocated. Reading is not the *prelude to,* but the *substitute for,* action; vicarious, armchair experience is less threatening than facing the decisions necessary for change (1973b, pp. 298-299). Certainly the widespread popularity of simple living ideas seems to have made little difference in the consumption styles of most of the population.

The theme of voluntary simplicity holds an especially powerful appeal for middle-class professionals torn between the need for more and the need for less as they try to manage the complexity of their lives. As with most calls for change, however, the desire for simple, painless maxims drives this massive quantity of literature. Irony abounds as self-styled experts in simplicity write books, circulate newspapers and magazines, develop web sites, and travel the country presenting symposiums, consuming fuel and resources in the process, thereby reinforcing the importance of money, space, mobility, and other non simple practices. The irony is reinforced as the media technology that has developed around the desire for wealth, that is the proliferation of materials, seminars, books, and guides advising people how to get rich, is now employed to help people simplify their lives. In the case study to follow, the television program *The Good Life* depends upon a complex media organization and a profusion of technology, including the equipment required to film a television series, although such is carefully kept out of camera range, rendering invisible its intrusion on the pristine natural settings in which the program is usually filmed.

Equally ironic is that this effort at simplicity must be *voluntary,* the result of a choice to renounce affluence and artificiality. The poor, who live lives of enforced rather than voluntary simplicity, are deprived of the moral value of such lives, voluntary simplicity being the prerogative of those "free to choose their standard of living" rather than the sordid poverty of those on the lower socio-economic rungs of the hierarchy (Shi, 1985, p. 7). "Selective indulgence" is the theme of much of the current literature. As MonDesire (2000) notes, "The nostalgic urge for a simple life by and large emanates from people who've never had to duck a landlord on the first of the month, never had to wait in the rain for a packed city bus that rides on by, never had to slide the money for a half-gallon of milk under the narrow slot in a grocery store's bullet-proof window" (p. 19A).

Overall, the simple life, 1990s style, appears dictated by personal needs and is framed almost entirely in the desire for fulfillment and personal growth. Converts do not renounce consumerism for religious reasons, for political dedication, or as a result of an environmental conscience. The quest is personal not political; secular rather than religious; self instead of other-centered. As defined by the oxymoronic *Simple Life Corporation*, the concept means a journey, an awakening to self and one's inner needs, the removal of things that distract one from "finding" oneself, including not only possessions but activities, relationships, and duties. A *Cathy* cartoon strip neatly sums up the ironies. The script reads: "The simple life: Discard the day planner, disconnect call waiting, unplug the TV, cancel all subscriptions, say 'no' to invitations, clear closets and cupboards of everything but the bare essentials, and travel to a cool, quiet place that inspires possibility. The Mall" (Guisewite, 2000).

HGTV'S *THE GOOD LIFE*

A variety of texts could be used to exemplify the rhetoric of voluntary simplicity, for example, internet web sites, books, advice columns, sermons, and instructional seminars, for it is the interaction of these aspects of popular culture that constructs and supports the ideologies of simple living. For this chapter, a Home and Garden network (HGTV) half-hour series entitled *The Good Life* was chosen and the analysis included more than twenty episodes aired over a period of two years. Although the stories vary—there are former lawyers, professors, journalists, models, executives, importers, even oil riggers—they are all variations on a theme. All articulate a core vision of what it means to live the good life. The stories, in fact, are strikingly similar despite the assurance that the good life is different for every individual. In these dramatic presentations the cultural drama of "less is more" plays out against its counter, "more is better." The stories are introduced as examples of people ("people just like you and me" the narrator assures us) who have left highly paid, highly stressed jobs in the city and relocated to a more natural environment to live a simpler and therefore better life. The verbal and visual dramas provide standard, mutually reinforcing formulas as viewers follow the stories of people who have changed their lives, following their dreams to the good life. Although viewers experience visual and verbal dramas simultaneously, in this chapter visual and verbal dramas are each considered first as a separate domain of meaning, and then considered together to point out how each complements the other as they construct the meanings of *The Good Life*.

THE VERBAL DRAMA OF *THE GOOD LIFE*

The verbal drama of *The Good Life* is a classic example of Burke's dramatistic process of guilt, repentance, and redemption. This well-known cycle of cleansing, drawn from religious rhetoric, is appropriated by Burke as a critical strategy for understanding how both social and personal change takes place symbolically. In this drama, conflicts of motives construct hierarchies, which in turn create various sorts of guilt. These shortcomings, when recognized, require change or redemption. Burke argues this process as fundamental to human communication. Thus in any situation, a critic can profitably look for the guilt, that is, the shortcoming, inadequacy, inconsistency, need for closure, that is the impetus for communicating. In the inevitable socioeconomic hierarchies, those with more are guilty of their excesses, those with less, of their lack of prestige or attainments; and each must seek to be redeemed via explanation and justification. In any social structure characterized by hierarchies, says Burke (1966), "Those 'Up' are guilty of not being 'Down,' those 'Down' are certainly guilty of not being 'Up' " (1966, p. 15). These are not necessarily conscious emotions or explicit rhetorical strategies but are inherent motives or "patterns of action" that drive explanations, justifications, comparisons, identifications, divisions. In *The Good Life*, these implicit motives become an explicit motif or narrative form.

The Good Life features such salvation stories as its fundamental script. Participants guilty of the sin of overwork at high-stress professions and refugees from frantic urban lifestyles repent of their erring ways and seek redemption. Nature is, as we will see, the primary agency of purification. Thus each episode of *The Good Life* turns on a conversion experience, as overworked suburbanites discover that something is missing in their lives and embrace change. At the root of their desires is a need for purification, through nature, from the guilt of consumerism. They repent, turn from their current way of life, and become new people, born again to a supposedly simpler existence, closer to nature, and implicitly, closer to God. Edye Ellis, the host and guru of the program, serves as an evangelist for this lifestyle change, exhorting others to follow in the footsteps of those whose conversion story was featured in this week's program. As with the self-help genre that infuses this portrayal, there is the "before and after" theme characteristic of any narrative of change (weight loss, addiction recovery, relational renewal, or political or religious conversions, to mention a few examples). The story each week follows the standard form of conversion testimony, from guilt to repentance to redemption.

Establishing guilt. The narrative begins with attention to the pathology of the participants' old way of life, by implication a "bad life." They describe their former lives as filled with stress, complexity, urban crowding, and long daily commutes, as they recount long hours on the job, mourn their disconnect from nature, and describe familial relationships in peril. The resulting self-diagnosis is described as a loss of self, identity, and meaning. They are no longer satisfied with the success they sought, the prestige gained, or the possessions accumulated by climbing the ladder to the top of their professions. "There must be something better" is the mantra of these seeking souls. For example, a former university dean tells of the day he discovered that he "had everything he wanted but didn't want anything he had" and vowed to quit his job and change his life.

Evincing repentance. The conversion always involves *risk* as well as renunciation. Penitents must pay the price by taking an economic or social risk, giving up something, either something *actual* (e.g., a high salary, social prestige) or *potential* (e.g., the chance for advancement). The "no pain, no gain" formula is reminiscent of the stories of risk-taking in pursuit of wealth. The definitions of risk, however, are comfortingly middle class, attractive to those who know they can somehow recover what may be lost. Thus they risk investing their savings in a business, in a move from a familiar location, by leaving their circle of friends, by choosing to live in a smaller space, or by making do with fewer possessions in their quest for something better. Although there is an attempt to maintain suspense, risk remains little more than a minor and temporary challenge to their middle-class values and identities. For example, a former journalist risks his savings to open a bakery in a small town, a Texas landscaper invests his life savings to convert a rural hotel to a bed-and-breakfast, a Chicago lawyer abandons his practice to open a restaurant.

Seeking redemption. Once willingness to risk is established, the redemptive moment of the narrative occurs, a turning point of almost mystical quality. Some penitents drive down a country road and find at the end a location where they are "meant to be." Or they may discover a small town and feel instantly as if they were born there. Almost always this redemptive moment involves some contact with the earth, or with nature in some form. This mystical moment is also a pivotal point at which penitents can surrender and embrace the salvation of the good life or draw back from the risk and remain doomed to its alternative. Following the muse involves, above all, the search for a location where a good life is possible. Few manage the conversion without some physical move, most frequently from urban to rural, large town to small town.

Thus, communion with nature is essential to the good life, whether from a cabin in the woods, a farm, the rural charm of a small town, or even a tranquil garden in a suburban back yard. Also essential to the conversion experience is a new occupation compatible with the conversion values. Work in some form is essential; few remain idle. Entrepreneurship is especially attractive, satisfying the yearning to be one's own boss, control one's own time. Artistry is likewise a key to the good life (writing, crafting, achieving creative fulfillment and frequently making money from the endeavor). The new occupation or avocation often requires some contact with the earth, from growing one's own food to using natural products to make beautiful and artistic creations.

A constant redemptive theme is the search for ideal relationships, for people with whom one can live the good life. Some converts bring intact families in need of renewal via simplicity; some seek change because of broken relationships and look for new, like-minded friends and/or life partners. Problems in previous relationships are linked to the values and practices of the old life (to date we have seen no programs about those whose relationships have broken up as a result of converting to the simple life). The search for self is paramount, however. As the old life is stripped away, as old locations, occupations, and relationships are replaced, the unique authentic self of the convert is revealed, hidden below the artificiality of the old life. The needs that were ignored in the complexity of urban professional life can now thrive and grow. Hidden skills and talents are uncovered: a professor discovers he is an artist, a former model becomes a world-class chef, others find amazing abilities to sculpt, create music, take prize-winning photographs.

Bearing witness. The final turn of the salvation drama is the evangelical responsibility of the convert. All participants devoutly affirm that they are now living the good life, lives of "deep fulfillment" as one declares. To a person, they express no regrets or nostalgia for the life left behind. The gains are far greater than the losses, the satisfaction worth the risk. They encourage others to make the same choice, again emphasizing choice and reinforcing the voluntary nature of their life change. The host completes the narrative with an altar call for conversion as she addresses viewers directly: "You too can have the good life." Like these inspiring stories, renewal begins "one step at a time."

Nature's role as commodity is evident in the consumerist attitude of selecting and owning an appropriate natural setting or backdrop for living the simple life. Control of life choices remains central; the stories turn on the volunteerist motive. The centrality of voluntary choice is significant. It implies that what has been surrendered can, if desired, be reappropriated. Participants stress they could have continued, even succeeded, in their former circumstances but chose to change their lives, always for personal and relational reasons. Thus choice implies a way out if the rigors of simple living are too great and smoothes a path back into the former lifestyle. The factors that support the ability to choose simplicity (money, education, social class) are also the very attributes necessary to success in a consumer society; thus these important qualities remain the property of the individual, to be played out as desires dictate. The sense of entitlement or ownership of nature as well as the implicit dependence on the attributes of consumerism continue to reinforce the orientations of the "old life," undermining the claims of conversion to simplicity.

THE VISUAL DRAMA OF *THE GOOD LIFE*

In this analysis of the visual drama of *The Good Life*, another dimension of Burke's dramatism is used, focusing on how various elements are presented visually as the substance or grounding of the good life. Burke's pentad is built upon the concept of substance, the symbolically constructed foundation or basis on which various aspects of the drama are played out. Burke (1973a) identifies five major orientations that compel the human drama—scene, act, agent, agency, and purpose (1973a, pp. 21-23). Humans use symbol systems to constitute their situations and contexts, their identities and differences, their shared pasts and futures, their needs, goals, desires. In the process, they construct compelling explanations of the human condition—narratives of human agency, of the constraining power of natural conditions, of being bound or liberated by ideas, of individual desire or cooperative action that overpowers restraints. Burke (1973a) argues that these orientations and the tensions among them, e.g. the struggle between the power of will (agent) and the power of situation (scene), are necessary to any well-rounded explanation of "what people are doing and why they are doing it" (1973a, p. xv). This perspective seems ideal for exploring the visual drama of *The Good Life* because of the overwhelming visual power of the physical settings as the essence or substance of the good life. We concentrate on the primacy of the scenic in the visualizations of the good life but the other terms are ever present and inevitably accessed in understandings of the visual drama presented in the program.

Nature as scene. The visual drama powerfully constructs the scenic dimension of the good life, both the foundational substance that grounds this life and the context, that is, the physical spaces or places in which the good life can be lived. Nature is a major component of both the grounding and the setting of a good life. But this scene is not raw and unruly nature. It is a nature ordered, controlled, and structured into the perfect setting for the values and qualities of the good life. This nature of pristine mountains, meadows, streams and oceans is a nature without heat, humidity, drought, cold, damp, mosquitoes, snakes, storms, or blight. Thus the camera pans over beautiful views, bountiful gardens, wildlife, forests, landscaped lawns, even occasional swimming pools and guest houses. Nature here is a visual feast, with shots carefully chosen to exclude power lines, cellular towers, jet contrails, litter, dams, encroaching urbanization, highways, and other visual blights from human development. Likewise the cameras, trucks, and other equipment necessary to filming are carefully kept out of camera range, as noted above, ignoring the irony that their presence destroys the very tranquility they are attempting to capture.

As the scene of the good life is visualized, it is done in true Burkean fashion by referencing what it "is not" in order to substantiate what is "is." Shots of the "old life" of stress and complexity, pollution and gridlock, are juxtaposed with those of the "new life." Nature thus is instantiated as both the substance that generates the good life and the setting or scene in which such a life is possible. (Of course, by implication, the scenes of the old life become places where a good life is not possible.)

Style as scene. There is another component to the scene, however, overlapping and extending the emphasis on nature. If the good life is grounded in nature, it is also rooted in the stylistic, an element necessary to separate the middle-class good life from the inadvertent and unavoidable simplicity of poverty and lower-class existence. Burke (1984b) defines style as a moral dimension of symbolizing that involves doing or being "right," that is, appropriate to the situation. It is "an elaborate set of prescriptions and proscriptions for 'doing the right thing' . . . a complex schema of what-goes-with what carried through all the subtleties of manner and attitudes" (1984b pp. 268-269). Those scenes and agents imbued with style determine the "correct" use of commodities. While most folks dress themselves, set their tables, and decorate their homes, to do so with style requires a knowledge of the nuances of social correctness as well as a flair for originality within the bounds of appropriateness. Thus style is an option for those with money and good taste, setting them apart from those who must take whatever is available at a price they can afford.

In *The Good Life*, nature as chief commodity must be stylized, made appropriate to the scene. Just as the natural beauty of the outdoors is configured into an aesthetic backdrop for the good life, the interiors of the simple but tasteful abodes are charmingly decorated with arts, crafts, and fabrics that utilize nature in elegant and artistic ways. Edye Ellis, the host of the program and the Martha Stewart of simple living, provides an enduring aura of taste, elegance, and aesthetic appeal. Cameras linger on Edye as she poses with flower arrangements, room decor, gardens, beautiful views, and tasteful accessories that embed style into the substance of the good life.

"Doing" nature with style: Constructing agents. Thus, these two components, nature and style, combine to produce the grounding for the good life. The scene, however, requires agents appropriate to that scene, generated by and imbued with its qualities. As Burke (1973a) explains: "It is a principle of drama that the nature of acts and agents should be consistent with the nature of the scene" (1973a, p. 3). As the verbal narrative stresses, converts to the good life must experience a rebirth, a reawakening of appreciation for nature and their own artistic abilities. The visual drama chronicles this rebirth. We see photos of the subjects as children, growing up, engaging as adults in the "bad life," juxtaposed with shots of new converts enjoying the good life. The visual connection between "what I was and what I am" constructs a new identity forged by their identification with the scene.

As noted above, converts to the good life almost always discover hidden artistic talents that can only now be developed. Abilities to paint, sculpt, photograph, decorate, or do crafts emerge as if by magic, as the substance of the good life draws these forth from participants. They thus possess the necessary style to be appropriate agents in the good life drama, style being a latent quality called forth by their participation in the scene. We often see participants actually constructing, physically and metaphorically, their placement in the new location. Often at the end of the program, the camera integrates agent and scene, as it lingers on converts engaged in the daily routines of the good life, for example, walking in the woods or by a lake, taking in a natural panorama from a deck, working in the garden, creating artistic objects from natural products, tastefully decorating their homes, or taking photographs of nature. The visual message is: "This is the good life and we now belong here, we have grown from and are now situated in this place, like the mountains and trees that surround us."

The snake in the garden: Commodity as agency. The visual drama has another component, however, one that challenges and ultimately overpowers the Edenic visions of the good life, infusing both scene and agent with the values of commodity culture—advertising. According to Burke (1973a), agency is the manner or means by which action is possible (1973a, p. xv). Advertising thus is implicitly the agency or means by which a good life is possible. As with all television programming, advertising is a vital ingredient of the program, and becomes part of the visual flow of meaning. The viewer can validly assume that the products advertised are by implication those necessary for, or at least compatible with, the good life. Television programming constructs a flow of meaning, evoking "subtle associations between aspects of the show and the commodity" presented in the commercials (Budd, Craig, & Steinman, 1999, pp. 153-154). Thus as visuals of Nature are juxtaposed with repeated ads for luxury automobiles, vacation cruises, and investment opportunities, the program implicitly argues that expensive commodities, consumed with style, are essential to the good life. In fact, these commodities and the wealth they imply are instantiated as the agency or means through which the good life is attained, making this a life framed by, surrounded by, and energized by consumer culture.

Style therefore is the essential quality that links nature and consumer culture. Living with nature appropriately requires style, just as style requires appreciation of the finest commodities that only money can purchase. The good life, then, uses consumption (with style) as agency to bridge the fundamental disjunction that has always rested at the heart of this culture's vision of the good life, the term that connects the "less is more" and "more is better" versions of the good life. As visualized in this program, the good life apparently means being able to drive up to your rural abode in your new Lexus, booking a Caribbean cruise from your rustic living room when you need a break from simplicity, and taking it for granted that you have a right to consume both nature and commodities as long as you do it with style.

INTERACTION OF THE VISUAL AND VERBAL DRAMAS OF *THE GOOD LIFE*

Obviously the verbal and visual dramas are interdependent, both needed to define the good life. If one considers the verbal narrative the dominant narrative—and that is only because our tools for dealing with words are more familiar—the visual narrative reduces and expands, abstracts and concretizes the verbal. Together the verbal and the visual dramas reside in the tensions between stability and change. If the verbal drama is the story of change, of agential choice shaping, molding, creating the desired environments for one's salvation, the visual drama privileges scenic power, as stable enduring nature embraces the prodigal, restores those who dwell therein to the timeless serenity of the universe. The incompleteness of each makes space for the other; in their contradictions lies satisfactory completion.

The verbal drama of choice includes no admission that the lifestyle of consumption being renounced bears any responsibility for misuse of nature. The visual narrative presents a static, ever-stable natural beauty, for example, pristine mountains, streams, and meadows unaffected by human excess and mismanagement. As noted, nature is visual art work, purchased and now possessed via the risks taken. In no sense is it an active entity. This visualization of nature energizes the verbal, temporal drama of human quest. The eternal ever present backdrop of nature becomes an object of desire in the temporal formula, placed back in eternal timelessness at the end. Each narrative (spatial and temporal) supports and constrains the other. The visual reduces nature to an aesthetic that complements the verbal drama's definition of nature as a choice of lifestyle, implying that a beautiful environment exists to satisfy human desires but failing to assign any responsibility for preserving that environment.

HGTV's *The Good Life* is one example, among many, of current visions of simple living. It is particularly striking because it embeds so many values in one compact package and presents so many seemingly oppositional ideas in a coherent verbal and visual narrative. This version of the good life provides vicarious atonement, offers the chance to reform without serious sacrifice. Its pathology is that it allows no serious economic, social, or environmental issues to emerge. It reduces complex, potentially tragic consequences of policies and practices to matters of individual preference, stylistic choices, aesthetic visions. Here the good life is about following one's own dream, discovering one's inner self. It is individualized as the freedom to "do what I want, when I want," as a number of participants observe. There are no stories of failure, no acknowledgment of social responsibility, no sympathy for those who cannot choose. It maintains the myth of infinite possibility for all, defining simplicity not as a moral alternative or environmental necessity but as a trendy lifestyle, allowing the viewer to forget that only the fortunate few can choose to leave a mess they have helped to create and maintain for a flight to rural, unspoiled areas.

By implication, the good life takes place in select localities, in rural, sparsely populated, attractive, and relatively unspoiled places such as the slopes of the Rockies, the foothills of the Appalachians, the ocean, lakefront, or bayou, in quaint New England towns, in other rural and unspoiled beauty spots of the nation. The visual component strengthens the aesthetic and grounds it in nature in ways the verbal cannot. Most examples presented in *The Good Life* require money, influence, and taste as the converts attempt to create a lifestyle of elegance and beauty in a new setting. Great emphasis is placed on improving communication in families and relationships; nature is the mystique that makes this possible. The work ethic is retained but relocated to include contact with nature. Each episode ends with an altar call, "You too can have the good life."

Thus, the good life utilizes natural environments as a stage-set for a lifestyle that continues to valorize commodity culture. Nature, in fact, is the foremost commodity; in order to live the good life it must be purchased, modified, and controlled. Nature and simplicity must be managed with the same skills and dedication that former professional careers were managed. As Burke (1973b) observes, the vision of the good life was built around the

ideal of the 'live-wire' salesman, with culture taken to mean the maximum purchase of manufactured commodities. . . . Out of books, out of delightful moments in one's personal life, out of sporadic voyages, out of *vacational* experiences as distinct from *vocational* ones, people got visions of a noncompetitive structure of living, a "good life" involving gentle surroundings, adequate physical outlets, the pursuit of knowledge, etc., and the very slogans of the commercial ethic assured them that they were "entitled" to all this. (1973b, p. 248)

CONCLUSION

Voluntary simplicity in 2002, then, appears to reinforce the dictates of simple living while wrapped firmly within commodity culture, defining it primarily as a psychological search for self-actualization in which nature becomes a resource for purchase. It calls us not to change our ways but to dabble in self-fulfillment, while continuing on our present course of over consumption and self-indulgence. By reducing the issues to individual conversion experiences, there is no need for national repentance, for a brake on conspicuous and wasteful consumption of resources. As this example illustrates, the simple life discourse is framed in and contained by assumptions and connections to consumption. It is constructed in the language of a consumer society. It is not a call for change but a powerful endorsement of the status quo. The cultural myth of success, the "divine right" to consume the world's resources, the unwillingness to acknowledge that the environment is not merely a backdrop or stage-set for our consumption of goods and enactment of trendy lifestyles, makes many current odes to simplicity, the "less is more" narratives, merely alternate versions of the "more is better" stories.

One program from one genre of popular culture—television entertainment—says little except when, as with *The Good Life*, its assumptions and expectations are deeply embedded in American culture. The program draws from and reinforces the powers of consumerism and the inevitable subsuming of environmental concerns to consumerist values. When these same assumptions, expectations, and values are evident across various genres of popular culture they become an uncritical and unconscious dimension of our cultural reality. Popular culture thus implicitly assures us that we are entitled to a good life, whether one of economic complexity or voluntary simplicity, and offers us nature for sale, an environment to be purchased and used in the search for personal fulfillment.

REFERENCES

Budd, M., Craig, S., & Steinman, C. (1999). *Consuming environments: Television and commercial culture*. New Brunswick, NJ: Rutgers University Press.

Burke, K. (1966). *Language as symbolic action*. Berkeley: University of California Press.

Burke, K. (1968). *Counterstatement*. Berkeley: University of California Press.

Burke, K. (1970). *Rhetoric of religion*. 2nd ed. Berkeley: University of California Press.

Burke, K. (1973a). *Grammar of motives*. 2nd ed. Berkeley: University of California Press.

Burke, K. (1973b). *Philosophy of literary form*. 3rd ed. Berkeley: University of California Press.

Burke, K. (1984a). *Attitudes toward history*. 4th ed. Berkeley: University of California Press.

Burke, K. (1984b). *Permanence and change*. 4th ed. Berkeley: University of California Press.

Burks, D. (1991). Kenneth Burke: The agro-bohemian "Marxoid." *Communication Studies, 42*, 219-233.

Dudgeon, C. (Executive Producer). *The Good Life*. Knoxville, TN: Home and Garden Television (HGTV). http://www.hgtv.com

Television (HGTV). http://www.hgtv.com

Guisewite, C. (2000, June 24). Cathy Cartoon. *Omaha World Herald*.

Horovitz, B. (2000, June 1). Simplesells: Chic back-to-basics explosion carries hefty load of irony. *USA Today,* p. 1A+.

MonDesire, D. (2000, June 9). How hard should we strive for simple life? *USA Today*, p. 19A.

Shi, D. E. (1985). *The simple life: Plain living and high thinking in American culture.* New York: Oxford.

What is the Simple Life? (2000, July 5). *Simple Life Corporation.* http://members.aol.com/simplfe/spirit.html.

7

An Analysis of the "Tree-Hugger" Label

Mark DeLoach, Michael S. Bruner, and John S. Gossett

Public discourse has both a grammar and a rhetoric (Burke, 1945, 1950). The grammar has to do with the usage of words and the history of uses. The rhetoric is concerned with the conflict between terms. This chapter on environmental rhetoric and popular culture has its origins in a conversation among the authors about anti-environmental discourse. In this chapter, it is postulated that anti-environmental discourse ridicules environmentalists as "tree-huggers" to delegitimize and dismiss the rhetoric of environmental advocacy. Our subsequent investigation of newspaper stories reveals that the tree-hugger label is much more complex than our initial formulation.

Before revealing what we discovered in the newspaper accounts, three issues that bear on the larger question of the relationship between environmental rhetoric and popular culture are addressed. Herndl and Brown, for example, assert that environment "is the product of discourse about nature" (1996, p. 3), and that rhetorical analysis might elucidate the discourse (p. 5). We argue, first, that the relationships between words and meanings are in flux. Gary Snyder, therefore, recommends: "We have faith in 'meaning' the way we might believe in wolverines—putting trust in the occasional reports of others or on the authority of once seeing a pelt. But it is sometimes worth tracking these tricksters back" (1990, p. 8). This chapter tracks the grammar and the rhetoric of the tree-hugger label in popular newspaper accounts, yet the struggle over meanings and the difficulty in trying to "fix" meanings are more evident than ever before.

Laclau and Mouffe are relevant here, when they propose that "[t]he practice of articulation, therefore, consists in the construction of nodal points which partially fix meaning...." (1985, p. 105). One task attempted in this study is documenting the struggle over the meanings of the tree-hugger label. At the same time, nodal points to make intelligible references to current uses and contexts have been constructed.

A second issue that cannot be fully addressed in this chapter is the relationships between words and images. In his 1999 book, *Image Politics: The New Rhetoric of Environmental Activism*, DeLuca takes on the task proposed by Szasz (1995, p. 57): "[w]e need to find a way of thinking about opinion formation that recognizes the distinctiveness of a process that relies more on the image than the word, a process that is more figural than discursive, a process that creates 'meanings' in which the cognitive content is under-articulated and is dominated by highly charged visual components." DeLuca asserts that "the primary rhetorical tactic of radical environmental groups is staging image events" (1999, p. xii). If DeLuca's argument has merit, then a focus on two words seems quaint. However, words and images cannot be separated completely, nor will words be pitted against images. The tree-hugger label is so graphic and so concrete that it almost dissolves the distinction between image and word.

A third area that requires much more analysis than can be undertaken here in this chapter is the proper understanding of culture. Cantrill argues that language, in general, or environmental discourse, in particular, speaks of the society in which people live. Our "rhetorical choices are rooted in the tacit understandings that ground human conduct and distinguish one culture from another" (1996, p. 167). Cantrill, further, admonishes us "to consider the possibility of having to reckon with *multiple* cultures in any given society" (1996, p. 168). We agree with Cantrill and suggest adopting Brummett's phrase: "overlapping popular cultures" (1991, p. xxi, emphasis added).

This chapter also offers a brief commentary on the question: What is the relationship between the media and popular culture? If culture is what is (a) deeply felt, (b) commonly intelligible, and (c) widely accessible (Carbaugh, 1988, p. 38), then popular culture may emphasize the third component—widely accessible. In Root's terms, popular culture is "accessible to the broadest spectrum of the society" (1987, p. 10). Brummett advances this line of analysis one step further, when he points out that popular culture is the "cutting edge of culture's instruments" (1991, p. xxi). Popular culture, therefore, is rhetorical, by definition. Popular culture is worthy of study, because the struggle to define who we are is ongoing and may be influenced by our analyses and behavior.

Newspaper accounts were chosen for study for two reasons. First, newspaper accounts represent a large and accessible data base. Second, while television is a dominant force in popular culture, we cannot overlook the influence of "hometown" newspapers. In fact, the very notion of "hometown" dovetails nicely with the "commonly intelligible" dimension of the concept of popular culture. In addition, many engaging case studies of environmental rhetoric focus on hometown (or local region). For example, Ruud and Sprague (2000) look at the tensions between the cultural worlds of loggers and environmentalists in a *community* in Northern California. They report that their focus groups revealed "divergent codes" in the two groups. These divergences sometimes become public on newspaper editorial pages and in letters to the editor.

The present study is based on a Lexis-Nexis database search for uses of the label tree-hugger, along with some current materials and some historical materials dating to 1977. Three hundred uses of the term *tree hugger* appear during the Spring 1999 period selected for analysis. The newspapers from which citations were drawn include The *Buffalo News*, The *Chattanooga Times*, The *St. Louis Post-Dispatch*, The *Salt Lake City Tribune*, The *San Francisco Chronicle*, and The *Washington Post*.

The chapter is divided into five sections. Each of the first four sections is devoted to a different use of the tree-hugger label. The final section, offers some comments on environmental advocacy and suggestions for future research and application.

REDUCTION TO ABSURDITY

The first use of the tree-hugger label is *reduction to absurdity*. This mocking use of the label is an informal version of the *Reductio Ad Absurdum* (R.A.A.), a technique for reducing an argumentative position to two mutually contradictory statements. While the formal version of the R.A.A. has been useful in mathematics (Manicas & Kruger, 1968, p. 113), an informal form of the R.A.A. is evident in public discourse that discredits environmental advocacy. In short, the tree-hugger label is used to reduce environmentalists and environmental advocacy to absurdity.

The most-studied linguistic form in public discourse, arguably, is metaphor. Claims about the power of metaphor to influence daily life range from modest to sweeping (Bosman, 1987; Bosman & Hagendoorn, 1991; Graesser, Mio, & Millis, 1989; Lakoff & Johnson, 1980; Mio & Katz, 1996). An interesting line of research links metaphor to learning (Pugh, 1989; Pawlowski, Badzinski, & Mitchell, 1998). The conclusion that metaphors play an important role in how people make sense of the world is widely accepted.

A similar claim can be made about fallacies, such as the informal R.A.A. Fallacies in public discourse are another way that people make sense of the world. A fallacy, therefore, is not simply a logical mistake. Nor is it enough for environmentalists to point out the logical mistakes in the reasoning of opponents. A fallacy can be a popular culture mechanism by which arguments are advanced and perceptions are promoted (Crosswhite, 1995). What is at stake is establishing a legitimate alternative discourse in the public sphere, as well as the characteristics or quality of that discourse (Olson & Goodnight, 1994; Riley, Klumpp, & Hollihan, 1995).

The following examples document the general usage of the R.A.A. to ridicule environmentalists and environmentalism:

Ever since [1969], and especially on April 22, "Earth Day" the Earth has been portrayed as a doomed victim of human greed and carelessness—which only *hair-shirt austerity* [emphasis added] can heal. (Matt Ridley, as quoted in The *Daily Telegraph* (London).

If public enthusiasm for Earth Day has waned, part of the reason is the Earth is doing pretty well. The Earth and its inhabitants are a lot more resourceful than the environmental groups gave them credit for. . . . Environmentalists warned that *we would run out of resources* [emphasis added]. (Jonathan Adler, as quoted in McCain, The *Washington Times*).

However, unlike some of my more extreme counterparts, I don't think that *rolling back civilization a few hundred years* [emphasis added] is the solution. (Brian Dipert, as quoted in *Information Access/Cahners Publishing*, wire release).

Ridley's use of the phrase "hair-shirt austerity" and Dipert's image of "rolling back civilization" are more than exaggerations. The informal R.A.A. makes environmentalists and their positions appear unrealistic and foolish. In Adler's opinion, environmentalists are wrong in their predictions. Worse, they are so wrong as to be absurd.

The public discourse surrounding the spotted owl controversy (Agrawal, 1999; Lange, 1993) is another example of the use of the informal R.A.A. in anti-environmentalist rhetoric. The central issue for E. O. Wilson and other prominent environmentalists is the preservation of habitat. In the case of the spotted owl in the Pacific Northwest, the point is to save old-growth forests. However, the informal R.A.A. is used to characterize and undermine the position of environmentalists. Agrawal provides a useful summary: "The philosophy of environmentalism has unfortunately been characterized as privileging sequoias and *spotted owls over human life*" [emphasis added] (1999, n.p.). The informal R.A.A. (that spotted owls are more important than people) obscures the primary argument about habitat preservation, and facilitates the dismissal of the environmentalists' position.

We characterize this usage as an *attack discourse*. Note the aggressive tone in the following three examples:

It absolutely infuriates me that *those damned tree-huggers* [emphasis added] would place this regulation in jeopardy (Jim Payne, as quoted in Tansey and Heredia, The *San Francisco Chronicle*).

Hooooeee! Will *those tree-huggers be steaming* [emphasis added] when they see you driving down the road! [in the new Ford Excursion, a large sport utility vehicle]. (Kevin Cowherd, writing in The *Baltimore Sun*).

By the end of the week, several district employees confirmed that administrators had mocked team members for months, calling them "tree huggers" and "crazed environmental communists." (News story by Greg Gittrich in The *Daily News of Los Angeles*, May 17, 1999).

This attack discourse can be used to delegitimize an individual as well as a position. For example, in newspaper accounts, former Vice President Al Gore often is ridiculed as a tree-hugger. Here is one example: "[a]ccording to what I'd read, the wacky crackpot tree huggers were really only gathering in Detroit so that wacky crackpot tree hugger presidential candidate Al Gore could use the occasion to further his ambitions" (Lee Anderson, *Chattanooga Times and Free Press*, May 5, 1999). Persons who argue for the protection of the environment are targeted as tree-huggers. In protest over the rebuilding of a road in a Nevada national forest, loggers, ranchers, and miners carried signs that attacked individuals who sought to protect the national forest. These signs targeted tree huggers as "the other red meat" (Sonners, 2000, B10). David Brower, former executive director of the Sierra Club, is referred to as "the George Patton of the environmental movement," the "Archdruid," and the "ultimate tree hugger" (McManis, 1999, p. 1). DeLuca (1999, p. 8) cautions that the aggressive tone can spill over into violence, such as in the clashes between Earth First! and Wise Use.

The phrase tree hugger has been used as a negative epithet as well. Camilla Herlevich, a land trust director in North Carolina, compared advice from tree-huggers to more valuable advice from accountants, noting: "It's one thing for a bunch of tree huggers to tell them (land owners) what to do; it's another for your accountant to say it" ("Tax," 1999, p. 6A). As mentioned above, Jim Payne, of the Paper, Allied-Industrial, Chemical and Energy Workers International Union, blamed tree-huggers for opposing a regulation favored by the union, pointing out: "It absolutely infuriates me that those damned tree-huggers would place this regulation in jeopardy" (Tansey & Heredia, 1999, p. A23). Tom Long, a columnist for The *Detroit News*, wrote in his column, "On Monday, I decided to wander over to Cobo Center to see what the wacky crackpot tree huggers who'd shown up for something called the National Town Meeting for a Sustainable America were doing" (1999, p. G1).

The tree-hugger label has been used to attack other social movement groups. Members of the animal rights movement, for example, who argue for protection of animal rights under the law, have been attacked as "tree hugging, fur-loathing vegetarians" (Abel, 2000, A12). Groups are often accused of being dominated by tree-huggers. For example, state Republicans argued that the Missouri Conservation Commission could "become dominated by 'tree huggers and Bambi lovers' who adopt the very policies that rural lawmakers are now trying to avoid" (Wagar, 1999, p. B3). The Sierra Club has been targeted by Arizona State Senator John Huppenthal as "a bunch of tree-hugging liberals" and "people who practice the fake environmental stuff" (Thomason, 1999, p. EV1). Senator Jesse Helms (Republican-North Carolina), in response to a proposal presented to him to promote global trade rules, questioned its validity by stating, "What's this 180 pages of 'NAFTA' on steroids' that some tree hugger's giving me?" (Peterson, 1999, p. A1).

Whether the tone is passively aggressive or overtly aggressive, the informal reduction to absurdity public rhetoric is an obstacle to environmental advocacy. Further study of the tree hugger-label in public discourse now leads to the conclusion that the label has at least three other broad categories of uses: in self identification, in description, and in moderating positions.

SELF-IDENTIFIER

The tree-hugger label originally referred to the National Park Service Rangers assigned to the Washington, D.C. area parks (Whitehead, 1977, p. 1). The term was used to distinguish the park rangers from the park police, who were known as "tree fuzz" (Whitehead, 1977). It was not until the appearance of a Heritage Foundation report in 1982 that the term was used in a negative light. The report, which evaluated the Reagan administration's first year in office, noted that conservationists were to be referred to as "prairie fairies and tree-huggers" ("Sound," 1982, p. D1). Another Heritage Foundation report, entitled *Mandate for Leadership*, argued that the Department of the Interior had been controlled by "biological types, prairie fairies, and tree-huggers" (Gilbert, 1983, p. 66).

The early years of the Reagan administration saw a movement away from the label as a rather neutral descriptor toward an increased negative connotation. The debate over the management of natural resources was characterized by a polarization of the pro-environmentalist forces and the administration officials, who were committed to breaking down the government's environmental bureaucracy. Jay Hair, then the executive vice-president of the National Wildlife Federation, noted that right-wing groups had referred to the federation as "posy pickers and tree huggers" (Dornan, 1983, p. n). When Anne Burford, President Reagan's appointee as Environmental Protection Agency chief, resigned under pressure, she believed that her managerial style was not supported by the Eastern press. She stated: "So whoever is the administrator of the EPA at least has to come off stylistically as a prairie fairy or a tree-hugger in order to get over that barrier that the eastern press corps demands, that you be emotive about the environment" (Hall, 1985, p. A4). An understanding of the historical uses of the label allows us to understand the self-identifier use more completely.

The use of the label as a self-identifier by environmentalists, ironically, may serve to delegitimize their own discourse. The term invites reduction to absurdity, because the term is too literal. The mental imagery is too concrete. Perry Young, a columnist for the *Chapel Hill Herald*, noted: "Being one of the biggest tree-huggers in three counties, I was overwhelmed with guilt when folks up and down Henderson Street began to ask me why 'they' cut down that beautiful old oak tree at the corner of Henderson and Rosemary streets" (2000, p. 4). Gerry Rising wrote in The *Buffalo News*, "But we also love our environment. Especially at this time of year, this time of renewal, we don't mind being called 'tree huggers.' We want to protect our wonderful surroundings. To do so we must take action now" (1999, 4B). Dorothy Coens, an advocate for the protection of National Historic Landmarks, boasted, "When I was on the County Board, they used to call me a tree-hugger, but I don't care" (Smith, 1999, 1C). Leslie Carothers, an environmentalist in Hartford, Connecticut, described herself when she noted, "I don't mind being called a tree-hugger. The environmental movement, by any standard, has been a success. So, as long as you get results and clout, I don't mind" (Seremet, 1999, D1). Grace Stock, an Audubon Society spokesperson, described a reaction to a pipeline project. She said, "I thought it needed more than just us tree-huggers because it affects the whole county" (Reeder, 1999, p. 1B). C. B. Livingston, a citizen of Fayetteville, Georgia,, wrote of himself, "I am a conservative tree hugger who is extremely distressed by what I see happening in Fayette County. While most of us recognize the importance of the loss of the rain forest, we seem to be oblivious to the mass destruction of the land in our own community" (Livingston, 1999, p. 6JM). Even Will Clay Ford, Jr., the chair of Ford Motor Company, is a "self-professed tree-hugger" (Incantalupo, 1999, p. D3).

It is possible that self-identified tree-huggers can deliver positive results for the environment. Henry County, Georgia, Commissioner Gary Freedman, "a self-described 'tree hugger,' " helped pass a tree protection proposal for the county (Banks, 2000, p. 2J). Business leaders, attempting to create a positive corporate image, can also take on this positive self-identifier. Ed Boyce, CEO and founder of Innsbrook, a Warren County, Missouri, resort community, noted: "I'm kind of a tree-hugger. I was one before it became politically correct" (Sealey , 1999, p. 1). Greg Callaway, of Callaway Development Corporation, believes that his company has "got kind of a reputation as being tree huggers" (Bush, 1999, p. 1H). A group in Porter Township, Michigan, known as the "Tree Huggers" has planted a number of trees in their township with funds derived from a local electrical cooperative grant ("Porter," 1999, p. D7).

Despite these successes, the tree-hugger label as a self-identifier is problematic. Whereas the label tree-fuzz, used by the National Park Service Rangers, is neutral and ambiguous, the label tree-hugger is not neutral or sufficiently ambiguous to transcend its literal use. Therefore, the tree-hugger label has serious defects and is not likely to create a more general, positive public discourse.

DESCRIPTOR OF OTHERS

The most literal application of the tree-hugger label in recent history is to Julia Butterfly Hill. On December 10, 1997, she took up residence in a redwood tree, which she named Luna, to prevent a logging company from cutting the tree and other trees in the area. She did not come down until December 18, 1999. Hill, who has engaged in a campaign to save California forests, has been portrayed as a tree-hugger. She once remarked: "No question the media attention has been hard on me. Some of it has hurt. But the good thing is that the scrutiny has made sure I walk my talk" (Krum, 1999, p. 6). What is interesting in this quotation is that Hill does not focus on the use of the tree hugger label as a descriptor, but as a motivator. The final section of this chapter discusses her case in more depth.

The tree-hugger label is often used to describe groups at odds with other groups. James F. Quillinan, a cofounder of a conservation club in Wisconsin, pointed out the relatively obvious proposition that "hunters and tree-huggers are at odds with each other" (Kuhns, 1999, p. 2). In a controversy over Long Island development programs, *Newsday* reported, "Preserving the East End is no longer a traditional battle between tree-hugging environmentalists and bulldozer-driving developers. Tourism and the second home market—and the related six-figure summer rentals in the Hamptons—depend on preserving the environment, which may act as its own development deterrent" (Freedman, 1999, p. A13). In the context of logging, Fisher argued "Too many in the timber industry have taken the position that an unlogged forest is necessarily an unhealthy forest, while too many in the tree-hugging groups have talked, and acted, as if logging on public land is something to be fought wherever it is proposed" (1999, p. 1F). In Tennessee, politicians are confronted with the tensions between environmentalists and lumber company representatives. Legislators take tension into account when they consider legislation. Anderson noted: "Considering all of the competing interests, Tennessee legislators are facing a number of proposals that deserve careful debate and fair consideration. There is natural tension between 'tree huggers' and 'chip mill' clearcutters" (1999, p. B7). We note in these examples how the tree-hugger label serves as a label, a convenient way to categorize and refer to groups of people.

The use of the label as a descriptor of others, then, sometimes is relatively uninteresting, because the label is a kind of synonym for "environmentalist." At other times, the descriptor seems more politically charged. If the struggle over meanings is historical and political, as well as grammatical, then these points of political tension are critical. What may be fascinating in this regard is to trace who applies the label, to whom, when, under what circumstances, and toward what end. In such an analysis, the tree-hugger label's relationship to *power* will become clearer. For example, if we use Hariman's (1995) "status-sensitive rhetorical theory," then we might conclude that the tree-hugger label functions not so much to describe as to marginalize and to conceal marginalization.

"TREE-HUGGER" AS A MODERATING DEVICE

The fourth use of the tree-hugger label found in the newspaper accounts included in this study is as a *moderating device*. The term tree-hugger has become more widely used today as an attempt to make one's position seem more moderate. Some advocates defend their position as less radical than "tree hugging." This moderating device has the possible rhetorical advantage of gaining support from individuals in favor of environmental protection, but at the same time leaving open lines of communication to other groups. Scott Hamilton, who moved to the state of Washington to live near mountains, argued that he was a "moderate tree hugger." He noted: "I believe in clean water. I'm a tree hugger. I'm nowhere near as militant as some of these other people. I believe a developer who buys land has a right to make money off it. I also believe a developer should be more sensitive to retaining trees and protecting water than he is typically" (Lindblom, 1999, p. B3). Riverside County (California) Supervisor Bob Buster is another example of an individual who had originally been perceived as an environmentalist, but who had overcome that reputation. One fundraiser described Buster as "a great combination of intelligence and integrity. Bob was perceived as a tree-hugger. He got a bad rap coming in" (O'Leary, 1999, p. B01).

In both of these cases, a moderate tree-hugger characterization is juxtaposed with a more radical variant in order to gain rhetorical advantage in the public sphere. The underlying logic seems to be that extremism is bad.

This kind of use of the tree-hugger term as a moderating device in public discourse has been a relatively recent phenomenon. According to Rall, "corporate America has retired the 'tree hugger' rhetoric in favor of quiet lobbying behind the scenes to fend off congressional attempts to reduce air pollution" (1999, p. 4D). Jean Dubail, in The *Cleveland Plain Dealer*, said of biomass programs, "This is not some pie-in-the-sky idea cooked up by granola-munching tree-huggers; nine states already have adopted such requirements" (1999, p. 11B). Rich Hood, the editorial page editor for The *Kansas City Star*, wrote, "I don't believe I qualify as the stereotypical tree-hugger because I realize that trees have many utilitarian uses, from fruit-bearing to lumber to simple shade. I'm fond of wood-working" (1999, p. K3). In an attempt to compromise between environmental interests and development, Thousand Oaks (California) Councilman Andy Fox argued, "I am not a big tree-hugger. I'm a by-the-numbers guy. I'm just doing my job trying to reach an identified goal for the city" (Griffith, 2000, p. B1). Economist David Woltz attempted to justify his advocacy for green solutions to problems, stating: "I'm not a tree-hugger, but we do have a planet of a finite size. If we don't watch our land and resources, it's going to cost us money" (Pearce, 1999, p. D1). Again, this use of the term is linked to reasonableness and good business sense.

More examples indicate how widespread this use of the label is. Justifying his support for grease-eating technology, Environmental Biotech Inc. founder Bill Hadley initially supported the technology for its environmental benefits, but noted, "I'm not a tree hugger" (Hielscher, 1999, p. 12). The group "Save Our Cumberland Mountains," a Tennessee protection group, attempted to moderate their appearance by claiming, "We're not tree-huggers. We don't say you can't cut down any trees. We are concerned because Tennessee has no regulations or registration required for timbering" (O'Neal, 1999, p. B1). A Washington County, Minnesota, project to create a green corridor along the St. Croix River gained support from members of the community through the same sort of argumentative approach. John Baird, a Stillwater, Minnesota, resident, noted "It isn't just tree-huggers that are after this. It is people who are interested in selling property" (Kaszuba, 2000, p. 1A). Andrew George, director of the Southern Appalachian Biodiversity Project, believed that "Environmental issues are received better by the public now than they ever have been. It's not just an issue of tree huggers and oxygen huggers, we all live on the planet" (Davis, 1999, B3). Dennis Phillips, the president of the Belgrade (Maine) Regional Conservation Alliance, noted in regard to a land trust program, "Without seeming like a tree-hugger, we need to set aside land for recreation and wildlife habitat. Obviously, people need a place to live, but we also need open space for recreation. There just has to be a balance" (Cooper, 1999, p. A1). Santa Susana Knolls, California, resident Holly Huff believed that "I'm not some radical tree hugger. I just love trees.

I'm just real concerned—all my life I watched trees go in the San Fernando Valley. There's no point in cutting down these trees" (Bartholomew, 1999, p. B1). In some of these cases the tree-hugger label is linked to lobbying for a certain quality of life. Moderate environmentalism is acceptable, apparently, if it ensures a green belt in one's neighborhood.

Politicians have attempted to use the term tree-hugger as a moderating device in their discourse. Describing Woody Snell, a developer who won a seat on the Cobb County (Georgia) Soil and Water Board of Supervisors, Steve Visser noted: "Snell said he is neither a tree-cutter nor a tree-hugger, but an engineer who will work to make sure developers start practicing conservation methods that protect topsoil and water quality. He promises them a healthy profit at the same time" (1999, p. 4B). State Senator David Magnani (Massachusetts), who argued for stricter pollution regulations, stated, "If people think I'm a flake or a tree hugger, then they're not paying attention to science. We are polluting our own nest" (Parent, 1999, p. 1). Even real estate agents have used the term tree-hugger to describe themselves in an environmentally positive fashion. John Kline, an Iowa developer, described his efforts to protect the environment: "We've been known to move streets to try to save a tree. I'm as close to a tree hugger as a real estate agent can be" (Lopez, 1999, p. 4). We note in several of these examples an attempt to link the moderate form of the label to science and relegate the extreme form of the term to impracticality.

In the following examples, note how far speakers will go to distance themselves from the tree-hugger label. In a statement about his positive feelings toward the Alaskan environment, Michael Foster, a vocational rehabilitation counselor who had recently moved to Alaska, noted:

Let me preface my remarks by stating that I am not a tree hugging, granola munching, hemp wearing environmentalist. I will eat granola however, if it contains chocolate chips and marshmallows. I have not adopted a spotted owl, and don't care to. I've never been involved in Greenpeace, the Sierra Club, or any environmental organization or cause. (2000, p. 8B)

Denis Hebert, Bath (Maine) city superintendent of cemetery and parks, said of the Forestry Committee's efforts in his town, "I couldn't do this without them. I just don't have enough manpower. They've been called tree huggers, but I would take exception to that. They temper their love for trees with the knowledge that trees have to share space with humans" (Hoey, 1999, p. 1B). In an attempt to sound more moderate, Donna Lopinto, a member of an ad hoc citizens' environmental group in New York State, characterizes the group as "not just tree huggers or sandal wearers or all of one kind" (Brenner, 1999, p. 14WC). What emerges in these examples of discourse, as well as in some of the previous examples, is Burke's process of identifications and divisions. Note that the speakers divide vocations and avocations into two sets. Those described in a positive tone are accountants, engineers, politicians, real estate agents, and scientists. Those described in a negative tone include "flakes," granola eaters, members of environmental organizations, and, of course, tree-huggers.

IMPLICATIONS AND CONCLUSION

This analysis of 1999 newspaper accounts indicates that the tree-hugger label is used in at least four ways: (1) as an informal Reductio Ad Absurdum to attack and ridicule environmentalists as absurd, (2) as a self-identifier, (3) as a descriptor of others, and (4) as a moderating device to gain rhetorical advantage, often to promote a business or "scientific" perspective. While it is useful to track and report on these four competing discourses, another critical task is to explore the implications of these findings. How these discourses might influence environmental advocacy is particularly interesting.

Earlier this chapter illustrated why the tree-hugger label has serious liabilities for effective environmental advocacy. The tree-hugger label is too graphic, too concrete, to become the basis of a widespread and positive discourse. The graphic, visual nature of the tree-hugger label lends itself to reduction to absurdity. Very few persons actually hug trees. Therefore, the image seems comic. A more ambiguous, open, and flexible label has greater potential for positive, popular use in the future.

By way of contrast with the tree-hugger label, in the following case a derisive nickname now is used with apparently minimal negative consequences. The case is that of General John J. Pershing. Early in his career as an officer in the U.S. Army, Pershing was assigned to the 10th Cavalry, the now-famous "Buffalo Soldiers." These troops were African American, or "black" soldiers, who after the Civil War were active in service in the western United States. Following his time with the "black" 10th Cavalry, Pershing was assigned to the U.S. Military Academy at West Point and reported for duty in June 1897. Pershing, a tough disciplinarian, became one of the most disliked officers on the staff at West Point. According to Vandiver's account, "unpopularity won a nickname for Pershing, one born in racist contempt. The cadets knew he belonged to the 10th Cavalry and so began to call him 'Nigger Jack.' In time it softened to 'Black Jack,' but the intent remained hostile" (1977, p. 171). Because the U.S. Army, and especially the officer corps, was a small community in that era, most insiders would know the meaning of the nickname. What is of concern in the present study is that a nickname "born in racist contempt" lost its harsh meaning and was transformed into a badge of honor. In the case of Pershing, several factors explain the transformation of the "Black Jack" nickname.

First, the meaning of the word black can be ambiguous. *Webster's Seventh New Collegiate Dictionary* lists more than a dozen definitions. Over the course of eighty years, the ambiguity inherent in this wide range of meanings facilitates the transformation of the meaning of the nickname. Second, with the passage of time, the origins of the nickname became more and more obscure. To understand that the nickname was a racist taunt, a listener in the year 2002 would have to know Pershing's background with the 10th Cavalry or have access to sources present at West Point in 1897. Then, too, an individual would have to have specific knowledge about the Buffalo Soldiers. Finally, the context for the discourse would have to permit the public use of racist language. These conditions, taken together, constitute significant barriers for constructing a univocal or dominant meaning, something that is possible, even likely, with the tree-hugger label. Some persons might think that the nickname "Black Jack" refers to a popular Las Vegas card game. Others might take the nickname to be a commentary on Pershing's demeanor, that he was tough or harsh. It also is perfectly plausible to believe that the nickname Black Jack is very positive, given the renewed interest in the Buffalo Soldiers and the acclaim given to them today. For all these reasons, the nickname Black Jack today is not linked to racism at West Point, whereas the tree-hugger label cannot escape its specificity.

Let us turn now to the case of the most literal of tree-huggers, Julia Butterfly Hill, whom we mentioned previously in this chapter. To what extent can Julia Butterfly Hill's very physical example of environmental advocacy grow into a positive, popular discourse? Media coverage of Hill's protest may qualify her as a popular culture figure (Achenbach, 1999, p. A1). She certainly is an icon among environmental advocates. DeLuca sees Hill's significance partly in the fact that she "sees the world from the tree's point of view and 'becomes' the tree" (1999, p. 56). At another point DeLuca writes: "Through inhabitation, a space that is interchangeable with many others becomes *this* place that is irreplaceable in its particularity" (1999, p. 161). Perhaps we now have moved from the label tree-hugger to an *experience*.

Brummett may be relevant here. He offers a way of understanding the relationship between the tree-hugger "text" and the individual decision maker. He suggests that we "move the site of struggle from the text, which is merely product, to the logics that create texts, and to choices among and awareness of those logics and how they position us as subjects" (1991, p. 89). Brummett uses the phrase "the ways in which culturally grounded forms could be used to order a person's experience" (1991, p. 196). What Brummett goes on to emphasize in this passage is everyday experience. He states: "Symbolic struggle over how to order and understand experience is the dimension of everyday life where rhetoric is at work" (1991, p. 196). Here, a "chicken-*and*-egg" model is suggested for linking text and experience. Popular culture influences how we order our experience, but our experience also orders how we are influenced by popular culture.

It is unlikely that Hill would sit in a tree for two years without some prior experience with nature. It is just as unlikely that a young person today will copy Hill's exploit without some prior connections to nature. Or, to be fair, a young person might emulate Hill if the emphasis were on ordering experience as *exploit*, because exploits are very much a part of youth popular culture today. In fact, those interested in environmental advocacy can influence young people in two ways.

First, advocates for the environment can employ a public discourse that characterizes Hill's actions and environmental advocacy, in general, as an exploit and as heroic. Second, the experience of the ages teaches us that environmental spirituality and advocacy grow out of deep, lived connections to nature. Advocates for the environment, therefore, need to intensify work with children. As parents, Girl and Boy Scout leaders, camp counselors, science teachers, sponsors for Future Farmers of America and 4H, and as nature center interpreters, environmental advocates can help young people to experience spaces that might become special places.

As for more traditional scholarly activity, both scholars and practitioners in the area of environmental rhetoric and popular culture may want to study other labels in popular culture, such as the term "hippies," and their connection to experience. It might be instructive to explore the links between labels, experience, and social movements (Libby, 1998; Peterson, T. R., 1997). Future studies could examine the relationship between power and the ability to define oneself in the environmental context. Particularly with the use of the term tree hugger, it is important to remember the power associated with personal experience and with the ability to define oneself.

REFERENCES

Abel, D. (2000, February 4). Lawyer leads fight for animal rights; "I know it's easy to make fun of what I do." The *Commercial Appeal* (Memphis, TN), p. A12.

Achenbach, J. (1999, April 30). Giants in the earth; In California, ancient redwoods make a last stand. The *Washington Post*, p. A1.

Agrawal, Y. (1999, March 18). Moving beyond the spotted owl. *Harvard Crimson*, np.

Anderson, L. (1999, May 5). For sensible forestry policy. The *Chattanooga Times and Free Press*, p. B7.

Anderson, A. & Custen, G. F. (1998). *Media, culture, and the environment*. New Brunswick, NJ: Rutgers University Press.

Banks, B. (2000, January 6). Proposed tree law gets planners' nod. *Atlanta Journal and Constitution*, p. 2J.

Bartholomew, D. (1999, April 23). Eucalyptus trees to stay for now. *Ventura County Star*, p. B1.

Bosman, J. (1987). Persuasive effects of political metaphors. *Metaphor and Symbolic Activity, 2*, 97-113.

Bosman, J. & Hagendoorn, L. (1991). Effects of literal and metaphorical persuasive messages. *Metaphor and Symbolic Activity, 6*, 271-292.

Brenner, E. (1999, May 9). Town houses may rise where Indians once made their homes. The *New York Times*, p. 14WC.

Brummett, B. (1991). *Rhetorical dimensions of popular culture*. Tuscaloosa: The University of Alabama Press.

Burke, K. (1945). *A grammar of motives*. New York: Prentice Hall.

Burke, K. (1950). *A rhetoric of motives*. New York: Prentice Hall.

Bush, R. (1999, May 5). Leaders looking at tree ordinance. *San Antonio ExpressNews*, p. 1H.

Cantrill, J. G. (1996). Gold, Yellowstone, and the search for a rhetorical identity. In C. G. Herndl & S. C. Brown (Eds.), *Green culture: Environmental rhetoric in contemporary America* (pp. 166-194). Madison: The University of Wisconsin Press.

Carbaugh, D. (1988). Comments on "culture" in communication inquiry. *Communication Reports, 1*, 38-41.

Chang, B. (1992). Empty intention. *Text and Performance Quarterly, 12,* 212-227.

Cooper, M. (1999, June 14). Guardian of the woods Rome man strives to set aside land for public use. *Kennebec Journal,* p. A1.

Cowherd, K. (1999, March 18). You wanted roomy? Now you've got it. The *Baltimore Sun,* p. 1F.

Crosswhite, J. (1995). Is there an audience for this argument. Fallacies, theories, and relativisms. *Philosophy and Rhetoric, 28,* 134-145.

Davis, T. (1999, April 23). WNC observes Earth Day with a variety of events. *Asheville Citizen-Times,* p. B3.

DeLuca, K. M. (1999). *Image politics: The new rhetoric of environmental activism.* New York: Guilford Press.

Dipert, B. (1999). Earth in the balance. Information Access Company, 44, 31.

Dornan, G. (1983, February 5). No title. United Press International, BC cycle, n/p.

Dubail, J. (1999, April 29). Puny guys losing in struggle with electric utilities. *The Plain Dealer,* p. 11B.

Fisher, J. (1999, May 9). Finally, in north central Idaho, a light in the forest. *Lewiston Morning Tribune,* p. 1F.

Foster, M. (2000, January 19). "Hey, flickers, keep your butts in your ashtray." *Anchorage Daily News,* p. 8B.

Freedman, M. (1999, May 17). The east end is at a crossroads: Protect open spaces or spur further growth. *Newsday* (New York), p. A13.

Gilbert, B. (1983, September 26). Inside interior: An abrupt turn. *Sports Illustrated, 26,* 66.

Gittrich, G. (1999, May 17). Critics claim LAUSD ignoring safety issues. The *Daily News of Los Angeles,* p. N1.

Graesser, A. C., Mio, J., & Millis, K. K. (1989). Metaphors in persuasive communication. In D. Meutsch & R. Viehoff (Eds.), *Comprehension of literary discourse: Results and problems of interdisciplinary approaches* (pp. 131-154). New York: Walter de Gruyter.

Griffith, A. (2000, February 6). Reaching for a plateau: Land swap would preserve open space. *Ventura County Star,* p. B1.

Grossberger, L. (1999, May 31). Media person. *Mediaweek,* np.

Hall, H. B. (1985, June 13). Burford attributes downfall at EPA to management style; "News media want a tree-hugger," she says. The *Washington Post,* p. A4.

Hariman, R. (1995). Status, marginality, and rhetorical theory. *Quarterly Journal of Speech, 72,* 2-17.

Herndl, C. G. & Brown, S. C. (Eds.). (1996). *Green culture: Environmental rhetoric in contemporary America.* Madison: The University of Wisconsin Press.

Hielscher, J. (1999, May 24). Grease-eating specialists. *Sarasota Herald-Tribune,* p. 12. Hoey, D. (1999, May 15). Bath starts arbor week events today. *Portland Press Herald,* p. 1B.

Hoey, D. (1999, May 15). Bath starts Arbor week events today. *Portland Press Herald,* p. 1B.

Hood, R. (1999, April 11). A pox on needless tree-killing. The *Kansas City Star,* p. K3.

Incantalupo, T. (1999, April 2). Dreamboat or tanker Valdez? *Newsday* (New York), p. D3.

Kaszuba, M. (2000, February 2). Washington County moves ahead with unique green-space proposal. *Star Tribune,* p. 1A.

Krum, S. (1999, April 5). Life in the leaves. *The Guardian* (London), p. 6.

Kuhns, L. (1999, May 17). Lake Butte des morts devotees trigger conservation effort.

Milwaukee Journal Sentinel, p. 2.

Laclau, E. & Mouffe, C. (1985). *Hegemony and socialist strategy: Towards a radical democratic politics*. London: Verso.

Lakoff, G. & Johnson, M. (1980). *Metaphors we live by*. Chicago: University of Chicago Press.

Lange, J. (1993) The logic of competing information campaigns: Conflict over old growth and the spotted owl. *Communication Monographs, 60,* 239-257.

Libby, R. T. (1998). *Eco-wars: Political campaigns and social movements*. New York: Columbia University Press.

Lindblom, M. (1999, June 4). Commitment his middle name—Newcomer's opposition to development refueled anti-growth movement. *Seattle Times*, p. B3.

Livingston, C. B. (1999, May 6). We're destroying our community. *Atlanta Journal and Constitution*, p. 6JM.

Long, T. (1999, May 5). Gore's visit isn't the only issue for local ecology people. The *Detroit News,* p. Gi.

Lopez, A. (1999, May 14). Trees can add value to your home. The *Des Moines Register,* p. 4.

Manicas, P. & Kruger, A. N. (1968). *Essentials of logic*. New York: American Book Company.

McCain, R. S. (1999, April 22). Planet's day in the sun: Earth Day has lost some luster, but is praised for aiding the environment. *Washington Times*, p. A2.

McManis, S. (1999, April 23). This Earth Day put on your walking shoes. The *San Francisco Chronicle*, p. 1.

Mio, J. S., & Katz, A. N. (Eds.). (1996). *Metaphor: Implications and applications*. Mahwah, NJ: Lawrence Erlbaum.

O'Leary, T. (1999, May 20). Developers' help builds for Buster. The *Press-Enterprise* (Riverside, CA), p. B01.

Olson, K.M. & Goodnight, G.T. (1994). Entanglement of consumption, cruelty, privacy, and fashion: The social controversy over fur. The *Quarterly Journal of Speech, 80,* 249-276.

O'Neal, M. (1999, May 4). Legislature to consider regulating timber industry. The *Chattanooga Times and Free Press*, p. B1.

Parent, R. (1999, April 11). Magnani wants SUV controls; Bill calls for limits on pollution from big vehicles. *The Boston Globe*, p. 1.

Pawlowski, D., Badzinski, D., & Mitchell, N. (1998). Effects of metaphors on children's comprehension and perception of print advertisements. *Journal of Advertising, 27,* 83-98.

Pearce, J. (1999, May 3). Eco-forum puts focus on Detroit; City hosts national town meeting on environment, growth. The *Detroit News*, p. D1.

Peterson, J. (1999, May 31). Trade's image takes beating among public. *Los Angeles Times*, p. A1.

Peterson, T. R. (1997). *Sharing the earth: The rhetoric of sustainable development*. Columbia: University of South Carolina Press.

Porter tree huggers plant 94 trees. (1999, May 14). *South Bend Tribune*, p. D7.

Pugh, S. (1989). Metaphor and learning. *Reading Research and Instruction, 28,* 97-103.

Rall, T. (1999, May 9). Getting warmer. Humanity toasts itself into extinction. *Las Vegas Review-Journal*, p. 4D.

Reeder, J. (1999, May 7). Gas pipeline backers set hearing in Fort Pierce. The *Palm Beach Post*, p. 1B.

Ridley, M. (1999, April 26). Comment: Acid test and yet, the earth is getting greener. The *Daily Telegraph* (London), p. 20.

Riley, P., Klumpp, J., & Hollihan, T. (1995). Democratizing the lifeworld of the 21st century: Evaluating new democratic sites for argument. In S. Jackson (Ed.), *Argumentation and values: Proceedings of the ninth SCA/AFA conference on argumentation* (pp. 254-260). Annandale, VA: Speech Communication Association.

Rising, G. (1999, April 19). Recommit to the environment this Earth Day. The *Buffalo News*, p. 4B.

Root, R. L., Jr. (1987). *The rhetorics of popular culture: Advertising, advocacy, and entertainment.* Westport, CT: Greenwood Press.

Ruud, G. & Sprague, J. (2000). Can't see the [old growth] forest for the logs: Dialectical tensions in the interpretive practices of environmentalists and loggers. *Communication Reports, 13,* 55-65.

Sealey, G. (1999, June 1). Innsbrook expansion plan nearly doubles home sites; Resort community makes room for more year-round residents. *St. Louis Post-Dispatch,* p. 1.

Seremet, P. (1999, April 27). In business to clean up: UTC's environmental chief thrives on change. *The Hartford Courant,* p. D1.

Smith, S. L. (1999, May 2). Van Hise Rock to be national landmark. *Wisconsin State Journal,* p. 1C.

Snyder, G. (1990). The etiquette of freedom. *The practice of the wild: Essays by Gary Snyder,* (pp. 3-24). San Francisco: North Point.

Sonners, S. (2000, February 4). 1,000 protest roads policy in Nevada. *The Desert News,* p. B10.

Sound and fury. (1982, January 29). The *Washington Post,* p. D1.

Szasz, A. (1995). *Ecopopulism: Toxic waste and the movement for environmental justice.* Minneapolis: University of Minnesota Press.

Tansey, B. & Heredia, C. (1999, April 23). Refinery gadflies asked to butt out; Cities devise safety rules without group's help. The *San Francisco Chronicle,* p. A23.

Tax incentives saving more land. (1999, May 25). *Morning Star* (Wilmington, NC), p. 6A.

Thomason, A. (1999, May 30). This pair really digs the public's stream beds. *Arizona Republic,* p. EV1.

Vandiver, F. E. (1977). *Black Jack: The life and times of John J. Pershing.* Vol. 1. College Station: Texas A & M University Press.

Van Eemeren, F. H., & Grootendorst, R. (1992). *Argumentation, communication, and fallacies.* Hillsdale, NJ: Lawrence Erlbaum.

Visser, S. (1999, June 10). Cobb election draws .07 percent of registered voters. *Atlanta Journal and Constitution,* p. 4B.

Wagar, K. (1999, April 30). Bill on wildlife petitions clears House but draws fire. The *Kansas City Star,* p. B3.

Whitehead, P. (1977, October 7). Getting away to admire the leaves. *Washington Post,* p. 1.

Young, P. (2000, January 8). Confessions of an errant tree hugger. *Chapel Hill Herald,* p.4.

8

From Loch Ness Monsters to Global Warming: Framing Environmental Risk in a Supermarket Tabloid

Donnalyn Pompper

News production is a vulnerable process that, when scrutinized, reveals much about the larger symbolic system of news in our culture. In particular, researchers have noted the pervasiveness of framing, or "selecting and highlighting some features of reality while omitting others" (Entman, 1993, p. 53), especially as used routinely by the news media. Surely such encoding is not the product of any conspiracy, but rather is the result of central cultural assumptions and journalistic practices rooted in organizational imperatives that tend to reproduce dominant ideology. This study content analyzed frames encoded in news texts about environmental risks involving air, water, and land protection, preservation, and restoration over a fifteen year period.

This focus is of interest because environmental awareness promoted by the news media (Lowe & Morrison, 1984) and legislation designed to protect natural habitat has grown over the last two decades in the United States and worldwide (Gare, 1995). Contributing to the urgency and complexity of the environmental issue is the lack of a global environmental ethic or a coherent international legal or regulatory regime (Kasperson & Kasperson, 1991) in spite of recent multinational environmental summits. Moreover, many have analyzed the 1960s and 1970s environmental movement (Bowman & Hanaford, 1977; Catton & Dunlap, 1980; Honnold, 1981; Milbrath, 1984; Hannigan, 1995), but subsequent decades have been scrutinized less.

There is much that we do not know about environmental risk issues affecting all current and future life on this planet and how we make meaning from the way these issues are represented. For example, many media-related studies of environmental issues have overlooked the cultural context by focusing exclusively on the communication process as a linear transmission (Hansen, 1991), and too many institutional risk analyses have ignored the social context of risk (Freudenburg, 1992). Also, there is a need to examine texts primarily used by readers who represent a lower socioeconomic bloc who feel marginalized by mainstream news media. Consequently, this study attempted to fill some of these gaps by building on an important body of work that has recognized weekly supermarket tabloids as worthy sites for popular culture study, and by narrowing the focus exclusively to environmental risk.

Even though Gitlin (1980) suggested that news frames fundamentally do not contradict dominant hegemonic principles, such as legitimacy of dominant social orders, Bird (1992) found that weekly supermarket tabloids purposively sustain a sense of popular antagonism toward dominant blocs. Therefore, this study further tested this later conclusion by using environmental risk news as the lens:

H: Tabloid newspapers use frames that emphasize opposition to dominant ideology when reporting environmental risk issues, as opposed to using frames which support the status quo.

Once the computer-assisted textual analysis (CATA) program[1] identified the news frames, traditional rhetorical analysis was used to qualitatively probe *National Enquirer* environmental risk texts. Overall, the overtly moral nature of the arguments raised in environmental risk issues seems to appeal to the news media (Hansen, 1991) and the frames they use in their stories are drawn from shared cultural narratives and myths (Gamson & Modigliani, 1989). Bird (1992) has related tabloids to folklore, suggesting that these newspapers are formulaic publications that rely on the same mix of stories shaped by an understanding of readers' narrative schemata. In this vein, the current study closely examined environmental risk news from 1983 to 1997 to learn more about how these issues are framed for a very specific audience. This analysis begins by exploring the framing literature, identifying dominant ideology in stories, and examining the significance of social risk.

FRAMING, STORYTELLING AND RISK

Over the past twenty years, framing has been recognized as a major theoretical concept in mass communication research (Goffman, 1974; Minsky, 1975; Tuchman, 1978; Gitlin, 1980; Gamson & Lasch, 1983; Rachlin, 1988; Graber, 1988, 1989; Gamson & Modigliani, 1989; Entman, 1993). Framing theory has been inspired by earlier work in philosophy, phenomenology, sociology, cognitive psychology, musicology, and semantics that looked at scripts (Schank & Abelson, 1977), prototypes (Rosch, 1975), paradigms (Kuhn, 1970), stereotypes (Fowler, 1991), and schemata (Schutz, 1945; Bateson, 1972; Cone, 1968; Rumelhart, 1980). Consequently, the framing concept appears in various traditions of scholarly inquiry and is visible in numerous scholarly journals, themed panels at academic conferences, and mass media textbooks. Following a comprehensive review of literature in search of studies involving framing, Entman (1993) resolved that frames occupy at least four locations in the communication process among – communicators, texts, receivers and culture worldview – and that frames can be used to define problems, diagnose causes, make moral judgments, and suggest remedies. In the current study, discovery of frames enabled textual analysis of a storytelling medium infrequently scrutinized relative to mainstream media.

In addition to its theoretical contributions, framing is a practical tool used in news work. Overall, journalism is a practice with a definable milieu that culminates in a manufactured product shaped by a complex, yet artificial or subjective, selection, collection, organization, and dissemination of data (Galtung & Ruge, 1973; Goffman, 1974, Darnton, 1975; Tuchman, 1978; Hall, 1979; Gans, 1979; Carey, 1986; Fowler, 1991). Journalists slice "strips" of the everyday world "from the stream of ongoing activity" (Goffman, 1974, pp. 10-11) and use frames to write efficiently, situate the players, and name the important points, angles, issues, and questions (Gitlin, 1980; Mencher, 1983). Some journalists may deny that they intentionally frame news, but many agree that they draw on collectively accepted images stored in the memories of audiences as a storytelling device. For example, framing a dictator as "another Hitler" lends deeper meaning to a story because it evokes images of genocide, persecution, and racial discrimination (Graber, 1989, p. 148). While framing has become a routine news practice, media critics ponder journalists' selection and salience of some issues over others – an intrinsic component of storytelling.

Looking at the unconscious way frames are used in storytelling lends insight into how dominant ideology shapes news texts. For several years, anthropologists and sociologists have studied storytelling as a means for perpetuating culture (Radcliffe-Brown, 1952; Mead, 1953; Levi-Strauss, 1964; Geertz, 1973), and many mass media scholars have characterized journalism as contemporary storytelling (Darnton, 1975; Barkin, 1984; van Dijk, 1988; Nord, 1989). Even though few mainstream journalists would classify journalism this way, analyses of news narratives, like other kinds of stories, reveal much about how our culture makes meaning (Park, 1940; Bird & Dardenne, 1988; Campbell, 1991). In this way, Carey (1974) described journalism as "a literary act, parallel to the novel, the essay and the scientific report" (p. 4). To better understand dominant ideology encoded in stories, it is relevant to turn to the work of scholars who have examined power relations and the mass media.

Researchers such as those at the Glasgow University Media Group (1976, 1980) and the University of Birmingham Centre for Contemporary Cultural Studies (Hall, 1979) viewed news as a mediated re-presentation of some slice of reality. These researchers' textual analyses are steeped in the theoretical foundations of Althusser (1971), a Frankfort School student in the Marxist tradition, who suggested that capitalism reproduces itself in ways more covert than overt. In other words, ideological state apparatuses such as an education system, a political system, and cultural systems such as the church and the mass media all enforce dominant ideology by structuring and reshaping consent and consensus.

Beyond these apparatuses, language itself is value laden. Thus, framing and dominant ideology seem to go hand in hand. Journalists produce stories relevant to particular conditions of social existence (Glynn, 1993) and in the process their use of framing promotes very specific worldviews. Mainstream newspapers are perceived as official, conventional, traditional, legitimate news purveyors that inform and are shaped by relatively powerful social blocs, thus advancing hegemony. Supermarket tabloids, on the other hand, entertain social blocs marginalized by class and education and in the process sustain a sense of popular antagonism toward dominant blocs. Many tabloid readers believe powerful institutions such as business, government, media, and scientists are "conspiring against the people" (Bird, 1992, p. 130). Thus, tabloid news stories often "interrupt certain circuits of socio-cultural power" because they know their readers relish stories that criticize official culture and question the normal social order and official knowledge systems (Glynn, 1993, p. 19). This makes tabloid newspapers a rich popular culture artifact.

Even though *Editor & Publisher* called the *National Enquirer* "the most accurate paper in the country" (Barber, 1982, p. 49) and *Newsweek* applauded the tabloids for increasingly covering "perfectly legitimate news" (Pedersen, 1996, p. 26), tabloids are characterized as second-tier media (Glynn, 1993; Hinkle & Elliott, 1989). It makes sense, however, to examine the *National Enquirer* as cultural capital circulated among an audience within lower socioeconomic strata in the hope of facilitating a more well rounded understanding of the public policy issue of environmental risk.

To more narrowly examine the universe of environmental risk issues, it is important to focus on risk as a prominent feature of contemporary politics and culture (Lowe & Morrison, 1984) and risk avoidance as a ubiquitous component of everyday living (Golding, 1992). Clearly, risk and the environment substantially intersect since the news media often link the two constructs by defining the environment as a social problem (Schoenfeld et al., 1979) and a public issue (Lowe & Morrison, 1984). Furthermore, the sheer magnitude of the complex debates are clearly consistent with journalists' perceptions of their role as a conduit for transferring information in society (Gans, 1979). Journalists attempt to take the technical language of risk analyses and transform it into comprehensible texts that the public can easily understand and use (Goodfield, 1983).

Meanwhile, many sources whom journalists consult when writing environmental risk stories define risk as merely the product of probability and magnitude without considering values, attitudes, social influences, and cultural identity (Renn et al., 1992). Freudenburg (1992) criticized many risk analyses as being too technical, because they ignored the social context of risk. Short (1984) urged a transformation of risk analysis by incorporating social science perspectives. This study's scrutiny of environmental risk stories created for a marginalized group, was designed to bridge this gap.

The next section examines how news media have addressed environmental risk.

NEWS COVERAGE AND ENVIRONMENTAL ISSUES

Mass media scholars have established that environmentalism has assumed the shape of a sociopolitical issue since the late 1960s (Schoenfeld et al., 1979), in part because of news media attention. But historically, environmental awareness has become a widespread social phenomenon among Western societies (Yearley, 1991). McConnell (1954) submitted that modern-day environmentalism stems from the conservation movement of the late nineteenth and early twentieth centuries. From the environmental protection, or ecology, movement of the 1960s, the fields of risk assessment and management have grown (Krimsky & Golding, 1992; Tiemann, 1987). Furthermore, environmentalism today represents people's grassroots response to the unregulated and adverse effects of modernity (Gare, 1995). In fact, Milbrath (1984) called environmentalism a permanent fixture of public life in modern industrial societies.

Over the years, the mass media have played a special role in arousing public concern about environmental quality (Mazur, 1990; Friedman, 1991), particularly since the Santa Barbara oil spill of 1968 (Murch, 1971). Overall media attention to the environment and the subsequent increase in citizen awareness of this issue are evident in a wide variety of texts: special programs aired on network television, environmental reporters hired by leading newspapers, green products' ecological features emphasized by advertising agencies, increased environmental paperback books, and publication of magazines devoting entire issues to nature protection (Rubin & Sachs, 1973; Schoenfeld, 1973; Hannigan, 1995).

The news media extensively have covered the environment over the past thirty years, primarily because specific events or problems often are negative, unexpected, rare, and less predictable than positive, normal, or status quo news (Galtung & Ruge, 1973). In fact, public interest in environmental issues remains high longer than with many other issues because such risks affect everyone, are highly dramatic/visual, and identify villains and victims (Downs, 1972). Consequently, the news media have been criticized for imposing their values through the selection of news (Gans, 1979; Tuchman, 1978), as well as promoting a "hazard-of-the-week syndrome" (Kasperson & Kasperson, 1991, p. 9). Cole (1993) called environmental news a "parade of newly discovered or newly assessed threats" (p. 9).

In sum, news media coverage of environmental risk has given rise to an extremely varied and productive research tradition. Despite the multifaceted nature of such studies, it is possible to identify a small number of central themes: (1) environmental risk has become a legislated (Gare, 1995) socio-political issue (Schoenfeld et al., 1979) and an integral component of modern life in industrialized societies (Milbrath, 1984); (2) the news media, as an institutional apparatus, mold social knowledge (Hall, 1979) and shape risk in and through processes of discourse (Stallings, 1990). Furthermore, people look to the news media as a primary source of environmental information (Nelkin, 1989, Dunwoody & Neuwirth, 1991); (3) the practice of framing in news production encodes values and culturally appropriate cues in news texts (Goffman, 1974; Graber, 1989; Entman, 1993). Specifically, environmental risk embodies conflict and is a specific area where storytellers have shaped social knowledge – especially in supermarket tabloids.

FINDINGS

Among fifteen years' worth of weekly *National Enquirer* newspapers, or 780 issues,[2] a census of 400 environmental risk news stories was gathered based on the presence of at least one key search word[3] and subjected to CATA. Five clusters of most-frequently-used words, or news frames, were discovered among[4] data were to test this study's hypothesis:

H: Tabloid newspapers use frames that emphasize opposition to dominant ideology when reporting environmental risk issues, as opposed to using frames that support the status quo.

Next, frames that emerged from CATA runs were qualitatively examined against *National Enquirer* stories for context and each frame was named (see Exhibit 8.1).[5] A rhetorical analysis of frames with examples from the newspaper's environmental risk stories follows.

Exhibit 8.1
National Enquirer **Environmental Risk News Frames**

Bureaucrats and Taxes
>   *Again, Food, Project, Taxes, Dogs, Without, Dollars, Environment, Declared, Government, Research, Study, National, Researcher, Washington, Work, Air, Taxpayers, NSF, Representative, Birds, Republican, Bureaucrats, Woman, Better, Place, Enough, Money, Down, Trees, Man, University, Cost, Workers, Fish, Incredibly, Grant, Put, Often, Traps, Federal, Waste, Thousands, World, Fumed, Long, Help, Need*

American Resourcefulness
>   *America, Good, People, Year, Animals, National Enquirer, Find, I, Can't, Spend, Life, Water, Day, Go, New, Used, Around, US, Big, Million, Few, Want, Free, Health, Away, Car, Cruel, Readers, Home, Time, Kill, Know*

Energy & Species
>   *Against, Land, End, Wild, Human, Learn, Little, Police, Almost, Director, Really, Wildlife, Once, Percent, Pay, Wife, Bill, Trash, Let, Species, Department, Far, Fuel, Garbage, Earth, Small, Fire, Town, Gas, Red, Oil, Slaughter*

Society and Health
>   *Area, Great, Doesn't, Never, Keep, Local, Next, Society, Cancer, Job, Children, Group, Feet, Right, Form, Took*

Elites and Destruction
>   *Bears, State, Stop, Experts, Family, Old, Began, Public, Officials, Save, Eat, Fight, House, Think, California, High, Lead, Professors, City, Scientists, Death, War*

BUREAUCRATS AND TAXES

This frame shaped stories about environmental risk issues and events in economic terms, not unlike those covered in mainstream newspapers. Instead of promoting hegemonic frames and suggesting that authorities have environmental risk situations under control, however, the *National Enquirer* told readers that government officials run amok frivolously spending the people's tax dollars. The words that shaped the "Bureaucrats and Taxes" frame were: *Again, Food, Project, Taxes, Dogs, Without, Dollars, Environment, Declared, Government, Research, Study, National, Researcher, Washington, Work, Air, Taxpayers, NSF, Representative, Birds, Republican, Bureaucrats, Woman, Better, Place, Enough, Money, Down, Trees, Man, University, Cost, Workers, Fish, Incredibly, Grant, Put, Often, Traps, Federal, Waste, Thousands, World, Fumed, Long, Help, and Need.* Stories that promoted a "Bureaucrats & Taxes" frame undermined authority, sensitizing readers to behind-closed-doors misappropriation of federal funds and wasteful spending.

This news frame clearly revealed the *National Enquirer*'s populist leanings, promoted political partisanship, and chastised the establishment. Glynn (1993) found that supermarket tabloid stories form an "opposition to the official cultures propagated by powerful classes and institutions" (p. 21). Indeed, there was nothing vague about the tabloid's criticism of grants awarded to university researchers and the federally funded National Science Foundation (NSF) in order to study behavior of trees, birds, dogs, and fish. Institutional authorities, or bureaucrats, often were called "bunglecrats" (Barr, 1989a, p. 44; Fenton, 1990, p. 45; Haley, 1990, p. 27; Milne, 1989a, p. 42; Plamann, 1993a, p. 17), "eggheads" (Barnhill, 1996, p. 14; Milne, 1995a, p. 14; Susman, 1989, p. 38), "pinheads" (Policy, 1983b, p. 35), and described as "slimy" (Milne, 1991, p. 26), "buggy" (Milne, 1989b, p. 43; Milne, 1992, p. 27; Nelson, 1989b, p. 39; Susman, 1990, p. 27), and "featherbrained" (Einstein, 1989a, p. 45; Milne, 1989c, p. 11; Milne, 1993, p. 12; Milne, 1995b, p. 30). Moreover, while Bird (1992) suggested that this supermarket tabloid tends to avoid "overtly political topics" (p. 29), environmental texts examined in the current study clearly identified the political

Exhibit 8.2
"Bureaucrats and Taxes" Representative Headlines

"Your cold cash goes to study penguins" (Policy, 1983a, p. 45)

"Outrageous! You're paying to study 35-million-year-old dead plants" (Barr, 1989b, p. 21)

"Your taxes go flying to study birds' sex antics" (Milne, 1995b, p. 30)

"*Enquirer* uncovered $2 billion in government waste last year" (Faucher, 1983, p. 33)

"Wow! Look at the wacky things your government is doing" (Levy, 1984, p. 47)

"Govt. blows $119 billion a year just to please a few people" (Coz, 1984, p. 13)

"Revolting! Military bigwigs waste $millions on batteries" (Capettini, 1988, p. 48)

---

party of specific Congressional representatives and senators who criticized their peers for misappropriating tax dollars for environmental research. The word *Republican* clustered within this frame. In numerous stories, Republicans demonized Democrats for wasting money.

Language used in headlines and in stories characterized by the "Bureaucrats and Taxes" frame cleverly poked fun at legitimate dominant social orders (see Exhibit 8.2). On behalf of readers, the *National Enquirer* creatively expressed outrage at government spending of thousands of dollars on incredible environmental projects and establishing federal celebrations promoted by powerful lobbies, such as Dairy Goat Awareness Week and Asparagus Month (Einstein, 1989b). This finding concurs with earlier rhetorical analyses of tabloid newspapers, particularly Bird's conclusion that the *National Enquirer* promotes a confrontational "us-against-them" theme (1992, p. 62).

In addition to scrutinizing tax expenditures for environmental research, the "Bureaucrats and Taxes" frame illuminated stories about spending abuses for environmental public works and military projects. Frequently appearing with such stories was a sig[6] identifying the topic "Bureaucracy Gone Batty," with a cartoonish graphic of a shocked man's face emerging from a paper heap. One article questioned why American tax dollars were sent to Mexico to bail out a failed, air-polluting copper mine in spite of high U.S. copper worker unemployment (DeConcini, 1983). Stories accused bureaucrats of nepotism in public works project funding (Coz, 1984), exposed bureaucrats' purchase of cars with funds earmarked for fighting animal cruelty (Magee, 1985), and accused EPA officials of driving in chauffeured cars at the taxpayers' expense (Capettini, 1986). Other exposés included stories about EPA officials who used tax money to create a country club out of a sewage plant (Einstein, 1985b), military spending on unnecessary environmentally hazardous batteries (Capettini, 1988), and building of a defective $12 million Arizona dam (Faucher, 1983).

The *National Enquirer*'s founder told *Newsweek* reporters in the 1970s that his supermarket tabloid offers "advocacy writing" and is "out to capture some of the old vitality of American journalism" (Peer & Schmidt, 1975, p. 62). Thus, the *National Enquirer* has positioned itself as a watchdog[7] that sniffs out and unabashedly ridicules government institutions for wasteful spending of Americans' tax dollars in the name of environmental risk.

AMERICAN RESOURCEFULNESS

While the *National Enquirer*'s environmental risk stories mocked elites, they concurrently celebrated average Americans' ingenuity and resourcefulness. An "American Resourcefulness" frame was shaped by the words: *America, Good, People, Year, Animals, National Enquirer, Find, I, Can't, Spend, Life, Water, Day, Go, New, Used, Around, US, Big, Million, Few, Want, Free, Health, Away, Car, Cruel, Readers, Home, Time, Kill, and Know.* Stories characterized by this frame sympathized with environmental risk victims and praised common people who helped neighbors and rescued injured animals. Readers also were offered practical, money-saving tips and uplifting advice for facing environmental risk and overcoming adversity (see Exhibit 8.3).

While mainstream media negatively depict hazardous mounds of solid waste, *National Enquirer* stories illuminated by the "American Resourcefulness" frame linked trash to heroism. News stories ranged from a Maryland mom of three who faced gender stereotype head on by working as a trash collector (Bolton, 1983),[8] to a California mayor who could do it all working as garbage collector by morning and legislator by afternoon (Fuller, 1987), to a Pennsylvania "lady mayor" who energetically swept the town herself (Rodell, 1995, p. 35), to a Swedish immigrant who built his house from recycled newspapers (King, 1996), and to a California recycling junkie (Smith, 1991). One feature simply told *National Enquirer* readers about valuables that can be found at a landfill (Ramirez, 1991) and how plunging six stories into a trash heap saved a two-year-old's life (Bolton, 1991b). Another story dubbed an 80-year-old man a "Good Samaritan" after he fixed trashed household items and gave them to the needy (Baker, 1983b, p. 45). Also, a whole town was applauded for teamwork when it cleaned up after itself during a budget crunch when city workers were laid off (Plamann, 1993b). Similar stories included a man who returned $8,100 found in the trash (Isenberg, 1994b), and a sanitation worker who returned a $4,000 ring lost in the garbage ("Trashmen," 1994). The "American Resourcefulness" frame accentuated the positives of environmental risk, for the trash contains surprises and brings out the best in people.

Other "American Resourcefulness" framed stories shared tales about nature as a source for cost-efficient solutions to environmental risk problems. For example, a 1984 *National Enquirer* story featured a clever Bureau of Land Management employee who supplied beavers with used tires for building a dam instead of using more conventional, costly means (South, 1984). The fashion industry also was applauded for turning trash into stylish clothing (Rodack, 1994) and Americans were congratulated for aluminum can recycling ("More," 1984). A California family fought a hefty power bill by going without electricity (Fuller, 1988), a group of Maryland homeowners built their own water system

Exhibit 8.3
"American Resourcefulness" Representative Headlines

"Mom of three cleaned up – as a trash collector" (Bolton, 1983, p. 14)

"Garbageman finds $200,000 prize in the trash" (O'Neill, 1995b, p. 7)

"How cheap are they? Thrifty New Englanders even use dirty diapers as fuel" (Smith, 1992, p. 10)

"Real American heroes" (McDonald, 1990, p. 33)

"What you can do to help clean up the environment" (Plamann, 1991a, p. 51)

"America is the greatest – Count your blessings, Americans! You live in a country where the quality of life is the best in the world!" (Wright, 1983, p. 39)

"Brigitte Bardot's desperate plea to *Enquirer* readers: Help stop this savage slaughter of helpless animals" (Gregory, 1993, p. 41)

(McCandlish, 1995), and high school students cleaned up a polluted trout stream (McDonald, 1990) and forest (Rodell, 1996a). Moreover, many stories offered readers toll-free telephone numbers and addresses for free environmental risk help. For example, readers were told they could conserve water by placing a water jug in a toilet tank (Plamann, 1991a), and were offered environmental risk information contact lists (Levy, 1983a). Bird (1992) analyzed supermarket tabloid newspapers' content using categories described by a former *National Enquirer* freelancer (Holden, 1977) and labeled some story themes as "rags to riches" (p. 56) and "volunteers and heroes" (p. 57). Such patterns are quite similar among environmental risk stories characterized by the "American Resourcefulness" frame discovered in the current study.

By default, the "American Resourcefulness" frame illuminated environmental risk stories that criticized non-U.S. residents, blaming them for draining U.S. financial resources, destroying the global environment, and torturing animals. Headlines such as "Uncle Sam, you are super . . . say experts after 18-month study of America versus the world" (Harrison, 1983, p. 29) advanced American culture and its value system, while denouncing others in strong ethnocentric views. For example, a *National Enquirer* feature blamed U.S. bureaucrats for funding a poorly constructed irrigation system in Asia (Gross, 1983) and officials were criticized for sending millions of dollars overseas to repair environmental damage (Einstein, 1986a).

Most dramatic of all stories illuminated by the "American Resourcefulness" frame were exposes that united and empowered readers to join write-in campaigns organized to end animal cruelty worldwide. Readers were encouraged to cut out and mail coupons printed as sidebars to protest animal abuse in military medical research, movie stunts, religious cults, peddling, gambling, rodeos, and other sports and activities. Condemned in particular were peoples of Australia, South Korea, Africa, Japan, Greece, and Russia. Such countries' governments and citizens were characterized in these ways: "sickeningly cruel owners of Japanese bear parks" (Plamann, 1992, p. 2) and "Australia's cruel harvest" (Einstein, 1983b, p. 18). The *National Enquirer* featured the animal rights activism of Hollywood actors, Paul Newman and Clint Eastwood (Solo, 1984), as well as Lou Ferrigno, Jamie Farr and Barbara Eden (Hunter, 1983), Eddie Albert and Rose Marie (Levy, 1983d), and Doris Day (O'Neill, 1983). Some reports turned a critical gaze toward U.S. animal abuses, as well (Fitz, 1991; McCandlish, 1992). For example, an investigation revealed that animal behaviorists broke live ducks' wings (Levy, 1983b). Throughout fifteen years' coverage analyzed in the current study, the *National Enquirer* routinely ran follow-up stories to applaud readers' write-in campaign successes in affecting legislative action (Cassels, 1984; Fitz, 1987, 1993; George, 1985; Grover, 1994; O'Neill, 1994). The "American Resourcefulness" frame simultaneously celebrated creative environmental risk solutions, promoted ethnocentric values, and empowered readers to participate in democracy and to right environmental wrongs.

ENERGY AND SPECIES

Throughout 1983-1997, many *National Enquirer* stories focused on energy production's impact on wildlife species and the state of natural resources, overall. An "Energy and Species" frame was shaped by the words: *Against, Land, End, Wild, Human, Learn, Little, Police, Almost, Director, Really, Wildlife, Once, Percent, Pay, Wife, Bill, Trash, Let, Species, Department, Far, Fuel, Garbage, Earth, Small, Fire, Town, Gas, Red, Oil, and Slaughter.* These stories sharply criticized industry and government officials for damaging the environment and for overstepping their authority, in contrast to people who live harmoniously with wildlife (see Exhibit 8.4).

Many *National Enquirer* stories shaped by the "Energy and Species" frame sympathized with citizens' burdens—paying for the energy industry's environmental cleanups and living with authorities' bad decisions. For example, taxpayers paid to clean up industrial pollution, including Exxon's 1989 Alaskan oil spill (Blosser, 1991; Coast, 1986) and contractors overcharged the government cleaning up toxic waste (Einstein, 1986b). Other stories accused the federal government of nepotism since oil companies bought oil-rich public lands for a fraction of their worth (Einstein, 1987). Industry and federal government elites also were blamed for killing birds, goats, and other wildlife species in the course of military operations and profit seeking (Grover, 1990; Nelson, 1989a) and for destroying Indiana lands while testing weapons ("Govt," 1991). Such stories underscored the divide between powerful authorities and citizens who pay the bills.

Furthermore, the energy industry was ridiculed for supporting ill-founded, wasteful, and dangerous energy production programs. Yet by contrast, average energy industry workers were portrayed as humanitarians. For example, the Department of Energy was mocked for turning dung into energy (Levy, 1983c), a gas-saving device polluted more than conventional systems (Einstein, 1985a) and damaged vehicles (McCandlish, 1991a), and the federal government acted

Exhibit 8.4
"Energy and Species" Representative Headlines

"Govt. foul-up sticks you with $31 million bill to clean up Exxon's oil spill" (Blosser, 1991, p. 36)

"A fuel-ish waste! Feds blow thousands on costly airplane tests" (Einstein, 1983a, p. 13)

"U.S. fishermen killing thousands of dolphins each year with bombs" (Nelson, 1989a, p. 61)

"An American success story: How we've saved many of our wild animals from vanishing forever" (Plamann, 1991b, p. 23)

"After 9 years of hell on a desolate island, family that was allergic to the world is cured - by fresh air!" (Pritchard, 1993, p. 39)

"The forest of miracles - where the mute speak, the blind see & the crippled walk again" (Blosser, 1996, p. 35)

---

too slowly to weatherize low-income homes (Latta, 1986). Conversely, fossil fuel workers pulled peers from peril and families watched their homes go up in flames following a refinery explosion (Brenna et al., 1984), a nuclear power plant employee risked radiation poisoning to save co-workers (Nuke, 1993), a New Jersey construction worker battled natural gas fumes to rescue a co-worker ("Construction," 1994), Illinois neighbors lived among fumes and a leaking petroleum refinery pipe (Fenton, 1991a), and residents living on a burning coal mine vowed to stick together rather than move to another town (Rodell, 1991, 1996c).

Several stories among those characterized by the "Energy and Species" frame championed many who squared off against the establishment to do right by protecting the natural environment. One story told of a woman who was fired for blowing the whistle on her boss after he had killed a federally protected bird (Krajewski, 1992). Other heroes included the "Bird Lady of the Rockies" who rescued 2,000 birds ("This lady," 1990, p. 55) and a grandmother who lived beneath a tree to save it from being cut it down (McDonald, 1993). Naturalists were celebrated, including Ladybird Johnson, who protected trees and wildflowers ("Former," 1996). Also, high school students turned a polluted creek into a trout stream (McDonald, 1990)[9] and a couple walked across the United States picking up trash (Fisk, 1995). Frequent updates provided the status on endangered species, including the American eagle (Plamann, 1991b; Pritchard, 1994) and America's 150 Loch Ness monsters (Fenton, 1993; McCandlish, et al., 1989).

Stories suggested that living and working in the natural environment are preferred to living in cities and working in offices and factories. For example, people escaped human society (Baker, 1984, Barritt, 1986) and the working world "rat race" to live closer to nature (Coz, 1988, p. 21; Levy, 1983e, p. 59), while people allergic to industrial chemicals were forced to become shut-ins (Pritchard, 1985; 1988). A follow-up story reported that a family's health recovered after living on a remote island (Pritchard, 1993). According to such stories, modern conventions are unnatural and false and wild species are natural and true. For example, a man used a tree to predict weather, refusing to believe scientists (Isenberg, 1996), a field guide used a "vision" instead of modern methods to find a grandmother lost in the woods (Smith, 1995a, p. 32), and Pacific Northwest farmers grew colossal vegetables without pesticides (Krajewski, 1983). Instead of using modern medicine, Bulgarians visited an ancient forest that healed the sick (Blosser, 1996) and Yugoslavians traveled to drink water from a well with curing powers (Cutter, 1995). In sum, all stories were bound by a central theme that nature is superior to modernity.

Other stories characterized by the "Energy & Species" frame criticized environmental regulations, as well as authorities' lack of common sense and out-of-balance priorities. For example, Philadelphia residents received bills even after a natural gas explosion destroyed their homes (Smith, 1994), a Colorado elementary school was forced to pay an energy tax for a small ethanol science experiment (McCandlish, 1988), and the benefit of designing cars to save gas was far outweighed by poor safety records (Einstein, 1988). Also, people were jailed for refusing to chop down trees, weed a garden, clean up garbage, and mow a lawn (Bolton, 1992; Mullins, 1991; Rodell, 1997; Smith, 1993, 1995b). Others faced fines for transforming a dump into a garden, picking up garbage, illegally dumping trash, refusing to clean up toxic waste, growing vegetables in a front yard, and throwing junk mail in the public trash (Fenton, 1991b, 1992; Fuller, 1990; Grover, 1993; Kaufman, 1990; Temmey, 1990; "War," 1992). Several people interviewed said they felt victimized by endangered species laws. For example, some were arrested for rescuing wildlife (Blackburn, 1993; McCandlish, 1993; Smith, 1996), building among endangered species ("Cheepers," 1991; Hoyt, 1989; Levy, 1988), and shooting an endangered grizzly in self defense (Isenberg, 1994a). Many other stories vilified environmental officials who senselessly harmed wildlife (Bolton, 1991a; Fenton, 1990; Rodell, 1996b), and were insensitive to the handicapped, women, and children (O'Neill, 1995a; Smith, 1996; "Town," 1991).

SOCIETY AND HEALTH

Another environmental risk news frame discovered among texts analyzed in this study underscored the *National Enquirer*'s role in providing readers with health tips. A "Society and Health" frame was shaped by the words: *Area, Great, Doesn't, Never, Keep, Local, Next, Society, Cancer, Job, Children, Group, Feet, Right, Form, and Took.* These stories were produced to help readers protect themselves and their children, and to promote good health in spite of cancer risks and other unhealthful environmental and workplace realities (see Exhibit 8.5).

Friendly self-help advice filled the *National Enquirer's* columns, empowering readers to eat well, live happily, and stay healthy. Stories educated readers as to which vitamins stave off pollution's harmful effects (Harrison, 1984, 1986), where to call for in order to test home carbon monoxide levels (Allison, 1996; McCandlish, 1989), what to look for in health food (Baker, 1983a), and why noise pollution can be harmful (Gregory, 1989). Other stories addressed how to thaw pipes without poisoning the family (Kohut & Sweet, 1996), avoid allergic

Exhibit 8. 5
"Society and Health" Representative Headlines

"Warning! Felt-tip marker fumes may be hazardous to your health" (Ramirez, 1985, p. 18)

"Survey of 1,040 doctors reveals 6 best ways to stay in good health" (Fenton, 1986, p. 15)

"Your dog could save our child from lead poisoning" (Plamann, 1994, p. 16)

"Secret investigation reveals Russian nuclear accident created monstrous animals" (Wilkins, 1990, p. 51)

"Bottled water is not safer than tap water – it may even be worse" (Policy, 1985, p. 7)

"Beware! Your carpet can make you sick – and even give you cancer symptoms" (Choueke, 1995, p. 4)

---

reactions to carbonless copy paper (Still, 1984), protect against the sun's rays ("Sunglasses," 1989), detect toxic seafood (Choueke, 1995; "New," 1993), and kill roaches without insecticides ("Simple," 1985). Overall, stories provided readers with health organizations' office hours and reassurance that safe air and water are within their reach.

Several stories shaped by the "Society and Health" frame specifically focused on society's avoidance of toxins and cancer. For example, stories identified the relationship between skin cancer and sun exposure due to a depleting ozone layer ("How," 1991; Stine, 1984) and examined women's odds of contracting breast cancer (Holeb, 1983; Ruehl, 1996). Other stories featured lists of the most risky cancer-causing occupations (Ruehl, 1984), warned readers of the hazards of cancer-causing agents in bottled water (Policy, 1985; Mullins, 1985; Ruehl, 1989) and pet flea dips and sprays (Fuller, 1994; Page, 1989), listed cancer-prevention techniques (American, 1986), and alerted readers about carcinogens in carpets (Choueke, 1995) and radon gas in the home (Allison, 1996). In addition to addressing physical harm caused by environmental factors, one *National Enquirer* story linked pollution to mental health, attributing criminal behavior to pollution (Young, 1997). Throughout such stories, cancer and other health risks were portrayed as a reality in a modern society. However, if *National Enquirer* readers were well informed, they could arm themselves, protect their families, and ensure healthy lives.

The *National Enquirer* also reported environmental risk from abroad – in the form of shocking tales of nuclear and chemical technology gone awry. One story, for example, linked fallout from the 1986 Chernobyl disaster to 40,000 American deaths (Still, et al., 1988). Fears of Third World misuse of Western technology have been well documented in news coverage analyses (Hansen, 1991). A Chernobyl-related *National Enquirer* story warned that "a shocking wave of weird mutated monster plants, farm animals and birds spring up in the condemned area around the Chernobyl nuclear plant" (Wilkins, 1990, p. 51). Such stories illustrated what Bird defined as "strange phenomena" (1992, p. 60) — stories most often printed in the *Sun* and *Weekly World News* tabloids—but sometimes appearing in the *National Enquirer*. Such stories exposed Cold War ideology, as found by earlier analysis of Chernobyl news media coverage (Patterson, 1989). Finally, readers learned how environmental risk affected military personnel abroad during wartime. A 1996 investigation, for example, told of a U.S. government cover-up after cancer-causing chemical weapons poisoned American G.I.s during the Gulf War (Fitz, 1996). Such stories underscored an ethnocentric theme, illustrating health risks associated with non-American use of technology.

In sum, the *National Enquirer* used a "Society and Health" frame to forge links between environmental risk and health, painting an optimistic picture complete with advice and assurance that Americans are better equipped to handle technology than most other nations.

ELITES AND DESTRUCTION

Environmental risk embodies conflict and is a specific arena where story-tellers have shaped social knowledge. In particular, supermarket tabloids rely on the news value, conflict, to promote counter-hegemonic, sensational, dramatic stories for a readership that enjoys ridiculing the establishment (Barber, 1982; Bird, 1992; Glynn, 1993; Holden, 1977; Peer & Schmidt, 1975). In the current study, the following words illustrated an "Elites and Destruction" frame: *Bears, State, Stop, Experts, Family, Old, Began, Public, Officials, Save, Eat, Fight, House, Think, California, High, Lead, Professors, City, Scientists, Death, and War*. This news frame questioned the authority, trustworthiness, and validity of decisions made by experts, state public officials, scientists, and professors—yet optimistically assured readers that the future would be bright (see Exhibit 8.6).

In particular, many *National Enquirer* stories shaped by the "Elites and Destruction" frame discredited science and technology as a means for under-standing the natural environment. For example, many stories mocked authorities' gloom-and-doom predictions about global warming, nuclear destruction and polluted air and water supplies as having "no basis in fact" and instead encour-aged readers to think positively and "make a positive future happen" (Stine, 1984, p. 58; "The truth," 1995, p. 17; Ramirez, 1994, p. 2). In fact, some stories listed experts' earlier predictions, calling them "wild and wacky" (Coffey, 1984, p. 57; Haley, 1984, p. 38). Acid rain was called "bunk" (Still, 1989, p. 52). One story cited a Houston researcher who called predictions for environmental destruction "all a pack of lies" (Goldstein, 1985b, p. 39). Another story about post nuclear disaster stated that "the so-called 'nuclear winter' would amount to nothing more than a little chill" (Ruehl, 1986, p. 32), and the greenhouse effect was dubbed a "greenhouse scare" (Ramirez, 1989, p. 24) because scientists use "faulty" thermometers (Downey, 1991, p. 35). Scientists who participated in the Biosphere project were exposed as a "greenhouse gang" of cult members (McCandlish, 1991b, p. 2). Furthermore, a list of think-tank members' problem-solving suggestions were ridiculed (Fenton, 1994, p. 42). Yet other features decried that "the world will be a great place to live in" (Ramirez, 1984, p. 9), pre-dicted that America will be "paradise" (Cassels, 1985, p. 20), and concluded that

Exhibit 8.6
"Elites and Destruction" Representative Headlines

"Bomb Alaska and Texas? 10 worst ideas in the history of science" (Fenton, 1994, p. 42)

"Oops! The experts goofed when they tried to predict the future" (Coffee, 1984, p. 57)

"Acid rain destruction is bunk, experts say" (Still, 1989, p. 52)

"Hooray for the future!" (Ramirez, 1984, p. 9)

"Fascinating book bonus brings good news to every American forget all those gloom and doom warnings—our future looks bright" (Stine, 1984, p. 58)

"Stunning story behind the biosphere ballyhoo" (McCandlish, 1991b, p. 2)

---

the United States is the "best place to live" (Montgomery, 1986, p. 6).

Several stories about death and war illuminated by the "Elites and Destruction" frame also undermined authorities' ability to make solid, sane environmental risk decisions. For example, one story cited historical examples of public officials' killing bears and other wild animals for crimes such as destroying crops (Goldstein, 1985a) and another story pondered why the government recycled a used nuclear bomb factory by selling it to a used car dealer—complete with instructions (McCandlish, 1994). Overall, allaying readers' doomsday fears by delegitimating authorities is consistent with this supermarket tabloid's goal in promoting populist messages.

DISCUSSION

To understand why the environment has become a prominent public policy issue at certain points in history, some researchers have suggested focusing on wider cultural resonances beyond mathematical probability and actuarial tables (Hansen, 1991; Rayner, 1992). The current study closely examined a nationally circulated newspaper produced for readers low on the socio-economic scale—a newspaper studied significantly less often than mainstream media—in order to discover how environmental issues are re-presented for non-elites. This study was designed to learn whether tabloid newspapers use frames that emphasize opposition to dominant ideology when reporting environmental risk issues, as opposed to using frames that support the status quo. Indeed, it was concluded that the *National Enquirer* produces a unique brand of environmental risk news for its readers, as illustrated in five news frames discovered by using CATA and illuminated using traditional rhetorical methods. When the five frames were examined in toto, consistent themes became apparent.

First, it is concluded that environmental risk stories promoted in the *National Enquirer* unified marginalized readers and provided a forum for solidarity against the establishment. Texts vilified government and industry elites, yet celebrated average, ordinary people (even wildlife) as victims who can be heroes and survivors. Journalism, like all literary acts, provides audiences with models for acting and feeling, or what Burke (1989) called strategies for selecting enemies and allies. In the *National Enquirer*, policy makers are the enemy, and neighbors, coworkers, outcasts, and helpless animals are the allies. Common citizens were portrayed as hard-working taxpayers with hearts of gold who earn little money and even less respect from elected officials who frivolously spend federal funds and abuse their authority. Discovering news frames enables a researcher to detect such dichotomies encoded in texts that can transmit and promote values (Bird, 1992), morals (Hansen, 1991), and cultural narratives (Gamson & Modigliani, 1989). Indeed, this supermarket tabloid newspaper unified groups subject to environmental risk policy and governance under power blocs.

Second, the *National Enquirer* empowered readers by featuring first-person accounts of successful environmental risk outcomes and encouraging readers to react to authorities' poor decisions, inexact research methods, and wasteful spending. News stories neither promoted passivity nor encouraged anarchy in response to this wide gap of difference between haves and have-nots. Instead, environmental activists inspired readers to write letters to their legislative leaders asking them to pass laws ending animal cruelty and other environmental injustices, and to heed the advice offered in the *National Enquirer*'s columns so that they might lead more fulfilling lives.

Furthermore, ordinary people were depicted as influential heroes who rise to the occasion in the face of extreme consequences—particularly where environmental risk and health intersect. According to stories, neighbors and coworkers help each other and offer advice to other *National Enquirer* readers, for all too often it is average taxpayers who must pay the price for industries pollution—whether it be in terms of clean-up costs or compromised good health. Moreover, the *National Enquirer* commended readers' resourcefulness and tenacity in living with environmental risk. Stories about trusting and relying only on people readers know filled the *National Enquirer's* pages—from community recycling campaigns to daring animal rescues. Readers were encouraged to deal with everyday problems and to hope for the best because America is the leading nation of the world and its citizens are intelligent, hard-working, creative, and morally superior.

Third, frames suggested that nature untouched by humans is preferable to civilization, concluding that industrialized society has failed miserably in its quest for the good life. According to *National Enquirer* stories, many people gave up on society and its conveniences in order to return to a simpler, higher quality, and more healthful lifestyle. Numerous first-person accounts offered advice on how to live harmoniously with nature and how to preserve wildlife by shielding it from industry and development. Technology, energy production, and medical advancements, according to texts, are a poor substitute for human intuition, honesty, and hard work. In fact, many texts predicted that science and technology's doomsday predictions should not be taken seriously.

Finally, news frames that emerged from *National Enquirer* texts suggested that there is a backlash associated with too much environmental risk regulation. This libertarian morality lesson questions the government's role as an environmental risk regulator. According to texts, common people can suffer dire consequences in the form of jail sentences and fines when too much regulation interferes with everyday living. Laws that prohibit people from cleaning up garbage, making an honest living, and growing a garden were characterized as silly and foolish. Such messages crystallized diminishing faith in the social contract —wherein citizens enable authorities to rule in exchange for protection.

Overall, the *National Enquirer* often featured the same environmental risk issues and events that many mainstream newspapers covered throughout 1983-1997. Yet, this supermarket tabloid promoted counter-hegemonic takes on environmental issues and events that positioned authorities and marginalized groups at opposite ends of a spectrum. Authorities were re-presented as authoritative, frivolous, and ineffective, and average people were re-presented as intelligent, frugal, and resourceful.

Thus, the framing concept has proven valuable in this study of environmental risk that examined connections among people, ideas, and values. More precisely, the relationship between words, meaning, and overall implications of hegemonic power relations is made clearer by refining content analysis techniques to more carefully measure nuances of meaning. This study's blending of quantitative and qualitative methods provided a solid approach to analyzing encoded messages in texts. Computer software programs can detect frames that may be difficult to identify using traditional approaches, and traditional qualitative rhetorical techniques provide context for the quantitative findings.

NOTES

1. Catpac (CATegory PACkage) software from Terra Research and Computing, Inc. is a set of unsupervised self-organizing artificial neural network (ANN) computer programs designed to perform semantic network analysis (Woelfel, 1998). Its strength lies in its ability to use a computer to read a nearly unlimited amount of text, reveal complex patterns associated with word clusters based on frequency and content, and graphically depict these patterns (Barnett, 1996; Woelfel, 1993). The neural model works by creating a words-by-words matrix called a WIN, or weight-input-network matrix. Catpac treats each word as a neuron as it moves a scanning window through text. Each window represents a "case," wherein neurons representing words are activated and then deactivated, decaying over time when the scanning window disappears (Woelfel, 1993). Neurons, or words, become positively interconnected in the network when they are simultaneously active in the window. The resulting words-by-words matrix of co-occurrences represents a compilation of the connection weights among the neurons, showing associations between all the words in a given text. The matrix then serves as a basis for further analysis, such as cluster analysis.

2. Contents of the *National Enquirer* were manually searched at the archives of the Library of Congress in Washington, D.C., because this information is not available electronically or indexed in any database. All news stories were scanned (or typed manually where text quality was poor) and saved as ASCII text.

3. A list of fifty-nine key search words was created by combining lists of key search terms used for earlier environmental risk news content analyses (Bowman & Hanaford, 1977; Downs, 1972; Lacey & Longman, 1993; Riechert & Miller, 1994, 1997). Obviously, key words used for the news story searches revealed some non-environmental risk stories. For example, the key word *environment* can be used to describe a work *environment* context. Similarly, the word *nuclear* might be used to describe a *nuclear* family. Such news stories are not relevant to the current study and were not included in analyses. Appropriate Boolean search syntax was used. To be classified as an environmental risk news story for content analysis, an article had to contain at least one of the following key search words: *Air, Atmosphere, Biodiversity, Chemical, Clean-up, Climate, Conserv!, Contaminat!, Danger!, Dump, Earth, Earth-Day, Ecology, Ecosystem, Endanger!, Energy, Environment!, Extinct!, Fertilizer, Forest, Fuel, Fungicide, Garbage, Glob!, Habitat Hazard!, Health, Herbicide, Insecticide, Jungle, Land, Litter, Natur!,Nuclear, Outdoors, Pesticide Planet, Pollut!, Power, Preserv!, Protect!, Quality, Rare, Recycl!,*

Resource!, Restor!, Risk, Safe!, Save, Scarce, Slaughter, Solid-waste, Species, Toxi!, Trash, Poach!, Poison!, Water, Wildlife.

4. To prepare for the cluster analyses that Catpac provides, numerous exploratory test runs were performed to choose among a variety of hierarchical clustering methods, text window sizes, and maximum number of words to be used in subsequent analyses. Decisions were reached about each of these options based on which selections yielded the most clean, detailed, and meaningful results. The centroid clustering method was selected for this study because clusters that emerged using this algorithm were most evenly distributed. During test runs, a scanning window size of five words produced the clearest clustering pattern. Also, 150 was the number selected for total unique words to be identified because early test runs showed that clusters emerging from analyses of fewer than 150 unique words were less useful, producing, for example, single-word clusters. Then, the entire corpus of stories underwent analysis by Catpac, which excluded certain articles, pronouns, prepositions, transitive verbs, conjunctions, and other non-content-bearing words as specified by the researcher such as articles. A list of frequencies of words used most often was computed first. Frequency is a measure of degree of concern or importance (Ogilvie et al., 1982; Stone, 1997). Next, the dendogram resulting from Catpac cluster analysis was examined as a graphic illustration of relationships between words. These word clusters then were interpreted as frames, in the sense that frames "are manifested by the presence or absence of certain key words, stock phrases, stereotyped images, sources of information, and sentences that provide thematically reinforcing clusters of facts or judgments" (Entman, 1993, p. 52).

5. In all dendograms, word cluster were defined as frames and assigned a name. In order to name the frames, it was important to closely scrutinize words that had clustered together as a result of the Catpac analysis, by looking for similarities, differences, and patterns. Frame names reflected themes arising from the majority of words in each cluster.

6. A sig, short for "signature," is used to identify topics, opinion pieces, briefs, and regularly appearing features (Harrower, 1991).

7. The term watchdog, as applied to the media, suggests that journalists monitor power structures on behalf of readers and is taught in many journalism classes as a guiding principle (Glasser, 1992).

8. This August 23, 1983, *National Enquirer* story, "Mom of 3 cleans up as a trash collector," featured a subhead, "Women in Men's Jobs." This newspaper frequently gender-stereotyped jobs.

9. As a sidebar to this 1990 story, the *National Enquirer* announced a new "Environmental Hero Award" to "recognize people who do their part to clean up America" with recognition in the tabloid and a $150 check.

REFERENCES

Allison, L. (1996, March 12). Danger! Your home can wreck your health - here's how to make it safe. *National Enquirer*, p. 34.

American Cancer Society's No. 1 plan to reduce your chances of getting cancer. (1986, March 18). *National Enquirer*, p. 26.

Althusser, L. (1971). *Lenin and philosophy.* London: New Left Books.

Baker, R. (1983a, March 1). Myths you shouldn't swallow about health food. *National Enquirer*, p. 22.

Baker, R. (1983b, August 9). Enquirer good Samaritan man, 80, turns trash from the dump into treasure for the poor. *National Enquirer*, p. 45.

Baker, R. (1984, April 17). Real-life Tarzan. *National Enquirer*, p. 62.

Barber, S. (1982, July/August). The boss don't like swindle make it robbery. *Washington Journalism Review*, 46-50.

Barkin, S. M. (1984). The journalist as storyteller: An interdisciplinary perspective. *American Journalism, 1*, 27-33.

Barnett, G. (1996). Chapter 5: Quantitative analysis of in-person interviews. In C. Barth (Ed.), *The practice analysis of management accounting*. Montvale, NJ: Institute of Management Accountants.

Barnhill, W. (1996, May 28). Do flies flirt? You're paying $258,000 to find out! *National Enquirer*, p. 14.

Barr, C. (1989a, January 10). *Enquirer* exposed $9.8 billion in govt. waste last year. *National Enquirer*, p. 44.

Barr, C. (1989b, August 22). Outrageous! You're paying to study 35-million-year-old dead plants. *National Enquirer*, p. 21.

Barritt, D. (1986, June 17). George Adamson, 80, is still battling to save his lions from poachers. *National Enquirer*, p. 19.

Bateson, G. (1972). *Steps to an ecology of mind*. New York: Ballantine Books.

Bird, S.E. (1992). *For enquiring minds: A cultural study of supermarket tabloids*. Knoxville: The University of Tennessee Press.

Bird, S. E. & Dardenne, R. W. (1988). Myth, chronicle, and story: Exploring the narrative qualities of news. In J. W. Carey (Ed.), *Media, myths & narratives: TV and the press* (pp. 67-86). Newbury Park, CA: Sage.

Blackburn, J. (1993, October 26). Woman handcuffed & jailed for saving this baby deer. *National Enquirer*, p. 2.

Blosser, J. (1991, July 2). Govt. foul-up sticks you with $31 million bill to clean up Exxon's oil bill. *National Enquirer*, p. 36.

Blosser, J. (1996, March 5). The forest of miracles - where the mute speak, the blind see & the crippled walk again. *National Enquirer*, p. 35.

Bolton, B. (1983, August 23). Mom of three cleaned up — as a trash collector . . . Women in men's jobs. *National Enquirer*, p. 14.

Bolton, B. (1991a, January 1). Cruel cop kicks tiny baby ducks to death. *National Enquirer*, p. 51.

Bolton, B. (1991b, October 1). Saved by the garbage. *National Enquirer*, p. 5.

Bolton, B. (1992, January 28). Arrested at gun point for cleaning up garbage. *National Enquirer*, p. 38.

Bowman, J. S. & Hanaford, K. (1977). Mass media and the environment since Earth Day. *Journalism Quarterly*, 54, 160-165.

Brenna, T., Cahill, L., Montgomery, C. & Wright, D. (1984, December 11). Blazing nightmare of the Mexico gas holocaust - survivors tell their stories. *National Enquirer*, p. 19.

Burke, K. (1989). *On symbols and society*. Chicago: The University of Chicago Press.

Campbell, R. (1991). *60 minutes and the news: A mythology for middle America*. Urbana, IL: University of Illinois Press.

Capettini, R. (1986, April 1). Taxpayers get taken for a ride! *National Enquirer*, p. 23.

Capettini, R. (1988, January 5). Revolting! Military bigwigs waste $millions on batteries. *National Enquirer*, p. 48.

Carey, J. W. (1974). The problem of journalism history. *Journalism History*, 1, 2-5.

Carey, J. W. (1986). Why and how? The dark continent of American journalism. In R.K. Manoff & M. Schudson (Eds.), *Reading the news* (pp. 146-196). New York:

Pantheon Books.

Cassels, M. (1984, April 3). 23,000 Enquirer readers protest gruesome slaughter of kangaroos. *National Enquirer*, p. 6.

Cassels, M. (1985, May 21). America will be a real paradise in 100 years. *National Enquirer*, p. 20.

Catton, W. R., Jr. & Dunlap, R. E. (1980). A new ecological paradigm for post-exuberant sociology. *The American Behavioral Scientist, 24,* 15-47.

Cheepers! $20 million mining machine forced to shut down by these birds. (1991, July 23). *National Enquirer*, p. 45.

Choueke, E. (1995, April 18). Beware! Your carpet can make you sick - and even give you cancer symptoms. *National Enquirer*, p. 34.

Coast Guard lets oil spillers stick taxpayers with $59 million tab. (1986, September 9). *National Enquirer*, p. 18.

Coffee, W. (1984, July 31). Oops! The experts goofed when they tried to predict the future. *National Enquirer*, p. 57.

Cole, L. A. (1993). *Element of risk, the politics of radon.* New York: Oxford University Press.

Cone, E.T. (1968). *Music form and the musical performance.* New York: W. W. Norton & Company.

Construction worker battles deadly gas to rescue co-worker. (1994, March 8). *National Enquirer*, p. 41.

Coz, S. (1984, May 22). Govt. blows $119 billion a year just to please a few people. *National Enquirer*, p. 13.

Coz, S. (1988, January 12). High-paid executive quits his job to run a small country inn. *National Enquirer*, p. 21.

Cutter, N. (1995, June 6). Thousands flock to tiny well with amazing power to heal the sick. *National Enquirer*, p. 33.

Darnton, R. (1975). Writing news and telling stories. *Daedalus, 104,* 175-94.

DeConcini, D. (1983, February 1). Bureaucracy gone batty! Government spends $50 million — to put more Americans out of work. *National Enquirer*, p. 13.

Downey, C. (1991, January 8). Is greenhouse scare hot air? Govt.'s new space-age thermometers are faulty - experts charge. *National Enquirer*, p. 35.

Downs, A. (1972). Up and down with ecology — the "issue-attention cycle." *The Public Interest, 28,* 38-50.

Dunwoody, S. & Neuwirth, K. (1991). Coming to terms with the impact of communication on scientific and technological risk judgments. In L. Wilkins & P. Patterson (Eds.), *Risky business: Communicating issues of science, risk, and public policy* (pp. 11-30). New York: Greenwood.

Einstein, P. (1983a, August 9). A fuel-ish waste! Feds blow thousands on costly airplane tests. *National Enquirer*, p. 13.

Einstein, P. (1983b, December 13). Enquirer readers help stop Australia's cruel harvest . . . lovable kangaroos slaughtered by the millions in orgy of senseless suffering. *National Enquirer*, p. 18.

Einstein, P. (1985a, August 6). Government blows $295,000 testing gasoline gizmo ex-President Ford liked. *National Enquirer*, p. 38.

Einstein, P. (1985b, November 12). This ritzy place is a sewage plant! . . . and your tax $$ are going down the drain to pay for it. *National Enquirer*, p. 18.

Einstein, P. (1986a, April 1). Uncle Sam spends over $2.6 billion every day — and here's where it goes. *National Enquirer*, p. 48.

Einstein, P. (1986b, November 18). Toxic $hocker! *National Enquirer*, p. 46.

Einstein, P. (1987, March 31). Government selling oil-rich land for $2.50 an acre. *National Enquirer*, p. 19.

Einstein, P. (1988, September 27). Shocking new study reveals – fuel-efficient cars save gas – but cost thousands of lives. *National Enquirer*, p. 25.

Einstein, P. (1989a, February 14). How does a goldfinch select a mate? You're paying 52G to find out. *National Enquirer*, p. 45.

Einstein, P. (1989b, July 18). Dairy Goat Awareness Week — Congress blows your taxes to pass laws for hundreds of silly holidays. *National Enquirer*, p. 22.

Entman, R. M. (1993). Framing: Toward clarification of a fractured paradigm. *Journal of Communication, 43*, 51-58.

Faucher, E. (1983, April 19). Enquirer uncovered $2 billion in government waste last year. *National Enquirer*, p. 33.

Fenton, S. (1986, July 15). Survey of 1,040 doctors reveals 6 best ways to stay in good health. *National Enquirer*, p. 15.

Fenton, S. (1990, September, 25). Bunglecrats poison thousands of fish - just so they can count 'em - they littered the shore for miles. *National Enquirer*, p. 45.

Fenton, S. (1991a, March 12). Town is a time bomb! *National Enquirer*, p. 2.

Fenton, S. (1991b, September 17). Litter lunacy! State bans Boy Scouts from picking up trash. *National Enquirer*, p. 35.

Fenton, S. (1992, July 28). Govt. demands $7.9 million from man who did nothing wrong. *National Enquirer*, p. 27.

Fenton, S. (1993, January 26). America has 150 Loch Ness monsters! & other amazing facts about the world we live in. *National Enquirer*, p. 14.

Fenton, S. (1994, July 5). Bomb Alaska and Texas? 10 worst ideas in the history of science. *National Enquirer*, p. 42.

Fisk, M. (1995, May 23). Couple walks clean across the U.S. picking up 3 1/2 tons of trash — & lots & lots of underwear! *National Enquirer*, p. 16.

Fitz, R. (1987, May 26). After Congressman asked for your help. *National Enquirer*, p. 26.

Fitz, R. (1991, May 14). You can help stop this sickening massacre. *National Enquirer*, p. 44.

Fitz, R. (1993, April 16). 25,000 Enquirer readers blast slaughter of defenseless bears. *National Enquirer*, p. 35.

Fitz, R. (1996, April 2). Gulf war GIs poisoned by American germ weapons - scientist blows lid off huge govt. cover-up. *National Enquirer*, pp. 26-27.

Fowler, R. (1991). *Language in the news: discourse and ideology in the press*. New York: Routledge.

Former first ladies are still making America great. (1996, August 27). *National Enquirer*, p. 19.

Freudenburg, W. R. (1992). Heuristics, biases, and the not-so-general publics: Expertise and error in the assessment of risks. In S. Krimsky & D. Golding (Eds.), *Social theories of risk* (pp. 229-249). Westport, CT: Praeger Publishers.

Friedman, S. M. (1991). Risk management: The public versus the technical experts. In L. Wilkins & P. Patterson (Eds.), *Risky business: Communicating issues of science, risk, and public policy*. (pp. 30-41). New York: Greenwood.

Fuller, C. (1987, October 27). He picks up garbage in the a.m. — runs country county government in p.m. *National Enquirer*, p. 30.

Fuller, C. (1988, November 8). Family jolted by hefty power bill so they pull plug for good. *National Enquirer*, p. 35.

Fuller, C. (1990, November 6). He throws junk mail in public trash bin & city threatens to fine him. *National Enquirer*, p. 5.

Fuller, C. (1994, October 4). New flea sprays kill pests without dangerous poisons. *National Enquirer*, p. 18.

Galtung, J. & Ruge, M. (1973). Structuring and selecting news. In S. Cohen and J. Young (Eds.), *The manufacture of news* (pp. 62-72). Beverly Hills, CA: Sage.

Gamson, W.A. (1989). News as framing. *American Behavioral Scientist*, 33, 157-161.

Gamson, W. A. & Lasch, K. E. (1983). The political culture of social welfare policy. In S. E. Spiro & E. Yuchtman-Yaar (Eds.), *Evaluating the welfare state: social and political perspectives* (pp. 397-415). New York: Academic Press.

Gamson, W. A. & Modigliani, A. (1989). Media discourse and public opinion on nuclear power: A constructionist approach. *American Journal of Sociology*, 95, 1-37.

Gans, H. (1979). *Deciding what's news*. New York: Pantheon.

Gare, A. E. (1995). *Postmodernism and the environmental crisis*. New York: Routledge.

Geertz, C. (1973). *The interpretation of cultures*. New York: Basic Books.

George, T. (1985, June 25). 10,080 angry readers protest cruelty to animals at rodeos. *National Enquirer*, p. 32.

Gitlin, T. (1980). *The whole world is watching: Mass media in the making & unmaking of the new left*. Berkeley: University of California Press.

Glasgow University Media Group (1976). *Bad news*. London: Routledge & P. Kegan.

Glasgow University Media Group (1980). *More bad news*. London: Routledge & P. Kegan.

Glasser. T. L. (1992) 'Objectivity and news reporting'. In E. D. Cohen (Ed.), *Philosophical Issues in Journalism* (pp. 176-185). New York: Oxford University Press.

Glynn, K. (1993). Reading supermarket tabloids as menippean satire. *Communication Studies*, 44, 19-37.

Goffman, E. (1974). *Frame Analysis: An Essay in the Organization of Experience*. Cambridge, MA: Harvard University Press.

Golding, D. (1992). A social and programmatic history of risk research. In S. Krimsky & D. Golding (Eds.), *Social theories of risk*, (pp. 23-52). Westport, CT: Praeger.

Goldstein, M. (1985a, July 9). Animals that were tried, jailed & even executed. *National Enquirer*, p. 35.

Goldstein, M. (1985b, September 3). These gloom and doom predictions are a pack of lies, says expert. America is better than ever. *National Enquirer*, p. 39.

Goodfield, J. (1983). *Reflections on science and the media*. Washington, DC: American Association for the Advancement of Science.

Govt. plan to save $6 million will cost over $6 billion. (1991, July 30). *National Enquirer*, p. 29.

Graber, D. (1988). *Processing the news: How people tame the information tide* 2nd ed. New York: Longman.

Graber, D. (1989). Content and meaning: What's it all about? *American Behavioral Scientist, 33*, 144-152.

Gregory, J. (1989, February 21). Noises you're not aware of can cause health problems. *National Enquirer*, p. 59.

Gregory, J. (1993, February 9). Brigitte Bardot's desperate plea to Enquirer readers: Help stop this savage slaughter of helpless animals. *National Enquirer*, p. 41.

Gross, M. (1983, November 8). Government pumps tax $millions down the drain in foreign countries. *National Enquirer*, p. 38.

Grover, W. (1990, January 30). Army docs torturing goats - helpless animals shaved & shot - just so surgeons can practice. *National Enquirer*, p. 39.

Grover, W. (1994, October 4). When Enquirer readers talk, people listen even in Russia! *National Enquirer*, p. 31.

Haley, L. (1984, May 15). Experts peered into the future 40 years ago & came up with wild & wacky predictions that bombed. *National Enquirer*, p. 38.

Haley, L. (1990, August 14). Govt. blows $160,000 to study grasshoppers' heads. *National Enquirer*, p. 27.

Hall, S. (1979). Culture, the media and the 'ideological effect'. In J. Curran, M. Gurevitch, & J. Woollacott (Eds.) *Mass Communication & Society* (pp. 315-348). Beverly Hills, CA: Sage.

Hannigan, J. (1995). *Environmental sociology: A social constructionist view*. New York: Routledge.

Hansen, A. (1991). The media and the social construction of the environment. *Media, Culture and Society*. London: Sage, 443-458.

Harrison, L. (1983, November 1). Uncle Sam, you are super . . . say experts after 18-month study of America versus the world. *National Enquirer*, p. 29.

Harrison, L. (1984, September 18). These foods can help stop pollution from harming you. *National Enquirer*, p. 32.

Harrison, L. (1986, July 22). Nearly half of water supplies in U.S. contain too much salt and it may be causing high blood pressure, expert warns. *National Enquirer*, p. 43.

Harrower, T. (1991). *The newspaper designer's handbook* 2nd ed. Dubuque, IA: Wm. C. Brown Publishers.

Hinkle, G. & Elliott, W. R. (1989). Science coverage in three newspapers and three super-market tabloids. *Journalism Quarterly*, 66, 353-358.

Holden, L. (1977, July). The incredibly rich tabloid market. *Writers Digest*, pp. 19-22.

Holeb, A. (1983, June 28). At last! We're winning the war against cancer. *National Enquirer*, p. 19.

Honnold, J. (1981). Predictors of public environmental concern in the 1970s. In D. Mann (Ed.). *Environmental policy formation* (pp. 63-75). Lexington, MA: DC Heath.

How the world is going to waste. (1991, February 11). *National Enquirer*, p. 37.

Hoyt, J. (1989, September 19). California landowners outraged as govt. bans all building to protect 100,000 rats. *National Enquirer*, p. 39.

Hunter, G. (1983, August 2). 55,000 Enquirer readers join battle to ban steel-jawed traps. *National Enquirer*, p. 39.

Isenberg, N. (1994a, September 27). He faces jail for shooting bear that attacked his dogs. *National Enquirer*, p. 19.

Isenberg, N. (1994b, December 27). He finds $8,100 at dump - and gives it all back. *National Enquirer*, p. 14.

Isenberg, N. (1996, February 20). He's the wizard of weather forecasts - thanks to a tree! He says it helps him make correct predictions 9 times out of 10. *National Enquirer*, p. 13.

Kasperson, R. E. & Kasperson, J. X. (1991). Hidden hazards. In D.G. Mayo & R. D. Hollander (Eds.), *Acceptable evidence: Science and values in risk management* (pp. 9-28). New York: Oxford University Press.

Kaufman, M. (1990, December 11). Man who turned dump into garden is saved from jail thanks to Enquirer. *National Enquirer*, p. 35.

King of recycling built house out of newspapers. (1996, November 26). *National*

Enquirer, p. 31.

Kohut, J. J. & Sweet, R. (1996, February 6). Dad poisons family trying to thaw pipes. *National Enquirer*, p. 15.

Krajewski, S. (1983, October 18). Wow! *National Enquirer*, p. 43.

Krajewski, S. (1992, March 17). I turned in a brutal bird killer and it cost me my job. *National Enquirer*, p. 21.

Krimsky, S. & Golding, D. (1992). Reflections. In S. Krimsky & D. Golding (Eds.), *Social theories of risk*. Westport, CT: Praeger.

Kuhn, T. S. (1970). *The structure of scientific revolutions*. Chicago: The University of Chicago Press.

Lacey, C. & Longman, D. (1993). The press and public access to the environment and development debate. *The Sociological Review, 41*, 207-243.

Latta, J. (1986, January 21). Govt. tries to save fuel but ends up wasting time & money. *National Enquirer*, p. 53.

Levi-Strauss, C. (1964). *The raw and the cooked*. New York: Harper & Row.

Levy, P. F. (1983a, January 25). Have a problem? Here's where to call for answers. *National Enquirer*, p. 28.

Levy, P. F. (1983b, February 22). Outrageous! Researcher cripples ducks — then turns them loose to die. *National Enquirer*, p. 4.

Levy, P. F. (1983c, July 5). Dung ho! Look where your taxes go. *National Enquirer*, p. 20.

Levy, P. F. (1983d, August 30). 91,000 outraged Americans speak up. *National Enquirer*, p. 37.

Levy, P. F. (1983e, September 13). Banker quits 40G job to live in the woods. *National Enquirer*, p. 59.

Levy, P. F. (1984, November 20). Wow! Look at the wacky things your government is doing, 700 pages of plans for a mousetrap — measuring noses of stewardesses. *National Enquirer*, p. 47.

Levy, P. F. (1988, February 16). Badly needed dam delayed to protect snakes that weren't even in danger. *National Enquirer*, p. 55.

Lowe, P. & Morrison, D. (1984). Bad news or good news: Environmental politics and the mass media. *The Sociological Review, 32*, 75-90.

Magee, M. (1985, April 30). Bureaucrats buy cars with $$ slated to fight animal cruelty. *National Enquirer*, p. 45.

Marx, K. (1964). The economic and philosophical manuscripts. In T. Bottomore (Ed.), *Karl Marx: The early writings* (pp. 61-219). New York: McGraw-Hill.

Mazur, A. (1990). Nuclear power, chemical hazards, and the quantity of reporting. *Minerva, 28*, 294-323.

McCandlish, J. (1988, October 25). Fuel-ish govt. tax wrecks a tiny school's project. *National Enquirer*, p. 30.

McCandlish, J. (1989, January 31). Warning - deadly carbon monoxide may be trapped inside your home - here's how you can find out. *National Enquirer*, p. 36.

McCandlish, J. (1991a, March 5). Hardly any gas-saving products really work. *National Enquirer*, p. 18.

McCandlish, J. (1991b, November 5). Stunning story behind the biosphere ballyhoo. *National Enquirer*, p. 2.

McCandlish, J. (1992, February 25). Big shame hunters. *National Enquirer*, p. 5.

McCandlish, J. (1993, March 16). Arrested, handcuffed & sentenced to jail for saving helpless animals! *National Enquirer*, p. 2.

McCandlish, J. (1994, December 27). Govt. blockheads sell nuclear bomb factory to used-car dealer — & even give him instructions. *National Enquirer*, p. 2.

McCandlish, J. (1995, April 25). Dig this! Folks build own water system & save a whopping $250,000. *National Enquirer*, p. 22.

McCandlish, J., Fuller, C., & Temmey, B. (1989, October 3). Strange monster in Canadian Lake - actual photos - video is so convincing govt. put creature on protected wildlife list. *National Enquirer*, p. 22.

McConnell, G. (1954). The conservation movement: Past and present. *Western Political Quarterly, 7,* 463-478.

McDonald, D. (1990, October 23). Real American heroes. *National Enquirer*, p. 33.

McDonald, D. (1993, April 13). Battlin' granny goes out on a limb to save a tree - she builds a home under it & guards it with her life. *National Enquirer*, p. 28.

Mead, M. (1953). The study of culture at a distance. In M. Mead & R. Metraux (Eds.), *The study of culture at a distance* (pp. 3-58). Chicago: University of Chicago Press.

Mencher, M. (1983). *Basic news writing.* Dubuque, IA: William C. Brown.

Milbrath, L. (1984). *Environmentalists: Vanguard for a new society.* Albany: State University of New York Press.

Milne, D. (1989a, January 11). How do frogs attract girlfriends? You're paying $46,000 to find out. *National Enquirer*, p. 42.

Milne, D. (1989b, February 28). You're paying $114,000 to discover how bugs nab spiders for dinner. *National Enquirer*, p. 43.

Milne, D. (1989c, August 29). How do ravens get dinner dates? It's costing you 50g to find out. *National Enquirer*, p. 11.

Milne, D. (1991, December 24). Slimy bureaucrats waste your tax $$ on earthworm study. *National Enquirer*, p. 26.

Milne, D. (1992, April 21). Buggy bureaucrats blow your tax $$$ — counting caterpillars. *National Enquirer*, p. 27.

Milne, D. (1993, October 19). Featherbrained feds blow your taxes studying bird habits. *National Enquirer*, p. 12.

Milne, D. (1995a, February 21). Government shells out $275,000 so eggheads can learn why some birds are unfaithful. *National Enquirer*, p. 14.

Milne, D. (1995b, October 10). Your taxes go flying to study birds' sex antics. *National Enquirer*, p. 30.

Minsky, M. (1975) A framework for representing knowledge. In P. H. Winston (Ed.), *The psychology of computer vision* (pp. 211-277). New York: McGraw-Hill.

Montgomery, C. (1986, March 4). News study reveals United States is the best place to live. *National Enquirer*, p. 6.

More than half of all aluminum cans were recycled last year. (1984, December 18). *National Enquirer*, p. 6.

Mullins, J. (1985, January 8). What you should know about bottled water. *National Enquirer*, p. 39.

Mullins, J. (1991, August 6). Wacky weed man is a thorn in the side of the neighborhood. *National Enquirer*, p. 40.

Murch, A. W. (1971). Public concern for environmental pollution. *Public Opinion Quarterly, 35,* 100-106.

Nelkin, D. (1989). Communicating technological risk: The social construction of risk perception. *Annual Review of Public Health, 10,* 95-113.

Nelson, J. (1989a, March 14). U.S. fishermen killing thousands of dolphins each year with bombs. *National Enquirer*, p. 61.

Nelson, J. (1989b, March 28). You're paying 25G to find out how dragonflies think. *National Enquirer*, p. 39.

New seafood safety hotline takes the worry out of eating fish. (1993, June 29). *National*

Enquirer, p. 54.

Nord, D. P. (1989). The nature of historical research. In G. H. Stempel & B. Westley (Eds.), *Research methods in mass communication* (pp. 290-315). Englewood Cliffs, NJ: Prentice-Hall.

Nuke plant worker risked cancer for sake of colleagues. (1993, January 5). *National Enquirer*, p. 40.

Ogilvie, D. M., Stone, P. J., & Kelly, E. F. (1982). Computer-aided content analysis. In R. Smith & P. Manning (Eds.), *A handbook of social science methods 2: Qualitative methods* (pp. 219-246). New York: Ballanger.

O'Neill, B. (1983, September 27). Letters of outrage pour in. *National Enquirer*, p. 30.

O'Neill, B. (1994, February 8). Voice of Enquirer readers is heard around the world. *National Enquirer*, p. 35.

O'Neill, B. (1995a, January 10). Park ranger seizes boy's school project. *National Enquirer*, p. 32.

O'Neill, B. (1995b, November 14). Garbageman finds $200,000 prize in the trash. *National Enquirer*, p. 7.

Page, C. (1989, April 11). Flea killer for your pets can make you sick. *National Enquirer*, p. 42.

Park, R. (1940). News as a form of knowledge. *American Journal of Sociology*, 45, 669-686.

Patterson, P. (1989). Reporting Chernobyl: Cutting the government fog to cover the nuclear cloud. In L. M. Walters, L. Wilkins & T. Walters (Eds.), *Bad tidings: Communication and catastrophe* (pp. 131-147). Hillsdale, NJ: Lawrence Erlbaum

Pedersen, D. (1996, March 11). Flash! The gutter press got it right. *Newsweek*, 26.

Peer, E. & Schmidt, W. (1975, April 21). The *Enquirer*: Up from smut. *Newsweek*, 62.

Plamann, S. (1991a, April 23). What you can do to help clean up the environment. *National Enquirer*, p. 51.

Plamann, S. (1991b, July 2). An American success story: How we've saved many of our wild animals from vanishing forever. *National Enquirer*, p. 23.

Plamann, S. (1992, March 31). Japan's secret shame — cuddly bears tortured and butchered — for fun — Bloodthirsty crowds cheer as zoo animals are forced to fight to the death. *National Enquirer*, p. 2.

Plamann, S. (1993a, January 5). Bunglecrats blow $180,000 of your taxes to learn if chimps can count. *National Enquirer*, p. 17.

Plamann, S. (1993b, March 9). Even the cops were fired in cash crisis, so citizens work for free to save town that went broke. *National Enquirer*, p. 14.

Plamann, S. (1994, February 8). Your dog could save our child from lead poisoning. *National Enquirer*, p. 16.

Policy, J. (1983a, January 25). Your cold cash goes to study penguins. *National Enquirer*, p. 45.

Policy, J. (1983b, March 29). Government pinheads fly away with your tax dollars. *National Enquirer*, p. 35.

Policy, J. (1985, December 31). Bottled water is not safer than tap water — it may even be worse. *National Enquirer*, p. 7.

Pritchard, C. (1985, September 17). Terrible allergy turns mom of 4 into prisoner of darkness. *National Enquirer*, p. 23.

Pritchard, C. (1988, October 18). A freak chemical accident makes this family — allergic to the modern world. *National Enquirer*, p. 5.

Pritchard, C. (1993, May 18). After 9 years of hell on a desolate island, family that was allergic to the world is cured - by fresh air! *National Enquirer*, p. 39.

Pritchard, C. (1994, November 15). I lived with an eagle for 10 years - and even slept in her nest. *National Enquirer*, p. 31.

Rachlin, A. (1988). *News as hegemonic reality: American political culture and the framing of news accounts.* New York: Praeger Publishers.

Radcliffe-Brown, A.R. (1952). *Structure and function in primitive society.* Glencoe, IL.

Ramirez, T. P. (1984, October 16). Hooray for the future! *National Enquirer*, p. 9.

Ramirez, T. P. (1985, August 20). Warning! Felt-tip marker fumes may be hazardous to your health. *National Enquirer*, p. 18.

Ramirez, T. P. (1989, December 19). Leading expert declares . . . greenhouse scare is hot air! *National Enquirer*, p. 24.

Ramirez, T. P. (1991, March 12). Whatta dump! *National Enquirer*, p. 38.

Ramirez, T. P. (1994, April 5). Why America is more beautiful than ever - our health is better, our homes are bigger, our air is cleaner, and much, much more. *National Enquirer*, p. 2.

Rayner, S. (1992). Cultural theory and risk analysis. In S. Krimsky & D. Golding (Eds.), *Social theories of risk* (pp. 83-115). Westport, CT: Praeger.

Renn, O., Burns, W. J., Kasperson, J. X., Kasperson, R. E., & Slovic, P. (1992). The social amplification of risk: Theoretical foundations and empirical applications. *Journal of Social Issues*, 48, 137-160.

Riechert, B. P. & Miller, M. M. (1994, July). *Magazine coverage of pesticide issues: The controversies, the concerns, the claimsmakers.* Paper presented at the Media and the Environment Conference of the Association for Education in Journalism and Mass Communication, Reno, Nevada.

Riechert, B.P., & Miller, M.M. (1997, May). *Competing views and news coverage in the case of wetlands: Frame mapping and the public issue landscape.* Paper presented at the 47th Conference of the International Communication Association, Montreal, Quebec.

Rodack, J. (1994, January 18). Today's newest fashions are made from trash. *National Enquirer*, p. 2.

Rodell, C. (1991, December 24). Holy smoke! Their town's on fire. *National Enquirer*, p. 7.

Rodell, C. (1995, May 2). Lady mayor runs a nice clean town. *National Enquirer*, p. 35.

Rodell, C. (1996a, April 16). He saved a forest at age 12 and now fights for animals. *National Enquirer*, p. 45.

Rodell, C. (1996b, June 18). Bambi shot dead! *National Enquirer*, p. 14.

Rodell, C. (1996c, November 20). Town's been on fire for 34 years but locals love it too much to leave. *National Enquirer*, p. 10.

Rodell, C. (1997, August 19). He goes to jail to save a tree. *National Enquirer*, p. 6.

Rosch, E. (1975). Cognitive representations of semantic categories. *Journal of Experimental Psychology, 104,* 192-233.

Rubin, D. M. & Sachs, D. P. (1973). *Mass media and the environment.* New York: Praeger.

Ruehl, F. R. (1984, March 27). New study reveals: Many jobs are health risks. Is yours on the list? *National Enquirer*, p. 62.

Ruehl, F. R. (1986, August 12). Scientists were wrong — new studies show we would survive nuclear war. *National Enquirer*, p. 32.

Ruehl, F. R. (1989, July 11). Fascinating facts about bottled water. *National Enquirer*, p. 12.

Ruehl, F. R. (1996, April 9). Don't worry! You're safer than you think. *National Enquirer*,

p. 14.

Rumelhart, D. E. (1980). Schemata: The building blocks of cognition. In R. J. Spiro, B. C. Bruce and W. F. Brewer (Eds.), *Theoretical issues in reading comprehension.* (pp. 33-48). Hillsdale, NJ: Lawrence Erlbaum.

Schank, R. C. & Abelson, R. P. (1977). *Scripts, plans, goals and understanding.* Hillsdale, NJ: Lawrence Erlbaum.

Schoenfeld, C. (1973). *Interpreting environmental issues.* Madison, WI: Dembar Educational Research Services, Inc.

Schoenfeld, A. C., Meier, R. F. & Griffin, R. J. (1979). Constructing a social problem: The press and the environment. *Social Problems,* 27, 38-61.

Schutz, A. (1945). *Philosophy and phenomenological research, 5,* 533-576.

Short, J. F., Jr. (1984). The social fabric at risk: Toward the social transformation of risk analysis. *American Sociological Review,* 49, 711-725.

Simple way to end roach problems without poison. (1985, January 15). *National Enquirer,* p. 18.

Smith, P. (1991, July 30). Recycling junkie doesn't waste a single thing! *National Enquirer,* p. 8.

Smith, P. (1992, January 21). How cheap are they? Thrifty New Englanders even use dirty diapers as fuel. *National Enquirer,* p. 10.

Smith, P. (1993, December 14). Jailed because I didn't mow my lawn! *National Enquirer,* p. 2.

Smith, S. (1994, August 9). Outrageous! Folks lose homes in gas blast & they're still getting gas bills. *National Enquirer,* p. 6.

Smith, P. (1995a, January 21). Trail guide's strange vision saves granny lost in wilds. *National Enquirer,* p. 32.

Smith, P. (1995b, November 7). 80-year-old hauled to jail in handcuffs for not weeding his yard. *National Enquirer,* p. 11.

Smith, P. (1996, October 8). Fowl! Cop tickets caring driver for stopping to help baby ducks. *National Enquirer,* p. 14.

Solo Syndication & Literary Agency, Ltd. (1984, April 24). Paul Newman & Clint Eastwood fight animal cruelty in movies, *National Enquirer,* p. 25.

South, J. (1984, January 3). A dam good idea, government puts beavers to work and saves you big money. *National Enquirer,* p. 59.

Stallings, R. A. (1990). Media discourse and the social construction of risk. *Social Problems,* 37, 80-95.

Still, W. (1984, June 26). 1 in 10 face health hazards from carbonless copy paper. *National Enquirer,* p. 16.

Still, B. (1989, November 7). Acid rain destruction is bunk, experts say. *National Enquirer,* p. 52.

Still, B., Nelson, J., & Herz, S. (1988, April 12). Controversial study claims — 40,000 American deaths are linked to fallout from Russia's Chernobyl disaster. *National Enquirer,* p. 3.

Stine, G. H. (1984, January 17). Fascinating book bonus brings good news to every American forget all those gloom and doom warnings — are future looks bright. *National Enquirer,* p. 58.

Stone, P. J. (1997). Thematic text analysis: New agendas for analyzing text content. In C. W. Roberts (Ed.), *Text analysis for the social sciences: Methods for drawing statistical inferences from texts and transcripts* (pp. 35-54). Mahwah, NJ: Lawrence Erlbaum.

Sunglasses not just for summer. (1989, April 18). *National Enquirer,* p. 10.

Susman, E. (1989, December 19). Govt. blows $98,000 to study why rats stomp their feet. *National Enquirer*, p. 38.

Susman, E. (1990, June 19). You paid $120,000 to find out tiny bugs run if big bugs chase 'em. *National Enquirer*, p. 27.

Temmey, B. (1990, December 11). Worker fined $88 million. *National Enquirer*, p. 19.

This lady is for the birds. (1990, September 25). *National Enquirer*, p. 55.

Tiemann, A. R. (1987). Risk, technology, and society. *Risk Analysis*, 7, 11-13.

The truth about the air we breathe. (1995, June 20). *National Enquirer*, p. 17.

Town spends $85,000 for ducks but turns its back on boy in wheelchair. (1991, August 13). *National Enquirer*, p. 23.

Trashmen to the rescue! (1994, March 15). *National Enquirer*, p. 37.

Tuchman, G. (1978). *Making news*. New York: Free Press.

van Dijk, T. (1988). *News analysis*. Hillsdale, NJ: Lawrence Erlbaum Associates.

War hero faces jail for growing vegetables. (1992, October 13). *National Enquirer*, p. 15.

Whorf, B. L. (1956). *Language, thought and reality*. (J. B. Carroll, Ed.), Cambridge: MIT Press.

Wilkins, P. (1990, March 20). Secret investigation reveals Russian nuclear accident created monstrous animals. *National Enquirer*, p. 51.

Woelfel, J. (1993). Artificial neural networks in policy research: A current assessment. *Journal of Communication*, 43, 63-80.

Woelfel, J. K. (1998). *User's Guide Catpac II Version 2.0*. Amherst, NY: Rah Press.

Wright, D. (1983, March 22). America is the greatest. *National Enquirer*, p. 39.

Yearley, S. (1991). *The green case*. London: Harper Collins Academic.

Young, R. S. (1997, August 26). New study reveals: Polluted drinking water can trigger criminal behavior. *National Enquirer*, p. 7.

9

A Faint Green Sell: Advertising and the Natural World

Julia B. Corbett

It is virtually impossible to think of any other message that is as pervasive, invasive, and ubiquitous as the advertisement. Of course ads are sandwiched between news and entertainment programming in the mass media, but there is also the ad on the bus bench and on the bus, on the telephone pole and billboard, on the sweatshirt, before the movie and on the popcorn bag, on "commercial free" radio, on cars and trucks, on Web sites, stuffed in bills and mailboxes, and on classroom walls. According to the American Association of Advertising Agencies, we are exposed to 3,000 advertisements each day, but we notice only 80, and have some sort of reaction to only 12 (Twitchell, 1996). But with daily repetition through multiple channels, the jingles and slogans of ads are on the lips of young and old, setting the trends for cars, clothes, and consumption. The advertisement is, without a doubt, the ultimate pop culture message.

In the 1980s, advertisers discovered the environment. When a revitalized environmental movement helped establish environmentalism as a legitimate, mainstream public goal (Luke, 1993), corporate America quickly capitalized on a lucrative market of "green consumers" (Ottman, 1993; Zinkham & Carlson, 1995). Marketers not only could create new products and services, they could also reposition existing ones to appear more environmentally friendly. What resulted was a flood of advertisements that focused on green product attributes, touting products as recyclable and biodegradable and claiming them good or safe for the environment. Increases in this genre were remarkable, with green print ads increasing 430 percent and green television ads increasing 367 percent between 1989 and 1990 (Ottman, 1993). The total number of products claiming green attributes doubled in 1990 to 11.4 percent from the previous year ("Selling green," 1991).

Virtually all of the existing research on so-called green advertising was conducted during this boom. Green advertising was defined by researchers as product ads touting environmental benefits or corporate green-image ads (Shrum, McCarty, & Lowrey, 1995; Banerjee, Gulas, & Iyer, 1995). Researchers also targeted and segmented green consumers (Ottman, 1993) and tested their motivations (Luke, 1993). Green appeals were categorized (Iyer & Banerjee, 1993; Obermiller, 1995; Schuhwerk & Lefkoff-Hagius, 1995) and consumer response to green ads analyzed (Mayer, Scammon, & Zick, 1993; Thorson, Page, & Moore, 1995).

By the late 1990s, advertisers announced the end of the green-ad boom. Advertising Age reported that as the country headed into the thirtieth anniversary of Earth Day, green positioning had become more than just a non-issue—it was almost an anti-issue (Neff, 2000). Marketers were launching a whole new class of disposable products from plastic storage containers to dust mops. There was a perceived decline in controversy over anti-green products such as disposable diapers, toxic batteries, and gas-guzzling SUVs (sport utility vehicles). In addition, only 5 percent of new products made claims about recyclability or recycled content, and the explosion of e-tailing added boxes, styrofoam peanuts, and air-puffed plastic bags to the waste stream. Green product ads in prime-time television, which never amounted to more than a blip, virtually disappeared by 1995, reflecting "the television tendency to get off the environmental bandwagon after it had lost its trendiness" (Shanahan & McComas, 1999, p. 108).

But Shanahan and McComas noted that their study—like virtually all research published during the green-ad boom—did not consider the most prevalent use of the environment in advertising: when nature functions as a rhetorically useful backdrop or stage. Using nature merely as a backdrop—whether in the form of wild animals, mountain vistas, or sparkling rivers—is the most common use of the natural world in advertisements. For all but the most critical message consumers, the environment blends into the background. We know that an advertisement for a car shows the vehicle outdoors and that ads for allergy medications feature flowers and "weeds." The environment per se is not for sale, but advertisers are depending on qualities and features of the non-human world (and our relationship to it) to help in the selling message. When the natural world is so depicted, it becomes a convenient, culturally relevant tool to which meanings can be attached for the purpose of selling goods and services. Although this intentional but seemingly casual use of the environment in advertising is by far the most common, it is the least studied by researchers.

Nature-as-backdrop ads also are notable for their enduring quality. Although the number of ads that focus on product attributes such as "recyclable" may shift with marketing trends and political winds, nature has been used as a backdrop virtually since the dawn of advertising. The natural world was depicted in early automobile ads ("see the USA in your Chevrolet") and Hamms Beer commercials ("from the land of sky-blue water") and continues to be a prominent feature in the advertising landscape. Nature-as-backdrop ads, therefore, provide an important record of the position of the natural world in our cultural environment and, as such, deserve scrutiny.

Advertisements are a special form of discourse because they include visual signals and language fragments (either oral or written) that work together to create messages that go beyond the ability of either individually. This chapter undertakes a critical analysis of the symbolic communicative discourse of advertising, viewing nature-as-backdrop ads as cultural icons of environmental values embedded in our social system. When ads present the environment with distorted, inauthentic, or exaggerated discourse, that discourse has the potential to foster inauthentic relationships to nature and influences the way we perceive our environment and its value to us.

Schudson (1989) argued that ads have special cultural power. In addition to being repetitive and ubiquitous, ads reinforce messages from primary institutions in the social system, provide dissonance to countering messages, and generally support the capitalistic structure that the advertising industry was created to support. This chapter will discuss how the ad industry developed, how ads work on us, and how ads portray the natural world . This chapter will argue, according to environmental theories such as deep ecology (Naess, 1973; Bullis, 1996), that the "green" in advertising is extremely faint by examining and developing six related concepts:

1. The business of advertising is fundamentally "brown," therefore the idea of advertising being "green" and capable of supporting environmental values is an oxymoron.

2. Advertising commodifies the natural world and attaches material value to non-material goods, treating natural resources as private and possessible, not public and intrinsic.

3. Nature-as-backdrop ads portray an anthropocentric, narcissistic relationship to the biotic community and focus on the environment's utility and benefit to humans.

4. Advertising idealizes the natural world and presents a simplified, distorted picture of nature as sublime, simple, and unproblematic.

5. The depiction of nature in advertising disconnects and estranges us from what is valued, yet at the same time we are encouraged to reconnect through products, creating a circular consumption.

6. As a ubiquitous form of pop culture, advertising reinforces consonant messages in the social system and provides strong dissonance to oppositional or alternative messages.

This analysis draws on the literature of advertising, environment, and communication and utilizes representative magazine and network television ads collected over the past three years to illustrate these points. Because past research on this type of advertisement is virtually non-existent, there was no attempt to conduct a scientific sampling. As an exploratory study, it was more appropriate to gather and analyze representative types and proportions of existing nature-as-backdrop ads. Obviously, in the last several years there have been an abundance of ads for the currently popular SUVs. Also noted were large numbers of ads geared toward recreational products and prescription drugs. Common ad features included animals and depictions of resources such as water and pristine landscapes.

THE "BROWN" BUSINESS OF ADVERTISING

1. The business of advertising is fundamentally "brown"; therefore, the idea of advertising being "green" and capable of supporting environmental values is an oxymoron.

Advertisements are nothing new to this century or even previous ones. There are plentiful examples in literature, including the works of Shakespeare, that peddlers have long enticed buyers by advertising (in print or orally) a good's attributes and associated meanings. After World War II, however, advertising found a firm place in the worldview of Americans. According to Luke (1993), after 1945, corporate capital, big government, and professional experts pushed practices of a throw-away affluent society onto consumers as a purposeful political strategy to sustain economic growth, forestall mass discontent, and empower scientific authority. Concern for the environment was lacking in the postwar posterity boom, at least until the mid-1960s when Rachel Carson sounded the alarm over chemicals and the modern-day environmental movement was born (Corbett, 2001).

To help alert consumers to new mass-produced goods, a new type of show called the "soap opera" was created for the relatively recent phenomenon of television. These daytime dramas were created for the sole purpose of delivering an audience of homemakers to eager manufacturers of household products, including soap. Advertisers realized that advertising on soap operas would help to establish branding, or creating differing values for what are essentially common, interchangeable goods such as soap.

Essentially, advertising was viewed as part of the fuel that would help keep a capitalist economy burning. Capitalism is a market system that measures its success by constant growth (such as the gross national product and housing starts), a system that many environmentalists recognize as ultimately unsustainable. You might even say that advertising developed as the culture that would help solve what some economists view as the central problem of capitalism: the distribution of surplus goods (Twitchell, 1996). Schudson (1989) concluded, "Advertising is capitalism's way of saying 'I love you' to itself." In a capitalist economy, advertising is a vital handmaiden to consumption and materialism. In the words of the author of Adcult, Americans "are not too materialistic. We are not materialistic enough" (Twitchell, 1996, p. 11).

The development of mass media, particularly radio and television, played an important role in delivering audiences to advertisers. By the mid-1980s, half of U.S. homes had cable, and the burgeoning number of channels allowed advertisers to target more specific audience segments. Advertisers and media programmers engage in a dance to fill each other's needs, each having a vested interest in constructing certain versions of the world and not others. According to Turow (1999), "the ad industry affects not just the content of its own campaigns but the very structure and content of the rest of the media system" (p. 194). At the same time, media develop formats and tones for their outlets and programming deemed to be most acceptable to the audiences that they hope marketers find most attractive. What this means for programming is that the upscale twenty-something audience—the most appealing segment to advertisers—will find itself represented in more media outlets than older men and women to whom only a small number of highly targeted formats are aimed. According to researchers of the green marketing boom, the segments of the population most committed to the environment do not belong to this twenty-something group (Ottman, 1993).

It is precisely the ability of advertisers and media programmers to tell some stories and not others that gives these entities power. "When people read a magazine, watch a TV show, or use any other ad-sponsored medium, they are entering a world that was constructed as a result of close cooperation between advertisers and media firms" (Turow, 1999, p. 16). Because all media provide people with insights into parts of the world with which they have little direct contact, media representations of the natural world to a largely urbanized population are highly significant. They show us, over and over again, where we belong in the world and how we should treat it. Yet, representations of the natural world are crafted for the sole purpose of selling certain audiences to advertisers.

The close cooperation between advertisers and media firms is understandable given advertising's financial support of media. For newspapers and some magazines, at least 50 percent of their revenue is from advertising; ad support approaches 100 percent for much of radio and television. By some estimates, advertisers spent $27 billion to support to television, $9 billion on radio, $46 billion on daily newspapers, and about $7 billion on consumer magazines (Turow, 1999, p. 13).

Given advertising's purpose of selling audiences to advertisers, is it even possible for any form of advertising–whether product ads or nature-as-backdrop ads–to be "green"? Dadd and Carothers (1991) maintained that a truly green economy would require all products to be audited and analyzed from cradle to grave for their environmental effects. Effects could include the resources used and pollution generated in the product's manufacture, energy used to produce and transport the product, the product's role in the economic and social health of the country of origin, investment plans of the company, and final disposal of product.

Applying this standard at the most basic level connotes it is an oxymoron to label marginally useful or necessary products (and the ads that promote them) as "green" or somehow good for the environment. Can an advertisement that encourages consumption of a product (or patronage of a company that produces the product) ever be green with a capital G? In his attempt to reconcile a brown industry with green ideals, Kilbourne (1995) identified three levels of green in advertisements. But even at the lowest level (defined as ads promoting a small "techno-fix" such as biodegradability) the message is still that "consuming is good, more is better, and the ecological cost is minimal" (p. 15). If an ad recognizes finite resources, it nevertheless views the environment purely as a resource, not as possessing intrinsic, non-economic value. Kilbourne concluded that from a purely ecological position, a truly Green ad is indeed an oxymoron: "the only Green product is the one that is not produced" (p. 16). Other researchers have likewise tried to categorize the green in advertisements (Banerjee et al., 1995). Adapting the deep and shallow ecology concepts of Naess (1973) to advertisements, they concluded that very few ads were "deep"—2 percent of television and 9 percent of print—defined by the researchers as discussing environmental issues in depth and mentioning actions requiring more commitment.

However, these attempts to make advertising fit a green framework simply illustrate how ideologically opposed advertising and environmental values are. Because advertising is the workhorse of capitalism and supports continually increased production, it is ideologically contrary to environmentalism, which recognizes that ever-increasing growth and consumption are inherently unsustainable. It matters not whether an ad boasts of recyclability or quietly features pristine mountain meadows in the background; the basic business of advertising is brown. Perhaps the only truly Green product is not only one not produced, but also one not advertised.

NATURE AS COMMODITY

2. Advertising commodifies the natural world and attaches material value to non-material goods, treating natural resources as private and ownable, not public and intrinsic.

Have you ever viewed a single advertisement and then rushed out to buy that product? Probably not. That is not the way that advertising generally works on us, especially not for national consumer goods. Advertising scholars argue that ads cannot create, invent, or even satisfy our desires; instead, ads channel and express current desires with the hope of exploiting them.

You may disagree that ads cannot create desires, particularly if you have ever found yourself yearning for a product that six months ago you did not know existed or that you "needed." But even if ads do not greatly corrupt our immediate buying habits, they can gradually shape our values by becoming our social guides for what is important and valued. According to Benton (1995), advertising displays values and signals to people what our culture thinks is important. Advertising is not capable of inventing social values, but it does a masterful job at usurping and exploiting certain values and not others. The prominent (though not monopolistic) role of advertising in the symbolic marketplace is what gives advertising "a special cultural power" (Schudson, 1989). In the words of one scholar, "Advertising is simply one of a number of attempts to load objects with meaning . . . it is an ongoing conversation within a culture about the meaning of objects." (Twitchell, 1996, p. 13).

The rhetorical challenge for an advertiser, then, is to load one product (even though numerous similar ones exist) with sufficient meaning so that the product appears able to express a desire. The natural world is full of cultural meaning with which to associate products, thereby attaching commodity value to qualities that are impossible to own. By borrowing and adapting well-known, stereotypical portrayals of nature, advertising is able to associate water with freshness and purity and weather as fraught with danger. If, for example, an ad wants to attach the value of "safety" to one particular car, it might demonstrate the car's ability to dodge "dangerous" elements of nature, such as falling rocks. On the other hand, if the ad wants to convey a truck's durability, it could just as easily attach a very different meaning to the same resource and say the truck is "like a rock." Neither product guarantees that you can buy safety or durability; both product ads merely expressed a consumer desire for them by associating a non-material good with a material one.

Animals in particular provide cultural shorthand for advertising. Animals, as popular symbols of the nonhuman environment, are a way for advertisers to link the perceived "personality" and stereotyped cultural value of the animal to the product (Phillips, 1996). In car advertising alone, ads compare vehicles to rams, eagles, wolves, cougars, falcons, and panthers. Some ads go so far as to portray the vehicle as an animal itself. An individual needs no direct experience with untamed environs to know what an eagle or cougar represents and is valued for.

The portrayal of animals in advertising need not be authentic or realistic for us to ascertain the value they represent. In a television commercial, two raccoons are peering inside a brightly lit living room window, "singing" a song from My Fair Lady. As the camera moves beyond the raccoons into the living room— where it appears the residents are not home—it focuses on the rocker-recliner. The raccoons sing, "All I want is a room somewhere, far away from the cold night air. Warm hands, warm feet . . ."

In this ad, the rocker-recliner you are enticed to buy has no direct or obvious connection to the natural world, but animals are very much part of the overall persuasive message. We are able to overlook the anthropomorphized singing raccoons because we have enough shared cultural meaning about raccoons and their behavior. We can decipher that these cute, mischievous "bandits" would like to "break in" to this warm room far away from the cold night air and maybe even snooze in that rocker. The intrinsic value of raccoons as a species has been usurped and exploited to demonstrate the comfort and desirability of a certain brand of chair.

Even if the original function of advertising was to market simple products such as soap, advertising now functions to market feelings, sensations, and lifestyles. According to advertisers, the consumption of an object often has more to do with its meaning than with its actual use (Twitchell, 1996). Discrete objects—whether cold medicine or fabric softener—are easier to sell if they are associated with social and personal meaning. The purpose of an ad is not to stress that the product functions properly, but that consumption of it will cure problems (Lasch, 1978), whether loneliness, aging, or even a desire to connect with the natural world. Advertising channels our psychological needs and ambitions into consumptive behaviors (Pollay, 1989). Price (1996) concluded that the success of the store The Nature Company depends "not so much what nature is as what nature means to us" (p. 189).

Take for example a series of print and television ads for a particular SUV that labeled the vehicle as "the answering machine for the call of wild." The print version tells us that "nature calls out for us" but with the vehicle's leather-trimmed seats, "civilization's never very far away." In television versions, we see the vehicle traveling over rugged terrain (but not the woman driving it) while an answering machine plays numerous messages from a worried mother and boyfriend to the woman who has escaped into the wild.

These ads do not focus on all the ways that this vehicle is superior to all the other very similar SUVs out there. The ads give us no reason to believe that the repair record, safety rating, price, or other important product attributes are some-how superior. Instead, these ads are selling meanings and values associated with the natural world. This product will reconnect you with "the wild," which appears to be missing in your life, and it will help you escape from your troubles and relationships. A rugged environment (yet one somehow made safer and more civilized by this SUV) is portrayed as the best place to find peace and this vehicle will take you there. (An ad for a very different type of product used the same slogan in a different way: "Radio Shack is answering the call of the wild with two-way personal radios." In the ad, "renowned wildlife expert" Jim Fowler uses the radio in a remote-looking location. "No matter where the wild calls you, you'll be ready to answer.")

Some scholars insist that advertising appeals primarily to personal dissatisfactions in our lives and insecurities over the ways and pace in which we live, not to our personal needs. In doing so, ads are carriers of anxiety that serve only to alienate us further (Lasch, 1978). In the SUV ads, the driver is not portrayed as using the vehicle for personal need, but for escape from relationship problems to an environment that is depicted as being free of all problems.

The rhetorical argument of commodification leads us to believe that we can solve problems and dissatisfactions with a purchase. We buy the peace and escape—represented by the wilderness and promised by the product—even though the product is incapable of fulling that promise. The intent of advertising, says Pollay (1989), is to preoccupy society with material concerns and to see goods as a path to happiness and a solution to problems (which is very brown thinking). In many of the appeals of nature-as-backdrop ads, the advertisements attempt to associate material goods with nonmaterial qualities that have disappeared from many people's lives, qualities such as solitude, wilderness, lush landscapes, free-flowing water, and clean air. In a print ad for L.L. Bean, we see a man wading across calm, milky blue waters to a small sailboat in early morning light. The caption reads, "Don't mistake a street address for where you actually live." Apparently this man cannot "live" in his everyday life—which we assume takes place in a far less serene setting—but must leave it to achieve qualities it lacks. Yet another SUV ad promises, "Escape. Serenity. Relaxation." Pristine mountain vistas and sparkling waters (usually devoid of people) allow us to romanticize about a life lost or connections broken. When such adventures are tied in such a way to products, that connection materializes a way of experiencing the natural world.

Commodification of what are essentially public resources–like milky blue waters– encourages us to think of resources as private and possessible. Ads may invoke public values of family, friendship, and a common planet as part of their message, but these values are put to work to sell private goods, a very capitalist principle. The satisfaction derived from these goods, even those that appear inherently collective such as water, is depicted as invariably private. This encourages "the promotion of a social order in which people are encouraged to think of themselves and their private worlds" (Schudson, 1989, p. 83), a very anthropocentric and narcissistic perspective. The environment, in many respects, doesn't function well as private space.

FOR THE PLEASURE OF HUMANS

3. Nature-as-backdrop ads portray an anthropocentric, narcissistic relationship to the biotic community and focus on the environment's utility and benefit to humans.

Another common feature in advertising appeals that utilize the natural world is self-absorption and narcissism. The word derives from Narcissus, a youth in Greek mythology who fell in love with his own reflection in a pool. The way in which advertising portrays this universal emotional type is as self-absorbed, self-righteous, and dependent on momentary pleasures of assertion. Narcissism in advertising often takes the form of outdoor adventure, as in this print ad: Two pickup trucks are parked on an expansive, rolling sand dune. In the open bed of each truck, a young man in a wet suit appears to be wind-surfing—through the manipulation of computer graphics. Water splashes around them in the air and onto the sand. The caption says the trucks are "built fun tough" and have "gallons of attitude." Of course we know this picture to be fake (although a similar juxtaposition of desert and water exists in human-made Lake Powell), but the picture tells us that these men are in it for the fun, for the adventure.

A narcissist is most concerned with pleasing himself or herself at the expense of others, and if we extend the analogy, at the expense of the environment. In terms of environmental ideology, a narcissist would be anthropocentric, believing that his or her own outdoor pleasure comes before that of other species and their needs. Ads that show people "conquering" natural elements are expressing me-first anthropocentrism. According to Lasch (1978), our culture is marked by an exaggerated form of self-awareness and mass narcissism, finely attuned (with the help of advertising) to the many demands of the narcissistic self.

Another example is a television ad that shows a young boy working through the pages of a puzzle book. He reads aloud, "Help the knight reach the castle," and with his crayon follows the winding path safely past the dragon to the castle. On the next page he reads,"Help the Jeep Wrangler reach the fishing hole." "Hmm," he says, grins, and makes a noise like a truck revving up. He draws a line straight across the puzzle book landscape, across two mountain ranges, a deep valley, and a patch of quicksand, ignoring the cleared path. As he smiles smugly, the announcer tells us that a Jeep is "more fun than you imagine."

Yet another truck commercial begins in a deserted mountain valley at twilight. Next, a gigantic booted foot with a spur crashes to the ground, reverberating all in sight. We then see that the foot belongs to a cowboy the size of Paul Bunyan. The message is that the human is essentially larger than life, dominating the entire landscape and all within it, as Bunyan did. Such exaggerated domination intentionally positions humans at the top of a pyramid, instead of belonging equally to a biotic community.

NATURE AS SUBLIME

4. Nature-as-backdrop ads idealize the natural world and present a simplified, distorted picture of nature as sublime, simple, and unproblematic.

As much as ads intentionally distort reality (in images such as wind-surfing in a truck or singing raccoons), they also present reality as it should be, a reality that is worth desiring and emulating (and owning). If you have backpacked or camped, you know that slapping mosquitoes, getting dirty, getting wet, and sweating are often part of the package. Such a real outdoor experience is unlikely to be depicted in advertisements (unless the product is for something like insect repellent). Instead, ads subordinate reality to a romanticized past, present, or even future. "Real" in advertising is a cultural construct: "The makers of commercials do not want what is real but what will seem real on film. Artificial rain is better than 'God's rain' because it shows up better on film or tape" (Schudson, 1989, p. 79). Advertisers do not intend to capture life as it really is, but intend instead to portray the "ideal" life and to present as normal and everyday what are actually relatively rare moments, such as a phenomenal sunset or a mosquito-less lake.

A great many nature-as-backdrop ads present the natural world as sublime, a noble place inspiring awe and admiration. As an exercise, my students draw their interpretation of a sublime place in nature, and invariably, similar elements appear in their pictures: snow-capped mountain peaks towering above pine trees and a grassy or flower-filled meadow, through which a clear creek or river flows. Sometimes, large mammals such as deer graze in the meadow. Humans are rarely present.

According to Oravec (1996), the sublime is a literary and artistic convention that uses a prescribed form of language and pictorial elements to describe nature, and that in turn encourages a specific pattern of responses to nature. Artistically, sublime representations can include blurring, exaggeration of detail, and compositional elements such as a foreground, middle ground, and frame. Settings are frequently pastoral or wild with varying amounts of human presence. There is a self-reflexive nature to the positioning, with the observer feeling both within a scene and also outside it, viewing the scene (and reflexively, the self) from a higher or more distant (and morally outstanding) perspective.

Oravec has called the sublime the founding trope in the rhetoric of environmentalism: "Sublimity has remained a touchstone or grounding for our public conception of nature and, through nature, of the environment" (1996, p. 68). As a conventional linguistic device, the sublime represents and encodes our understanding of the natural world. Because the sublime is associated with what is "natural," "the sublime connotes an authenticity and originality that is part of its very meaning; yet like rhetoric itself, it has a long-standing reputation for exaggeration and even falsehood" (p. 69).

The sublime is as much a part of advertising as it is of the artistic and literary realms. Advertising presents the natural world as pristine, simple, and not endangered, yet depictions are always contrived and often created. What appears as real rain is artificial, what looks like a natural wildlife encounter is contrived, and what appears entirely natural was created with computer animation and digital manipulation. The artificial seamlessly approximates the real in the sublime world of advertising.

Numerous vacation advertisements depict people in sublime settings, such as thin and tan couples on pristine white sand beaches, or peacefully cruising under sunny skies amid glaciers and whales. Vacationers in this idealized world never encounter anything other than perfect environmental conditions and enjoy these sublime locations unfettered by crowds.

A host of pharmaceutical ads likewise enlist nature backdrops as rhetoric for the sublime. One ad for an arthritis medication takes place in a pastoral setting assumed to be a park. The sun is shining, the park is empty except for the actors, there is no litter or noise, and even the dogs are exceedingly friendly and behaved. In another ad for what is presumed to be a mood-enhancer, a woman strolls slowly along a pristine, deserted beach in soft light, a contented smile on her face. In these instances, the sublime backdrop doubly represents the sublime state the person will achieve upon taking the medication. Many of these ads rely so heavily on the power of sublime meaning that the actual purpose of the drug is not stated, only assumed.

Other commercials depict the sublime after a product has changed problematic nature into idealized nature. Numerous ads for lawn care products and allergy medications first portray nature in a state of chaos or war, needing to be tamed and brought under control. One television ad for lawn chemicals showed a small army of men and supplies descending from the sky to tame and tackle nature. Some allergy commercials depict the flowers and weeds physically attacking people. But ah, after the product is introduced, unproblematic and peaceful nature returns.

When humans are introduced into sublime scenes, their representation is also idealized. Just as nature is presented as reality-as-it-should-be, people are presented as-they-should-be in a limited number of social roles. Therefore, people in ads are primarily attractive, young or middle-aged, vibrant, and thin, or they are celebrities with those qualities. The environments in which they live, whether inside or outside, are also limited to idealized conditions; no one has dirty houses or unkempt lawns, and no one travels through dirty city streets, encounters polluted rivers, or finds abused landscapes. In the world of advertising, there are no poor people, sick people, or unattractive people, and sometimes there are no people at all. For example, most car ads do not show anyone actually driving the vehicle through the tinted windows, and you hear only the disembodied voice of the announcer. The social roles played by advertising actors are easily identifiable—the businessperson, the grandmother, the teenager—but the actors are anonymous as individual people and portray only social roles tailored to specific demographic categories. The flat, abstract, idealized, and sometimes anonymous world of advertising "is part of a deliberate effort to connect specific products in people's imagination with certain demographic groupings or needs or occasions" (Schudson, 1989, p. 77).

Of course you recognize pieces of this idealized presentation of people and their environments, just as you recognize the utterly impossible pieces—a car parked on an inaccessible cliff or polar bears drinking Coke. We are not stupefied by a natural world that is unrealistic and idealized in advertising: in fact, we expect it.

A NATURAL DISCONNECT

5. The depiction of nature in advertising disconnects and estranges us from what is valued, and we attempt to reconnect through products, creating a circular consumption.

Some critics believe that advertising may be more powerful the less people believe it and the less it is acknowledged. According to Schudson (1989), ads do not ask to be taken literally and do not mean what they say, but "this may be the very center of their power" (p. 87). While we are being exposed to those 3,000 ads a day, we may carry an illusion of detachment and think them trivial and unimportant. According to some theories, though, it is very possible to "learn" without active involvement, a so-called sleeper effect. This myth of immunity from an ad's persuasion may do more to protect our self-respect than help us comprehend the subtleties and implications of their influence (Pollay, 1989). Although we may not think an ad speaks to us, its slogan may suddenly pop into our vocabulary—just do it, it does a body good, got milk? We may be unaware and uninvolved in front of the television, but the message of the ad may prove important at purchase time. According to Pollay (1989), advertising does more than merely stimulate wants; it plays a subtle role in changing habits.

Take the habit of drying your clothes, an activity that for many people throughout the world involves pinning clothes to a line in the backyard or between buildings. When I was a girl, I loved sliding between clean sheets dried outside on the clothesline and drinking in the smell. How do many people get

that same outside-smell nowadays? They get it with detergents and fabric soft-
eners with names like "mountain aire" and "springtime fresh" or with similarly
scented dryer sheets. Although perceived convenience and affordable dryers no
doubt helped change our clothes-drying habits, where did we learn to associate
the smell of outdoors with purchased products? Advertising.

The message in these product ads is that the artificial smell is somehow easier or superior or even just equivalent to the real smell in the natural world. It not
only commodifies something of value from the natural world, it gradually disconnects us from that thing of value. The more successfully ads teach us to associate natural qualities such as fresh air with products, the more disconnected we
become from what was originally valued. The more estranged from the original
thing of value, the more we may attempt to reconnect through products that
promise an easy replacement. When we become so estranged from the natural
world that we attempt to reconnect through products, a circular consumptive pattern is created – which supports the capitalist economy that advertising was created to support. If advertising tells us that non-saleable qualities of the outdoors
such as fresh air and natural smells are easy to bring inside, need we worry about
the condition of the real world?

Just as advertising can change habits, it can help create rituals and taboos. A
good example of a taboo largely created by advertising is litter. Through national advertising campaigns begun decades ago, litter was labeled as an
environmental no-no. While cleaning up litter makes for a visually appealing
environment, the automobiles from which the trash is generally tossed cause far
more environmental harm than almost all types of litter.

Advertising also works to create rituals. A ritual is created when we make
inert, prosaic objects meaningful and give them symbolic significance. Mistletoe
means little to us as a parasitic evergreen, but it is loaded with significance as a
holiday ritual about kissing. Whales mean more to us as communicative, spiritual symbols of the deep than for their inherent value and place in ocean ecosystems. Price (1996) concluded that Native American fetishes and baskets, which
have been ritualized by non-native populations (and appropriated by advertising), "associate nature nearly interchangeably with indigenous peoples" (1996,
p. 189). In a similar way, once a species or animal has been so ritualized, it precludes a more complete and accurate knowing of it and disconnects us.

Advertising, directly and subtly, idealizes and materializes a way of experiencing the world, including the natural world. It promotes products as the simple
solutions to complex dilemmas by tapping into our dissatisfactions and desires.
If you feel disconnected to the natural world, you can "solve" that with moun-
tain-scented laundry products, bear fetishes, and whale audiotapes, but these
purchases only increase the estrangement. If you need to escape modern life
yet want to feel safe and civilized while doing so, you can simply solve that by
taking a rugged SUV into the wilderness.

Yet environmental dilemmas are anything but simple, and wilderness is a
good example. A print ad features a four-wheel-drive car crossing a sparkling,

boulder-strewn stream and announces, "Coming soon to a wilderness near you." In this idealized portrayal, there is no mud being stirred up from the bottom of the stream, no dirt of any kind on the car, and of course, there is no visible driver. But in addition, "wilderness" is a rare commodity that rarely exists "near you," and by its very definition, includes few people and even fewer developed signs of people. In wilderness with a capital W, cars and all motorized equipment are forbidden. Setting aside an area as wilderness involves contentious negotiations and land-use trade-offs. But whether formally designated or not, experiencing wilderness is not the simple matter of materialization and driving a certain kind of car.

Another example of advertising portraying a complex environmental issue as simple and uncomplicated is the depiction of water. We see it babbling down brooks in beverage commercials, refreshing someone in a soap commercial, quenching thirst in ads for water filters and bottled water. Pure, clean, healthy— but simple? More than half the world's rivers are drying up or are polluted. Agricultural chemicals have seeped into many U.S. underground aquifers. Oil, gas, and a host of herbicides and pesticides wash off streets and lawns into waterways. Political and legal fights are waged over dams, diversions, and water rights. A host of bacterial contaminants have threatened water supplies and public health in major U.S. cities, and traces of antibiotics and other prescription drugs have been detected in some municipal water supplies. Clean water is definitely not a simple environmental issue.

ADVERTISING DOES NOT STAND ALONE

6. As a ubiquitous form of popular culture, advertising reinforces consonant messages in the social system and provides strong dissonance to oppositional or alternative messages.

For any societal element to wield power, it must exist in concert with other social institutions in a way that is mutually reinforcing. Advertising is layered on top of other cultural elements and bound up with other institutions, from entertainment and popular culture to corporate America and manufacturing. Each element is heteroglossic, continually leaking into other sectors, with advertising slogans showing up in both casual conversation and political speeches. The very ubiquitousness of advertising—extending beyond regular media buys to include placing products in movies, sponsoring sporting events, and the full-length infomercial—ensures its power and influence in numerous places and institutions.

For an example of this interwoven character of advertising and consumption with other elements of society, consider plastics recycling. We routinely see ads touting how certain products are recyclable or made from recycled items. Currently, the plastics industry is running an advertising campaign that reminds us of all the wonderful ways that plastic contributes to our lives. That means that multiple corporate public relations departments and public relations agencies are involved in getting mileage from the recycling issue. Public relations and advertising personnel have regular contact with media people in both the advertising and editorial sides, and the boundaries between news and advertising functions are becoming increasingly blurred (Stauber & Rampton, 1995). Meanwhile, giant corporate conglomerates have become the norm, putting journalists under the same corporate roof as advertisers and the very companies they attempt to scrutinize. For example, if a television station is owned by General Electric and is also receiving thousands of dollars in revenue from an ad campaign about the value of plastics, there is dissonance—whether acknowledged or not—for those TV reporters covering a story about environmental impacts and energy used to recycle plastic.

The hallowed halls of education are not immune from commercial messages, including those about plastic. Captive youngsters are a tempting market: more than 43 million kids attend schools and even elementary-age children exert tremendous spending power, about $15 billion a year (McNeal, 1994). Ads cover school buses, book covers, and scoreboards, and corporate flags fly next to school flags. The Polystyrene Packaging Council, like other corporations, has supplied "supplemental educational materials" free of charge to K-12 classrooms. Their "Plastics and the Environment" lesson teaches that plastics are great and easily recycled, even though most plastics are not recyclable for lack of markets. Consumers Union evaluated this lesson as "highly commercial and incomplete with strong bias . . . [T]he disadvantages of plastics . . . are not covered" (Zillions, 1995, p. 46). Another critic noted that when teachers use such materials, "American students are introduced to environmental issues as they use materials supplied by corporations who pollute the soil, air, and water" (Molnar, 1995, p. 70).

Beyond communication and education, legal sectors also get involved in advertising claims about recycled and recyclable plastic, and politicians know it is wise to support recycling as a generalized issue. Some municipalities sponsor curbside pick-up programs for plastic, and trash haulers and manufacturers run businesses dependent on recycling plastics. Recycling plastics not only creates new business opportunities, it also is philosophically consistent with a capitalist economy that is based on ever-increasing consumption. After all, the message of recycling is not to reduce or avoid consumption but essentially to consume something again. According to one critic in Harper's, oftentimes the new product created from recycled plastics is "the perfect metaphor for everything that's wrong with the idea of recycling plastics. It's ugly as sin, the world doesn't need it, and it's disposable" (Gutin, 1992, p. 56).

The vested interest of so many powerful social institutions makes it that much harder to separate the influence of one from another—such as advertising from news media—and to effect significant social change. It also makes the ubiquitous, repetitive messages of advertising reinforced and in a sense replicated, free of charge. Individuals or groups with oppositional messages about plastics would have to contend with what seems a united front about the place, if not the value, of plastic.

WORKING TOGETHER

Obviously, the six concepts presented here work in concert. Here is one final example of an ad that considers them together.

First, the visual of this television ad: A waterfall flows over the driver's seat of a car and a tiny kayaker (in relation to the size of the car seat) spills down the face of the falls. The scene quickly shifts to the kayaker (full-sized now and paddling away from us) amid glaciers. The next scene takes us into the car's back cargo area—still covered with water—and two orca whales breach in front of the kayaker, who pauses mid-stroke. (In all of these shots, we have never seen the kayaker's face; when he paddles away, his head is covered in a fur-lined parka that looks "native.") The next shot is a close-up of a paddle dipping into water shimmering with the colors of sunset and above the words "Discover Chevy Tahoe." The last scene shows the unoccupied vehicle parked on the edge of a stream in front of snow-covered mountain peaks. The accompanying audio includes Native American-sounding drum beats and a mixed chorus singing a chant-like, non-English song. Over this music, we hear the voice of a male announcer who quotes a passage from John Muir about how a person needs silence to get into the heart of the wilderness, away from dust, hotels, baggage, and chatter.

The meanings that these elements convey to us are multiple. Peace, serenity, at-oneness with nature, and a return to a simple yet sublime "native" existence are part of the promise of this vehicle. Native drums, whales, glaciers, paddling through still waters, and even the deep ecologist Muir are powerful, idealized, and ritualized symbols that are employed to market a feeling and a sensation. The seamless juxtaposition of scene both inside and outside the vehicle conveys that nature is transported effortlessly for you to experience these things directly, without leaving the safety and luxury of your car. The vehicle is the commodity to aid your escape to this sublime place, a place depicted as real yet entirely contrived, with kayakers spilling over car seats. The entire promise is one of self-gratification, helping the driver/kayaker travel to this idealized wilderness. Yet, if you truly want to heed John Muir's advice, silence is needed to get into the heart of the wilderness, not a noisy car. Hence if you buy into (pun intended) the vehicle being the solution (and not existing instead in your own life or soul) the result is further estrangement from the very thing desired and valued. Advertising, as a primary support system for a capitalist economy, can only transfer meaning and express latent desires—not deliver on any of these promises.

THE POWER OF A FAINT GREEN SELL

Advertisements that employ nature as a backdrop provide a record of the position of the environment in our cultural environment. These ads serve as cultural icons of environmental values embedded within the social system. Even if nature-as-backdrop ads do not generally give us the latest advertising jingles and slogans, the values of these pervasive, invasive, ubiquitous ads are heteroglossic, leaking into and influencing other elements of the social system.

The values that advertising communicates about the natural world revolve around an idealized and materialized environment. The idealized natural world of advertising is pristine, problem free, comfortable, accessible, and fundamentally uncomplicated, uncrowded, and uncompromised. It is replete with rare qualities such as open space, solitude, exotic wildlife, and clean water, yet disconnects those qualities from larger, complex issues that lack simple solutions. The idealized natural world of advertising is capable of solving our personal dissatisfactions and anxieties, and promises abundance, fulfillment, and peace. Advertising has fit the environment into modern society's story of frenetic escapism (Turow, 1999), positioning the natural world as the ultimate, utopian escape. Of course this is just as unrealistic an expectation as the satisfaction promised by products themselves; neither products nor the environment—not even a pristine, sublime one—can solve personal problems.

Advertising also presents the natural world as a material commodity. Advertising has played an enormous role in instilling a materialistic, consumer way of life (beginning as early as age four) and has hyped the private, individual gains to be made from what are more appropriately collective goods. Although we have a sense that "nature" somehow counters consumerism and is able to function as antonym and antidote to materialism (Price, 1996), it functions quite differently in advertising. Like the old ad slogan of Prudential Insurance, we are told that we can indeed own a piece of the rock—if we have the right vehicle and the right shoe to get us there, and the right lip balm and hand-held Global Positioning System to keep us safe when we are out there. Products somehow transport us to pristine nature and are capable of delivering all the non-saleable qualities that magically appear with them, such as risk-free adventure and serenity. As Price (1996) asked, "Is it possible that people in our culture have become so estranged from nature that their only avenue to it is consumerism?" (p. 197). As a pervasive cultural influence, advertising has played a large role in this estrangement. As discussed, simple products like fabric softener and dryer sheets commodify something of value from the natural world—clean, fresh-smelling air—and gradually disconnect us from that thing of value. There is little incentive to protect a public good such as clean air when we can purchase its facsimile as a private commodity.

Treating natural resources as private commodities reinforces an anthropocentric, narcissistic relationship with the natural world. The ad with the young boy and his puzzle book expresses these qualities. He uses a vehicle to conquer the environment and its "obstacles" such as mountains, displaying a me-first, adventure-seeking attitude that serves his own fun at the expense of other ecosystem elements. In this type of nature-as-backdrop ad, there is no intention of expressing an eco-friendly image. But the underlying eco-message is that the environment is there primarily for your pleasure and adventure.

But does an idealized and materialized representation of the natural world mean that ads have the power to somehow affect how we feel, believe, and behave in regard to their natural surroundings and resources? Not in isolation, of course. As noted, advertising exists in consort with and is reinforced by other social institutions. However, by its very ubiquitous, repetitive, and pervasive nature, advertising has a special cultural power (Schudson, 1989). Ads are our social guides for what is important, valued, and acceptable. For example, ads tell us it is now acceptable (plastics recycling notwithstanding) to buy a certain brand of plastic food container precisely because it is cheap enough to throw away and not wash and reuse. Ads for throw-away dust-mops, cloths, contact lenses, and aluminum foil deliver the same message.

As scholars argue, ads never intend solely to sell a product, but to sell you a meaning associated with it. The meaning conveyed by ads for products such as throw-away plastic containers is likewise anthropocentric and narcissistic; human convenience is the most important factor, and resource use is trivial. Even ads with obviously surreal or fictitious elements that do not ask to be taken literally still convey meaning about the natural world, which may be the very center of their power (Schudson, 1989). If we are exposed to 3,000 ads per day—even if we only react to a dozen—a lifetime of exposure means that it is virtually impossible to remain detached, immune, and oblivious to the portrayal of a nature from which we are increasingly detached. It is virtually impossible to study the effects of advertising because it is impossible to isolate advertising messages about the natural world when those very issues, products, and relationships are bound up culturally and socially with so many other institutions.

We cannot consider individually the impact of an ad for an SUV when it is sandwiched between a news story about EPA emission regulations, a weather report that refers to vehicle pollution as "haze," and pop songs about driving in your car. Herein lies another piece of the power of the faint green sell. Even ads that appear green and innocuous in their appeal leak into our lives and throughout our culture. If we could somehow isolate the advertisement from the culture in which it is embedded, the underlying message of an ad is still to sell, which renders the green component faint indeed.

REFERENCES

Banerjee, S., Gulas, C. S., & Iyer, E. (1995). Shades of green: A multidimensional analysis of environmental advertising. Journal of Advertising, 24, 21-32.

Benton, L. M. (1995). Selling the natural or selling out? Exploring environmental merchandising. Environmental Ethics, 17, 3-22.

Bullis, C. (1996). Retalking environmental discourses from a feminist perspective: The radical potential of ecofeminism. In J. G. Cantrill & C. L. Oravec (Eds.), The symbolic earth: Discourse and our creation of the environment. (pp. 123-148). Lexington: University Press of Kentucky.

Corbett, J. B. (2001). Women, scientists, agitators: Magazine portrayal of Rachel Carson and Theo Colborn. Journal of Communication, 51, 720-749.

Dadd, D. L., & Carothers, A. (1991). A bill of goods? Green consuming in perspective. In C. Plant & J. Plant (Eds.), Green business: Hope or hoax? Philadelphia: New

Society Publishers (pp. 11-29).

Fink, E. (1990). Biodegradable diapers are not enough in days like these: A critique of commodity environmentalism. EcoSocialist Review, 4.

Gutin, J. (1992, March-April). Plastics-a-go-go. Harper's, 17, 56-59.

Iyer, E. & Banerjee, B. (1993). Anatomy of green advertising. Advances in Consumer Research, 20, 484-501.

Kilbourne, W. E. (1995). Green advertising: Salvation or oxymoron? Journal of Advertising, 24, 7-20.

Lasch, C. (1978). The culture of narcissism. New York: W. W. Norton.

Luke, T. W. (1993). Green consumerism: Ecology and the ruse of recycling. In J. Bennett & W. Chaloupka (Eds.), In the nature of things: Languages, politics and the environment. (pp. 154-172). Minneapolis: University of Minnesota Press.

Mayer, R. N., Scammon, D. L., & Zick, C. D. (1993). Poisoning the well: Do environmental claims strain consumer credulity, Advances in Consumer Research, 20, 698-703.

McNeal, J. U. (1994, February 7). Billions at stake in growing kids market. Discount Store News, 41.

Molnar, A. (1995). Schooled for profit. Educational Leadership, 53, 70-71.

Naess, A. (1973). The shallow and the deep, long-range ecology movement: A summary. Inquiry, 16, 95-100.

Neff, J. (2000, April 10). It's not trendy being green. Advertising Age, 16.

Obermiller, C. (1995). The baby is sick/the baby is well: A test of environmental communication appeals. Journal of Advertising, 24, 55-70.

Oravec, C. L. (1996). To stand outside oneself: The sublime in the discourse of natural scenery. In J. G. Cantrill & C. L. Oravec (Eds). The symbolic earth: Discourse and our creation of the environnment. (pp. 58-75). Lexington: University Press of Kentucky.

Ottman, J. A. (1993). Green marketing: Challenges and opportunities for the new marketing age. Lincolnwood, IL: NTC Business Books.

Phillips, B. J. (1996). Advertising and the cultural meaning of animals. Advances in Consumer Research, 23, 354-360.

Pollay, R. W. (1989). The distorted mirror: Reflections on the unintended consequences of advertising. In R. Hovland & G. B. Wilcox (Eds.), Advertising in society. Lincolnwood, IL: NTC Business Books (pp. 437-476).

Price, J. (1996). Looking for nature at the mall: A field guide to the Nature Company. In W. Cronon (Ed.), Uncommon ground: Rethinking the human place in nature. (pp. 186-203). New York: W. W. Norton.

Schudson, M. (1989). Advertising as capitalist realism. In R. Hovland & G.B. Wilcox (Eds.), Advertising in society. Lincolnwood, IL: NTC Business Books (pp. 73-98).

Schuhwerk, M. E., & Lefkoff-Hagius, R. (1995). Green or non-green? Does type of appeal matter when advertising a green product? Journal of Advertising, 24, 45-54.

Selling green. (1991, October). Consumer Reports, 56, 687-692.

Shanahan, J., & McComas, K. (1999). Nature stories: Depictions of the environment and their effects. Cresskill, NJ: Hampton Press.

Shrum, L. J., McCarty, J. A., & Lowrey, T. M. (1995). Buyer characteristics of the green consumer and their implications for advertising strategy. Journal of Advertising, 24, 71-82.

Stauber, J., & Rampton, S. (1995). Toxic sludge is good for you! Lies, damn lies, and the public relations industry. Monroe, ME: Common Courage Press.

Thorson, E., Page, T., & Moore, J. (1995). Consumer response to four categories of "green" television commercials. Advances in Consumer Research, 22, 243-250.

Turow, J. (1999). Breaking up America: Advertisers and the new media world. Chicago: University of Chicago Press.

Twitchell, J. B. (1996). Adcult USA: The triumph of advertising in American culture. New York: Columbia University Press.

Zillions: For kids from Consumer Reports (1995). Captive kids: Commercial pressures on kids at school. New York: Consumers Union Education Services.

Zinkham, G. M. & Carlson, L. (1995). Green advertising and the reluctant consumer. Journal of Advertising, 24, 1-6.

10

Environment as Consumer Icon in Advertising Fantasy

Diane S. Hope

As a consequence of the mass media technologies of photography, print, film, television, and computers, the visual image has become ubiquitous in contemporary culture. Scholars have examined the proliferation and import of visual images from a range of disciplinary perspectives and concerns, and the prevalence of the mass-produced image as a defining characteristic of modern culture is commonplace (Berger, 1984; Burnett, 1995; Combs & Nimmo, 1993; Edelstein, 1997; Frank, 1997; Leeds-Hurwitz, 1993; Lester, 2000). Advertising has been an especially productive resource for the study of images in popular culture (Ewen 1976; Goffman, 1976; Goldman & Papson, 1996; Marchand, 1985, McAllister, 1996; McLuhan, 1951), for when corporate goals meld with aesthetics and design, advertising creates a visual rhetoric of specialized and significant influence.

This chapter examines print advertising displays that use visual icons from nature and earth to create particularly arresting images. Ads were selected in two categories: (1) *Nature ads* which feature portrayals of the natural world in relatively pristine conditions, for example, forests, canyons, landscapes, and seascapes, and (2) *Global earth ads* which feature images of the earth's globe in space. Although both categories included advertisements for a multitude of products or services, the nature ads were dominated by advertisements for tourism and automobiles. High-tech products and services dominated those print advertisements featuring the global earth.

In the world of images, competition for viewers' perceptual attention dominates advertising strategies. Whether in the form of television commercials, print advertisements, billboards, packages, wearing apparel, or Internet banners, advertising's images are specifically designed to differentiate themselves from all the other images in the viewer's sight.

Although advertising's content is more constrained than that of popular culture, the style of presentation is likely to be more perfectly wrought, with a more highly polished aesthetic surface. There must be no imperfections or unintended rough edges on a television commercial or magazine advertisement, or they will detract from the communication the advertiser is paying dearly to achieve. (Fowles, 1996, p. 14)

Advertising messages are heavily weighted by the stylistic presentations of images and words. The need to stand out in the contemporary visual landscape ensures that print advertising does not simply reproduce two-dimensional "copies" of products (Scott, 1994), as did much early advertising (Clymer, 1955; Ewen, 1976; Marchand, 1985), but rather invents rhetorical displays specifically designed to seize the attention of the viewer. In their important book, *Sign Wars: The Cluttered Landscape of Advertising* (1996), Robert Goldman and Stephen Papson conclude: "The dilemma faced by corporate advertisers today is how to cut through the [visual] clutter and get viewers to notice their message. Advertisers often respond with even more spectacular executions" (p. 27). Unlike verbal persuasion, in which appeals or arguments can be developed after the attention of the audience is secured, the rhetoric of advertising concentrates its form on winning the instantaneous decision of the viewer to pause and to look. Motivated primarily by the need to be distinguished from competing images, advertising appropriates visuals from wherever it wants: artful invention, cliché, and sensational picturing are equally mannered devices used to "hail" viewers (Goldman & Papson, 1996, p.2)—even for a fraction of a second, a focus that creates conventions peculiar to this singular rhetorical goal.

One of the conventional devices used in advertising images is to present eye-catching images of fantasy for private and collective consumption. Ernest G. Bormann's essay on fantasy theme analysis describes the creation of rhetorical visions in persuasive campaigns when verbal fantasy themes "chain out" through many channels of communication (1972). Advertising, too, contributes to shared rhetorical visions, but the channels of communication for print advertising are constrained. Print advertising must break through the clutter of images without the added value of sound or motion available in radio or television commercials. Absent the enhancements of music, voice, and action, print advertisements must condense the fantasy into a silent still picture or series of pictures, usually seen in the context of a magazine rife with competing images. By combining iconic images with pungent text, print advertising distills the presentation of fantasies that may seduce, amuse, titillate, or shock in order to get and hold attention. To accomplish this, advertising often appropriates powerful visual icons already at work in the cultural imagination. In print advertising, the aggregate accumulation of similarly pictured fantasies creates a rhetorical vision shared by a culture of consumers.

The analytical perspective used in this study is rooted in the concept of a *symbolic environment,* a term that is a productive analogue for the rhetorical critique of visual images in general and advertising images in particular. Kenneth Burke's insistence that "Man is the symbol-using (symbol-making, symbol-misusing) animal" grounds this approach (1968, 16). As Leeds-Hurwitz (1993) points out, communication scholars, especially rhetorical critics, assume a focus on symbols:

In fact, symbols have been so readily regarded as a traditional focus of attention in communication that they have often been taken for granted with details of definition, function, and use left uninvestigated (p. 28).

In understanding human action as shaped by hierarchies of symbol use, terms such as *symbol system, symbolic reality* and *symbolic environment* are used to explain the interconnected sets of symbols shared by a given culture. The term "symbolic environment" best describes the complex of symbol use, as the term allows analogous comparisons to other human environments. In this approach, the symbolic environment is one of four interconnected human environments, along with the manufactured environment, the social environment, and the natural environment. As people live within specific natural, manufactured, and social environments, so are we immersed within particular symbolic environments. Like other environments, the symbolic environment is at once a determinate and an expression of human habitation. Each of the four environments is necessary to culture, each can be traced through a dynamic ecological system, and all are interdependent with each other. Human actions (intended or not) in any one of the environments have consequences for each.

Comprising arbitrary symbols and signs, narratives and myths, the symbolic environment orders, defines, and gives meaning to human experiences of nature, artifact, and others through a cultural lexicon dominated by words and images. The symbolic environment is the cognitive space where meaning is assigned to human experience. "Through symbols people create a social reality for themselves, an overlay of meaning laid across the natural world" (Leeds-Hurwitz, 1993, p. 33). While experiences in the natural, manufactured, and social environments can give us relatively direct information, in the symbolic environment meanings are interpretive and constantly in flux. Of further significance to understanding contemporary commodity culture is the recognition that meanings in the symbolic environment are increasingly created by marketers, advertisers, and other corporate representatives with the singular goal of increasing profit and capital. The preface to McLuhan's early work, *The Mechanical Bride: Folklore of Industrial Man*, opens with a description of advertising more true today than when it was written in 1951: "Ours is the first age in which many thousands of the best-trained individual minds have made it a full-time business to get inside the collective public mind" (p. v). The way into the "public mind" is through the creation of stories, myths, icons, and fantasies that can become part of the symbolic environment. In the symbolic environment of popular culture commodity fantasies and their attendant meanings are a pervasive force. By examining the representative icons in images of print ads, a rhetorical vision of the consumer culture emerges. In the aggregate, the ads reveal a visual rhetoric that allows viewers to experience the beauty and bounty of the earth as a prize for consumption. Consumers are invited to enter the picture by virtue of their affluence. Whether presented as objects of love, worship, or exploit, nature and earth are offered to deserving consumers as a righteous reward. By combining icons laden with aspects of both religiosity and domination in a sensual display of color, light, and form, the fantasies propagate a visual oxymoron whereby a pristine earthly environment becomes a sacred icon of commodity culture. The fantasy's appeal provides consumers the means to deny the terrible dilemma of the commodity culture—the reality that over-consumption accelerates the pace of environmental degradation. Thus the fantasies portrayed in visual advertising are at the heart of a cultural vision in which an idealized natural earth is the righteous reward for consumption of commodities.

In a chapter titled "Green Marketing and the Commodity Self," Goldman and Papson (1996) discuss one of the ways by which images of the environment are transformed into "commodity signs" for elite consumers in an environmentally conscious time:

Prompted by the growth of the environmental movement and awareness that over-consumption contributes to environmental destruction, mounting criticism has been directed at advertising. Advertising has responded by developing what has come to be known as "green" or environmental advertising. By appropriating signifiers from nature and transforming them into commodity signs, advertising repositions "thoughtful" consumption as a solution to encroaching environmental disasters. We argue that environmental marketing legitimates consumption by buffering corporate practices from criticism and by alleviating the guilt associated with over-consumption by creating a distinction between good consumption and bad consumption. Ironically, advertising raids nature for the very signifiers it uses to justify continued incursions into nature. (pp. 187-188)

"Green" advertising appeals directly to environmental concerns of consumers. For example, concern for the natural environment makes its appearance in a General Motors ad for an electric car, EV1 ("Don't Worry," 1997). The page is dominated by an image of stunning sky and clouds, and features a scarecrow in a field "staring" at a yellow-hued road and the distant car. In part, the text reads, "Don't worry. The stares will stop. Someday." The land of Oz associations create a fantasy of landscape and future, and offer salvation through the wizardry of technology—the use of "worry" and "someday" in the text implies that all we have to do is wait and environmental problems will be solved. State Farm Insurance provides another example of green advertising, and presents a nostalgic tribute to the conservation hero John Muir ("His Blindness," 1997). "His blindness helped us all to see," the ad proclaims, and displays a photograph of Muir in a wilderness setting. The text tells the story of an industrial accident and Muir's temporary blindness, and goes on, "He became the first environmentalist and worked tirelessly to preserve the environment . . . he gave us a vision of the beauty that surrounds us all. . . . We all have our own vision of the future . . . and although State Farm can't predict the future, we can help you plan for it." The leap from John Muir's blindness to his environmental vision to investment management exemplifies the cynicism of green advertising. All we need is to keep on buying—and the future will be secure, the environment magically protected from our own habits of accumulation by past heroes and mythical legends.

But most advertisements create commodity associations with images of nature and the earth less blatant than the green ads described above. For consumption without guilt, consumers must pretend to believe that buying things is just a good thing to do—even without direct appeal to environmental issues. Nature signifiers used in many ads allow consumers to disconnect the "dirty" production of goods from the "pristine" natural world and bad consumption from good. Advertisers promote the pretense by offering commodity purchases as the solution to most problems. Fantasy images relieve consumers of responsibility for finding real solutions by appropriating powerful icons of nature and earth already at work in the symbolic environment.

Nature and earth iconography are rooted in conflicting American mythologies of earthy paradise and manifest destiny, now moved beyond this continent to domination of the globe itself. Images central to contemporary advertising present nature as a sacred and sensual paradise. Pictures of stunning landscape and pristine forest, lush blossom and stalking mountain lion associate commodities with a longing for the mystical promise of the unspoiled Garden of Eden. At the same time, other advertisements present images of the global earth as a power symbol of globalization and Western domination of the new economy, (the contemporary vision of manifest destiny). Powered by iconic representations of these twin mythologies, advertisements tap into strong emotional traditions in the American experience and work to deny consumer culpability for polluted and endangered nature. Images of earthly paradise and manifest destiny have long occupied a special place in the experience of the Americas and have traditionally served to cover the reality of destructive ecological practices with illusory fantasies.

As early as the fifteenth century, images of the pristine and the spectacular were used as rhetorical devices to persuade and to propagandize colonial adventures. Like contemporary ad makers, fifteenth-century hucksters of colonial paradise combined mystical and sensual images to mask the environmental consequence of appeals to human acquisitiveness. When European adventurers, businessmen, and royal company agents needed to raise money and to recruit settlers and workers for risky journeys to unknown and perhaps dangerous places, they wrote dazzling descriptions of the new world in pamphlets and circulars distributed throughout Europe. In her book *The Lay of the Land,* Annette Kolodny traces the sexual metaphors used to describe the land in the early writings (1975). Before the renderings of artists who would soon follow, the earliest adventurers wrote about the seductive power of the land in descriptions of its visual appeal. Christopher Columbus declared that the new world was "a land to be desired, and seen, it is never to be left" (quoted in Kolodny, 1975, p. 11). In 1632, Thomas Morton extolled New England as "Paradise . . . not to be paralleled in all Christendome . . ." and painted a sensuous picture of its "many goodly groues of trees; dainty fine round rising hillucks: delicate faire large plaines, sweete cristall fountaines, and cleare running streames . . ." He added, "The more I looked, the more I liked it" (quoted in Kolodny, 1975, p.12). Hundreds of published letters and written appeals attracted men and women adventurous or desperate enough to try to find the beautiful utopia. Promoters promised the wild beauty of the land and its rich bounty would make dreams of riches and paradise a common reality.

From the earliest descriptions, through to the pervasive mythology of the California gold rush and the Western adventure in nineteenth-century novels and twentieth-century movies, writers, painters, photographers and filmmakers reinforced the fantasy of unlimited bounty even as the beloved environment disappeared (Mitchell, 1996). The promise of quick riches and unlimited beauty and freedom describes the American experience. In "American Destiny or Manifest Mythology: Some Historical Considerations of the Western Image," John Wood (1997) considers the image of the West revealed in early photographs of settlers and adventurers who subscribed to the vision: "Nowhere was a mythology more manifest than on the frontier because nowhere was a mythology more needed. The mythology was manifest on their very faces and that mythology shaped their destinies" (p. 12). In hindsight we can see that the North American experience was shaped by conflicted dreams of an abundant, lush, and spectacular land that would reward its destroyers with riches. Such dreams and fantasies worked to push domination of the continent ever westward. It was a mythology, after all, propagated as a godly mission and a manifest right. Thus the attitude toward the natural environment combined religious aspects of paradise, seductive appeals to sensuality, and base impulses of greed and domination. The fantasy did not vanish but indeed has grown, fueled with images, verbal and visual, that have become cultural touchstones in the symbolic environment of the United States.

Perhaps no other reservoir of images has maintained the popular appeal as the lines written in 1893 by Katharine Lee Bates in her patriotic hymn, "America the Beautiful":

O beautiful for spacious skies, / For amber waves of grain, / For purple mountain majesties / Above the fruited plain! / America! America! / God shed his grace on thee / And crown thy good with brotherhood / From sea to shining sea!

Bates, professor of English Literature at Wellesley College during the nineteenth century, wrote the verses during her first trip west. The song's familiar combinations of beauty, religiosity, and manifest destiny in verbal descriptions of North America have entered the symbolic environment as sentimental visual icons on greeting cards, calendars, commercials, travelogues, videos, and advertisements. Less often visualized are the stanzas that bless incursions into the wilderness and material success:

O beautiful for pilgrim feet / Whose stern impassioned stress /A thoroughfare for freedom beat /Across the wilderness! /America! America! / May God thy gold refine / Till all success be nobleness /And every gain divine! / O beautiful for patriot dream / That sees beyond the years / Thine alabaster cities gleam / Undimmed by human tears! / America! America! / God shed his grace on thee / And crown thy good with brotherhood / From sea to shining sea! (Katharine Lee Bates)

The song is a standard of popular culture patriotism and wraps the ideology of manifest destiny, democratic ideals, and capital around images of the land as ever beautiful and ever bountiful. Advertising's use of the song's familiar images exemplifies a powerful rhetorical strategy.

Advertising appropriates images from songs, from art, from folklore, from fairytales, from movies, television, and journalism as well as from other ads in new combinations of representation. "No cultural analysis of advertising today can ignore the mercurial process of recombining meaning systems in order to generate additional value and desirability for brand-name commodities" (Goldman & Papson, 1996, p. 5). An examination of themes in specific ads demonstrates how "nature ads" and "earth ads" combine to create the environment as icon in consumer fantasy.

THE NATURE ADS

As do most symbols appropriated by advertising, images of nature work to strengthen the heart of the commodity culture. In the advertisements discussed here, viewers are invited to experience the natural environment in association with tourism or through the purchase of commodities. Images from the natural environment are used to create sensuous and beautiful visual displays. The ads present the natural world as the focus of our attention. They depict specific places or geographical features of great beauty as icons of paradise on earth, often using words and images that evoke love of the natural world and awareness of ecological problems.

Two interconnected fantasy themes dominate the advertisements and contribute to a rhetorical vision in which nature is a reward for consumption. First, the wonders of nature are always somewhere else—never where the viewer is, and second, the far-away nature is offered as a hiatus from real life and work. For example, American Airlines promotes itself with an image of quiet calm water. "A place to reflect" ("Place," 1995). The lush views of nature are offered as brief periods of calm: sensuous pleasure afforded by vacations from the serious world of work evoke the old meanings of paradise: life without toil, beauty without end. Advertisement copy for a cruise to Alaska speaks of the fantasy directly, "Somewhere between having a dream and having a plan" ("Somewhere,"1996). An advertisement for travel to Canada is most obvious in its positioning of nature as elsewhere, "You should come to our place," and highlights a red sunset over water and sky ("Canadian sunset," 1997). The sunset is a pervasive icon in many ads evoking peaceful vacation, exotic locales, and sensual experience. The Canada ad also features a bicycle, strongly indicating that the interlude is not part of the serious world of work. Nature is for fun, for relaxation, for romance, for getting away from it all. By implication, "it" is the urban environment of the work-a-day world. The fantasy that work is unconnected to the natural environment is an especially prevalent theme in consumer advertising and ad after ad features the contemporary signs of no-work: beach umbrellas, bicycles, and fishing poles from the manufactured environment; sunsets, palm trees, and waterfalls from the natural environment; and romantic (heterosexual) couples in various stages of nudity from the social environment. In most ads, nature and work are presented as absolute unrelated segments of life. Thus are connections between the natural world, work, production, and consumption denied—if nature is featured, usually work is absent.

An ad campaign promoting Puerto Rico as a vacation spot to be "discovered" well illustrates this vision. In one ad a full page image features a tropical waterfall of intense greens and dappled light. Slightly off center and very small to the viewer's eye a partially clothed man and women embrace at the foothills of the falls. Across the bottom of the page, a line of text describes and emphasizes Puerto Rico as close by, in fact, as a place within the United States. Superimposed on the right side of the image an arrangement of free verse evokes the sensual experience of "America's Rain Forest" with lush descriptions of tropical sights, smells, and sounds, evoking a fantasy of "nature's reality." Although the Puerto Rico tourism campaign touts the island as "near," in fact, the point of the ad is to promote travel to Puerto Rico because it is not near to where ad readers live and work. "Nature's reality" is a waterfall in Puerto Rico's tropical rain forest, and is displayed as an exotic habitation—best fit for romantic encounters ("Rainforest," 1996).

Another ad in the same Puerto Rico campaign emphasizes the second feature common in these images: scenes of pristine beauty are offered as respite from the everyday stress of work setting up the dramatic contrast, "daily life versus the natural world." In the second ad, a man and woman sit in beach chairs under an umbrella facing the ocean. The viewer sees only the backs of the chairs and the couple's clasped hands. The text reinforces the theme that nature is separate from work, is in fact a reward for a life of rigid, unhappy routine. "I go at my own pace. Eating is a function of desire not the ticking of the clock. I stroll down shimmering, pristine beaches. A different one each day. If I want. I decide." The significant implication is that no matter what we do in our daily lives, nature will be preserved for us somewhere else, obviating the connections of global ecologies, work, production, and consumption. The distancing of natural environments also precludes our serious attention to local ecologies. Nothing in these ads indicates that the natural environment is always with us, where we live and work, in the polluted river down the road, in the diminishing green spaces of our cities, in the toxic mix of chemicals in "our own backyards."

Thousands of print ads use images of nature to promote various products, frequently using "paradise" images of nature to frame the object of the ad (a commodity). Advertisements for Marlboro cigarettes are exceptional for their particularly stunning photos of the western landscape, and also because the cowboy is "working" while he inhabits a natural world ("Marlboro," 1997). The Marlboro images evoke awe, beauty, and romance—while recalling the themes of adventure, masculine control over nature, and manifest destiny.

Nature sells drugs for HIV, aftershave lotion, fashions, coffee beans, whisky, radios, IRAs, life insurance, allergy medicine, and tools. An ad for grapefruit juice is "reflective" (Goldman & Papson, 1996, p. 74-77) and pokes fun at spiritual nature themes in advertising by presenting an image of a woman drinking grapefruit juice in a golden field of wheat labeled, "Actual photo of woman in Nirvana." All of these images are part of our symbolic environment, endlessly repeated and rapidly re-created to catch the eye of the weary ad viewer. Nothing, however, equals the automobile ads, in sheer number or in the power of the images to mask ecological realities with fantasy.

Automobile ads provide an especially rich example of the transformational power of the symbolic environment to reshape the meaning of human experience. To see how visual images work in the symbolic environment, we can first briefly define the automobile in the manufactured environment, the social environment, and the natural environment before discussing specific advertisements for automobiles. In the manufactured environment, the car is a comparatively long-lasting, 3,000 to 5,000 pound machine built for private transportation, powered by gasoline, and manufactured primarily from metals, petroleum, and derived plastics. Additionally, the automobile's extensive use has led to the construction of millions of miles of cement and tarmac in highways. It has speeded the creation of suburbs, shopping malls, over-development, and urban sprawl.

In the social environment of human relationships, the car has observable consequences for cultural groups, community, sexual relationships, family, work, and class. Car ownership provides a clear class boundary, separating the non-car-owning poor from the middle and upper classes in suburban/urban divisions of community, employment, education, and leisure. The car allows its owner to live in one community, work in another, and play in many. In addition to routine transport to work, car ownership provides easy mobility and the luxury of privacy for a number of activities: sightseeing, outings, romantic encounters, and private, convenient travel to distant places, friends, and family. It is a moving dining room, concert hall, bedroom, and office.

But in the natural environment of earth and land, water and air, the car is a dangerous polluter, spilling carbon dioxide, carbon monoxide, nitrogen oxide, sulphur dioxide, hydrocarbons, benzene, methane, aldehydes, and other noxious substances into the air, resulting in ozone depletion, toxic smog, and global warming. Additionally, the construction and maintenance of roads and pavements cause extensive destruction of diverse ecosystems and contribute to the extinction of plant and animal species. Indeed, balancing the benefits of mobility and convenience against the costs in lives, health, money, and environmental damage, attitudes about cars are remarkably absent of dread, apprehension, or anxiety. Instead, cars engender feelings of power, playfulness, desire, and freedom. It is through the symbolic environment that the car is thus transformed. In the symbolic environment, the car is a mystical status marker attached to identity, earthly pleasures, and domination. In the fantasies of the commodity culture, paradise is as close as the nearest SUV.

When we examine automobile advertisements, it is clear that like tourist ads, car advertisements offer nature as a reward for affluence. And like the tourism ads, automobile ads promise adventure and romance in a personal playground called earth. But automobile advertisements go beyond the presentation of nature as a beautiful escape from the reality of work. In the symbolic environment of advertisements, the car is a heroic "god" to be worshiped by childlike suppliants. The realm of the religious or sacred is often symbolized by rays of light descending from the heavenly clouds that focus viewers' eyes on the holy vehicle. In these ads the religious symbolism is blatant and extreme. In a Jeep ad the sky radiates heavenly light beams which illuminate the car amid the canyons ("Jeep," 1997). To further extend the religious fantasy, the jeep sits majestically on an altar of rock, combining auto worship with sacred canyon views. A Lincoln ad again uses heavenly clouds and rays of light coming through the window to illuminate dashboard and leather seats ("It gets," 1997); in case we don't get the religious significance the copy makes it clear, "It gets into your soul . . . the V-8 engine invigorates your spirits." These ads feature nature as background for the single automobile. No stalled traffic lines approaching the Grand Canyon here; every auto is the only one on the road. Sky, rock, and rays of light combine with technology in sensual images that present the car as the ultimate object of our worship and desire.

Cars are spiritual vehicles that transform adults into children. Two Tracker ads are indistinguishable from each other and from scores like them: the car is a toy, "Go Out and Play," reads the text. Like small children in a sandbox, consumers are absolved of responsibility for care of the earth. An Infiniti image uses reflective humor to knowingly "wink" at the high status of the worshiped auto: the car resides in a tent while the owner camps out in the open ("Infiniti," 1997).

When pictures of commodities from the manufactured environment, such as automobiles, are associated with iconic representations of nature, the meaning of such objects is transformed. In an ad that promotes the Toyota Corporation, the car itself disappears; in its place is a cathedral of trees ("Trees,"1997). The corporation is thus represented as nature itself—paradise on earth, alive and growing. In using a powerful archetypal image, a natural forest sanctuary, the ad blurs the distinction among corporate ideology, natural environment, and religious sentiment. The fantasy theme reasserts the power of the mythology that an earthly paradise is always there waiting for discovery. All one has to do is buy.

THE GLOBAL EARTH

In 1968 a remarkable series of photographs presented new perspectives of the earth and immediately invited reappraisal of the human relationship to the planet. Images of earth photographed from the Apollo spacecraft signaled swift cognitive changes in understanding the planet's ecologies and atmosphere. At the same time, these images invited genuine emotional response and provided visual inspiration for the contemporary environmental movement. The words of Astronaut Edgar Mitchell best describe the spectacle as seen in the natural environment of space:

Suddenly from behind the rim of the moon, in long, slow-motion moments of immense majesty, there emerges a sparkling blue and white jewel, a light, delicate sky-blue sphere laced with slowly swirling views of white, rising gradually like a small pearl in a thick sea of black mystery. It takes more than a moment to fully realize this is Earth—home. My view of our planet was a glimpse of divinity. (quoted in Kelly, 1988, pp. 42-45; 52)

The language was religious, fearful, sensual, protective. Combined, the pictures and words together created a visualized discourse new to our culture—the global environment. And these early images of the earth were central to that discourse; widely reproduced on television, magazines, textbooks, and exhibits, the images became part of our symbolic environment. The "blue marble," "mother earth," or "spaceship earth" soon became the most appealing symbol of the environmentalist movement; it glowed from the cover of the Whole Earth catalog, billowed from Earth Day flags, and adorned campus dorm walls as poster-sized reproductions. The image of the earth was powerful, accumulating and incorporating meanings of spiritual awe, environmental awareness, and sensual beauty. Like most powerful symbols in commodity culture, advertisers found these images to be irresistible and soon appropriated the symbol of earth and its layers of meanings to sell commodities.

In an abundance of current magazine ads, the earth's globe is but a prop for assorted commodities. While images of the earth in space evoke environmental awareness, the ads are striking for their bold presentation of globalization as a visual metaphor. Fittingly, advertisements for high-tech commodities and financial services dominate this group of images. Like the eighteenth-century themes of manifest destiny, the fantasy theme emerging in these ads is about the righteousness of power. The visualization of globalization presents the icons of advanced economic technologies—computer screen, keyboard, high-tech systems—in juxtaposition with images of the global earth, creating a nearly perfect icon for manifest destiny in the age of the global economy. Finally, in perhaps its darkest aspect, the fantasy exonerates the 20 percent of the world's population in the commodity cultures who use 80 percent of the planet's resources. Global earth images in advertising do this by presenting technology, capital, and privilege as proof of the manifest right of exploitation.

Advertisements for Sun Microsystems, Sony, and Merrill Lynch typify the ads whose image and text appropriate symbols of power, conquest, and greed. The ads tap feelings of awe associated with the early photographs of earth and attach them to technological control, high status, and economic power. A large image of the earth's globe dominates the page advertising a camcorder in a Sony ad ("NASA," 1997). The product's technology is compared to satellite images of earth and found to be superior. Visually placing the product above the planet, the ad reduces the globe to a pedestal for advanced technology while poking fun at itself: "NASA may do a fine job up there, but it took Sony to conquer that space between your sofa and your TV." Sun Microsystems depicts the earth's globe as an image on a screen. The screen is being touched and encircled by a dozen or more hands, all appearing to be white: "One name stands for network computing experience world wide," reads the copy. "Our strength is networking people." The advertisement for Merrill Lynch directly appeals to economic globalization's power. In the image, the globe is reproduced as a mechanical toy held by and controlled by (white) human hands representing the company. Merrill Lynch is in total control and can open and close the greatly diminished planet at will. Lengthy text extols Merrill Lynch as a corporate ally whose thoughtful "intelligence" can find opportunity in the global world of competition through "worldly wisdom" ("Take on the world," 1997). These ads appropriate the symbol of the globe to signal both environmental concern and worldly conquest in a strong appeal to desires for power.

Advertising thus uses the environment as icon to evoke powerful mythologies of earthly paradise and manifest destiny. In combining images of nature and earth in fantasy themes, the symbolic environment of advertising creates a shared vision for the commodity culture. Multitudes of images sell an array of products and services by using images of nature and the earth. AT&T sells its technology through the display of a rather gaudy moonrise over the Grand Canyon, combined with sentimental copy evoking a childhood friendship.

Microsoft advertises a computer travel service, "Expedia," by combining images of mountains, sky, and clouds in an ego-gratifying appeal to Western adventures and technological control. The copy uses a linguistic metaphor of beef, meat high on the food chain and of particular controversy in environmental discourse: "Book a ride to the wild west, make it raw, well done or anything in between." The implication of rugged domination is clear and reminds us who is in control. The ad tells the viewer that the environment is there for the taking. Any way you want it, the land is yours.

This chapter has focused on fantasy themes in two kinds of advertising, those that use images of a pristine nature and those that feature earth's globe. Both types investigated here absolve consumers of responsibility for the ecological consequences of consumption. Although used to advertise a variety of commodities, images of a pristine nature are especially prevalent in tourism and automobile advertisements. In these ads the most frequent fantasy presents nature as somewhere else, distanced from everyday life and work—accessible and available as a reward to affluent consumers. The fantasy further enables consumers to deny connections between consumption and ecological degradation by evoking the powerful myth of earthly paradise in lush and sensuous images. Nature is exotic, preserved for the righteous, somewhere far away. Images of the earth's globe in space are dominated by commodities associated with advanced technology and high finance. Such images create a visual metaphor for globalization and evoke mythologies of manifest destiny, now expanded beyond the continent to the world. In these advertisements, elite consumers are rewarded with the opportunity to make more money by control of the planet earth.

An approach developed from the concept *symbolic environment* and used in this chapter allows critics to examine the rhetoric of visualizations. By using icons from the manufactured environment, the social environment, and the natural environment to create the symbolic environment, human experience is transformed. Advertising and commercials are but the most direct expression of the corporate culture's need to continually stimulate consumer spending. Commercial interests evident in the content of film, television, magazines, music, and press generate an endless stream of symbols and signs poured into the symbolic environment as strategic marketing (Frank, 1997). While art, literature, historical narrative, folk drama, and religion traditionally dominate the symbolic environment, the influence of advertising in the symbolic environment of popular culture is enormous. This chapter concludes that one of the most influential features of print advertising is the use of the environment as an icon in consumer fantasy—a fantasy with particularly troubling consequences for the planet.

REFERENCES

Barry, A. M. S. (1997). *Visual intelligence: Perception, image, and manipulation in visual communication.* New York: SUNY Press.

Bates, K. L. Falmouth Historical Society WebPage. (2000): http://members.aol.com/rfitzpa24/FHS/klb.htm

Berger, A. A. (1984). *Signs in contemporary culture.* London: Sheffield Publishing Company.

Bormann, E. G. (1972). Fantasy and rhetorical vision: The rhetorical criticism of social reality. *Quarterly Journal of Speech, 58,* 396-407.

Burke, K. (1968). *Language as symbolic action.* Berkeley: University of California Press.

Burnett, R. (1995). *Cultures of vision.* Bloomington: Indiana University Press

Clymer, F. (1955). *Historical scrapbook: Early advertising.* New York: Bonanza Books.

Coombs, J. E. & Nimmo, D. (1993). *The new propaganda.* White Plains, NY: Longman.

Don't worry. The stares will stop someday. (1997 April 28). *New Yorker,* p. 2-3.

Edelstein, A. (1997). *Total propaganda: From mass culture to popular culture.* Mahwah, NJ: Lawrence Erlbaum.

Ewen, S. (1976). *Captains of consciousness: Advertising and the social roots of the consumer culture.* New York: McGraw-Hill.

Fowles, J. (1996) *Advertising and popular culture.* Thousand Oaks, Ca: Sage.

Frank, T. (1997). *The conquest of cool.* Chicago: University of Chicago Press.

Goffman, E. (1976). *Gender advertisments.* New York: Harper Torch Books.

Goldman, R. & Papson, S. (1996). *Sign wars: The cluttered landscape of advertising.* New York: Guilford Press.

His blindness helped us all to see. (1997, November 3). *Newsweek,* pp.18-19.

Infiniti. (1997, July 28). *New Yorker,* inside front cover.

It gets into your soul. (1997, April). *Atlantic Monthly,* p.73.

Jeep. (1997, May 5). *Newsweek,* p.44.

Kelley, D. W. (Ed.). (1988). *The home planet.* New York: Addison-Wesley Publishing Company.

Kolodny, A. (1975). *The lay of the land: Metaphor as experience and history in American life and letters.* University of North Carolina Press.

Leeds-Hurwitz, W. (1993) *Semiotics and communication.* Hillsdale, NJ: Lawrence Erlbaum.

Lester, P. M. (2000). *Visual communication: Images with messages.* 2nd Edition. Belmont, CA: Wadsworth

Marchand, R. (1985). *Advertising the American dream: Making way for modernity 1920-1940.* Berkley: University of California.

Marlboro cowboy. (1997, July). *Spin,* inside front cover.

McAllister, M. P. (1996). *The commercialization of American culture.* Thousand Oaks, CA: Sage.

McLuhan, M. (1951). *The mechanical bride: Folklore of industrial man.* New York: Beacon Press Edition.

Miller, M. C. (1988). *Boxed in: The culture of TV.* Northwestern: University Press.

Mitchell, L. C. (1996). *Westerns: Making the man in fiction and film,* Chicago: University of Chicago Press.

NASA may do a fine job up there, but. (1997, November 8). *Newsweek,* p. 7.

Place to reflect. (1995, October 2). *New Yorker,* pp.6-7.

Rainforest - nature's reality. (1996, January). *Smithsonian,* p. 11.

Scott, L. M. (1994) "Images in advertising: The need for a theory of visual rhetoric," *Journal of Consumer Research, 21,* 252-273.

Sivulka, J. (1998*). Soap, sex, and cigarettes: A cultural history of American advertising.* New York: Wadsworth.

Somewhere between having a dream and having a plan, (1996, January). *Smithsonian.* p. 21.

Take on the world. (1997, May 5). *New Yorker,* inside front cover.

Trees. (1997, November). *Discover,* p.63-64

Wood, J. (1997). American destiny or manifest mythology: Some historical considerations of the Western image. In Wood, J., (Ed.). *The photographic arts.* Iowa City: University of Iowa Press.

Living Above it All: The Liminal Fantasy of Sport Utility Vehicle Advertisements

Richard K. Olsen, Jr.

American popular culture offers a long history of celebrating modes of transportation. From the pony express through the various planes, trains, and automobiles, each mode of transportation has captured the national imagination. Television programs and movies such as *Route 66*, *Knight Rider*, and *Smokey and the Bandit*, have made particular automobiles popular. The popularity of a particular model of vehicle such as the Mustang is not examined in this chapter, but rather an entire category of vehicles: sport utility vehicles (SUV). The SUV has become a dominant vehicle on both the physical and cultural landscapes of America. The popularity of SUVs and the way they have been portrayed in advertisements reveal a cultural stance regarding the environment and speak of what "wilderness" can mean in popular culture. The popularity of SUVs as well as some negative implications of that popularity are briefly reviewed here. The concepts of fantasy theme, dialectic, and liminality are introduced which will guide the analysis of SUV advertisements. This analysis of the advertisements from the vantage point provided by these concepts is used to demonstrate that the fantasy operating in many SUV advertisements attempts to position the SUV as a purchasable and permanent resolution to the dialectics inherent in our relationship with the environment. This chapter concludes with implications of how this fantasy informs the environment's definition in the arena of popular culture.

EVERYWHERE YOU WANT TO BE: THE RISING POPULARITY OF SUVs

Current Popularity of the SUV

In the early 1980s, there were a handful of SUVs to meet the demands of a small niche of drivers who needed the size and strength of a truck but the configuration of a van or station wagon. By 1996, however, there were over twenty-seven versions of SUVs, by 2000 that number almost doubled to forty-seven. While some figures suggest the SUV market is maturing and stabilizing, managers in vehicle design and marketing believe there is still more easy gold to be prospected. George Murphy, Ford's general marketing manager, is confident that "there are still a few opportunities to define a segment with a new vehicle" (Robinson, 1999, p. 16). Murphy expects the number of SUV models to increase to seventy by 2005, and other experts agree.

A large variety of vehicles already exist within the SUV category. Automakers as diverse as BMW, Mercedes, Toyota, Suzuki, Ford, and Chevy all have at least one entry in the SUV market. At one point, many of these entries were products of what is known as rebadging. Rebadging occurs when one manufacturer dresses up another maker's SUV and calls it their own (Isuzu Rodeo/Honda Passport). This practice is lessening, however, as each manufacturer creates its own models and seeks its own niche (Needham, 1996). At least one SUV, the Oldsmobile Bravada, has been specifically targeted toward female buyers. Advertising for the Bravada has included captions such as, "As a matter of fact, I do drive like a girl" (Halliday, 1999).

The popularity of SUVs is certainly not without controversy, particularly as SUVs continue to become bigger than the great outdoors they are ostensibly designed to roam. A strong appeal of SUVs is the perception that the bigger vehicle is the safer vehicle. *Sierra* writer Paul Rauber (1999) cynically called this doctrine the "survival of the fattest" (p. 20). Rauber notes that in many cases this is a misconception because many smaller cars score safer in crash tests than SUVs.

The poster child for the SUV arms (and leg room) race is the Ford Excursion. The Excursion measures nineteen feet long, weighs up to 8,500 pounds and gets ten to twelve miles per gallon. It has become the target of consumer and environmental groups alike due to its size and high fuel consumption.[1] Ford has replied that the Excursion's fuel efficiency qualifies it as a low-emission vehicle. Ford CEO William Ford has openly admitted that SUVs are harmful to the environment but that they are also Ford's most profitable product line. Over 90 percent of Ford's profits come from the SUV/light truck segment. William Ford's strategy to counter criticism by advocacy groups has been to openly admit the harm and to promise to commit significant funds to improve SUV environmental track records. Several environmental groups, including the Sierra Club, have rewarded his stance with guarded support (Welch, 2000).

GMC's response to the unveiling of Ford's behemoth that is one foot longer than a Suburban was "We set the benchmark for this type of vehicle. We don't intend to simply hand it over" (Nichol, 1999, p. 50). Fortunately, one report indicated that Suburban will become more refined, rather than larger, and will be marketed as the "sensible SUV" (Neil, May 29, 2000). Indeed, Dodge has tried to market its Durango as being in between the "toys and the tanks." However, the Durango's fifteen miles per gallon gas mileage undermines that claim a bit. There are some indications that the economics of fuel pricing could modify the

SUV industry. The Daimler Chrysler Corporation delayed if not abandoned its Jeep Commander concept, which was to be built on the Dodge Ram full-size pickup chassis, because of rising fuel costs (Welch, January 17, 2000). Some companies seem to be questioning their ability to sell such gas guzzling vehicles during a season of rising fuel costs.

Yet Toyota lumbered into the behemoth SUV category with its Sequoia model. The 2000 model boasted Excursion-like dimensions inside and out. In fact Ford vehemently contested Toyota's claims of equal interior storage, noting that the Expedition has 3.7 cubic feet more cargo space than the Sequoia if you use a U.S. and not a Japanese calculator (Mateja, 2000).

Impact of the SUV

The environmental impact of SUVs is multifaceted but largely predictable: more raw materials, more fuel, more impact on environment and infrastructure. However, this impact is difficult to quantify. How much additional erosion do we suffer because SUVs encourage off-roading and the tire tread is typically more aggressive than the thread of traditional tires? How much wildlife is harassed due to human/SUV presence?

The 1999 Ford Explorer weighed over 1,200 pounds more than the Ford Focus, a compact car. The 1999 Excursion was 4,639 pounds heavier than the Focus. The raw materials and manufacturing processes invested in the Ford Excursion and other large and/or luxurious SUVs are significantly higher than in standard automobiles. In addition, SUV gas mileage clearly suffers from the additional weight. While meeting government regulations for low emissions, the Excursion's ten miles per gallon does not compare favorably with Focus' twenty-eight miles per gallon, or even the Explorer's eighteen miles per gallon (Neil, 2000). Rauber (1999) offers compelling examples of the various hazards of SUVs:

The dangers caused by SUVs are not just to their own drivers or to others on the road. Half of all cars these days are gas-guzzling sport utes, minivans, or pickups, and the more fossil fuel consumed, the more global-warming gas is added to the atmosphere. In its life-time, a fuel-efficient Honda Civic emits 40 tons of carbon dioxide, a Ford Excursion 134 tons. The reason is the huge loophole in the CAFÉ law that requires fleets of passenger cars to average 27.5 miles per gallon, but allows light trucks an average of 20.7 mpg. (p. 21)

Such direct impact on the environment has led to some active protests against SUVs and their owners. Two mischievous Californians have printed up bumper stickers that read, "I'm changing the environment! Ask me how!" and have placed them on hundreds of SUVs in order to publicly shame the owners. The activists have even created a web site that tells the SUV owners how best to remove the bumper sticker and provides information and an opportunity to dialogue (Gaudette, 2000).

The resource-intensive and fuel-guzzling nature of SUVs could be avoided according to the Union of Concerned Scientists (UCS). The UCS redesigned a Ford Explorer to "shave 621 pounds, double its fuel economy and cut pollution by 75 percent" and claims that the UCS "Ford Exemplar" could be built with current technology" ("Memo," 2000, p. 2). In addition, some changes are already on the way. Rules requiring improvement in gasoline quality as well as SUV and light truck emissions standards are scheduled to phase in between 2004 and 2009 (Kruger, 1999). These changes will likely raise both gasoline prices and SUV prices.

Another hazard SUVs present is less obvious. A recent traffic patterns study found that several types of motor vehicles slow down traffic due to slower acceleration and the tendency of other motorists to give these vehicles more space. The primary offenders are SUVs, trucks, and minivans (Bradsher, 2000).

However, none of these factors are likely to deter the SUV hold on automobile makers or the national imagination. A Cox news service (February 16, 2000) story offered anecdotal evidence that SUV owners will keep their SUVs but alter their driving habits in light of higher gas prices (p. 6C). In addition, an increase in SUV production costs can be covered easily by manufacturers, because the profit margins for these vehicles is quite high. For example, the Excursion brings fifteen to twenty thousand dollars' profit per sale, which will continue to make it a dealer favorite and allow its retail price to remain fairly stable despite modest increases in manufacturing costs (Neil, 2000).

The SUV is a popular, controversial and perplexing breed of vehicle. SUVs are not designed for suburban life, yet most are driven in suburbia; they are not very maneuverable in parking lots, nor are they very zippy on on-ramps. They are not fuel-efficient. Many also have greater potential for rolling-over. While they are often safer in accidents involving smaller vehicles, they have not been proven safer in general than other types of vehicles. So why have they become so popular? Why are there over fifty varieties with more coming every day?

The "Western Cowboy" myth could offer one explanation of their popularity. Certainly the four-wheel drive, ground clearance, and very name—sport *utility* vehicle—capture the American "can-do" attitude and spirit of adventure and exploration. These vehicles, however, are not marketed solely—or even primarily—on their utility at all. While no single study could fully explain their popularity[2], a significant contributor to their success can be revealed in the underlying liminal fantasy of many SUV advertisements. These ads perpetuate a particular view of nature and our relationship to it. The meanings promoted by these ads are important because, as Mead (1934) and others have argued, we react to things on the basis of what they mean for us. The SUV choice is often a symbolic, not a pragmatic, one. An examination of SUV advertisements using the concepts introduced in the following section provides clues to their popularity.

ENJOYING THE VIEW: GAINING PERSPECTIVE THROUGH CRITICAL CONCEPTS

In a number of SUV ads, the SUV owner and his vehicle stand alone atop a pristine vista enjoying views rarely seen by man generally and never by the own-ers of a mere car, or even another brand of SUV. Just as these jean-clad souls and their bandana-wearing dogs need an SUV to assume that vantage point, so we too need a little help in gaining perspective. Three critical concepts are used here to provide such a view: fantasy theme, liminality, and dialectic. Some presupposi-tions about the rhetorical analysis that guide's this project are briefly laid out as well.

Martin Medhurst and Thomas Benson (1991) identify three positions one can take on the rhetorical analysis of mediated artifacts. First, one can draw a strict line between the rhetorical and the poetic. Second, one can examine the rhetorical dimensions of artifacts. Third, one can assume, along with Kenneth Burke, that rhetoric is inherent and intrinsic, that is, that every human activity is thoroughly if not entirely rhetorical because of human nature and the human con-dition. Rather than align with a particular school, Medhurst and Benson argue for an eclectic critical practice that "should be judged by the insights and under-standings it affords the reader . . ." (p. xviii). This approach often uses a variety of tools to focus primarily on illuminating the artifact rather than refining theo-ry. This chapter embraces that eclectic and pragmatic perspective; it also acknowledges the value of artifact-oriented analysis. Leff (1980, 1986), Darsey (1994), and Foss (1990) have, in various ways, taken rhetorical scholarship to task for being preoccupied with advancing and refining theory and method rather than understanding the artifacts under analysis. While this chapter invokes several theoretically rich concepts, those concepts are subordinate to the goal of understanding the artifact at hand. The concepts are tools to help explain the cul-tural phenomenon of the SUV.

Fantasy Theme

Earnest G. Bormann (1972/1995) argues that fantasy themes, and the result-ing rhetorical vision they chain out to create, are powerful contributors to group identity:

Individuals in rhetorical transactions create subjective worlds of common expectations and meanings. Against the panorama of large events and seemingly unchangeable forces of society at large or of nature the individual often feels lost and hopeless. One coping mechanism is to dream an individual fantasy, which provides a sense of meaning and sig-nificance for the individual and helps protect him from the pressures of natural calamity and social disaster. (p. 245)

Individuals often coalesce around an idea or drama. Thus, the overall label for Bormann's project is called *symbolic convergence*. A key communication variable that contributes to this convergence is the fantasy theme. Fantasy themes dramatizing messages and expresses group ideals. Foss (1996) wrote that it is "a word, phrase, or statement that interprets events in the past, envisions events in the future, or depicts current events that are removed in time and/or space from the actual activities of the group" (p. 123). Bormann, Knutson, and Musolf

(1997) suggested that groups resonate with particular fantasies because (1) the fantasies express a shared psychodynamic concern, (2) the fantasies provide an indirect way of engaging a problem or issue that is too intense to engage direct-ly, and (3) the "conscious artistry with which the message was designed and delivered was a factor in whether or not it was shared" (p. 256). The recognition of artistry is an important extension of Bormann's system and will feature promi-nently in the analysis that follows.

This chapter treats the dramas embedded in the SUV advertisements as fan-tasy themes, since the advertisements are meant to appeal to individual con-sumers and not to be the basis of any large-scale collective action. The imbedded fantasy themes are also arguments because they seek to gain our adherence and ultimately guide our attitudes, beliefs, and behaviors.

Dialectic

The second concept that informs this analysis is the dialectical perspective of relationships as articulated by William K. Rawlins (1992) and Leslie Baxter (1988). *Dialectic* is a "tension between two or more contradictory elements in a system that demands at least temporary resolution" (Littlejohn, 1992, p. 280). A key insight to take from Littlejohn's definition is that most resolutions are tem-porary—despite the fantasy presented in SUV ads. This is consistent with Baxter's (1988) reminder that despite the various uses of the term *dialectic* "the two features that are common across various dialectical theories are *process* and *contradiction*" (p. 258). Rawlins' examination of friendships revealed two gen-eral classes of dialectics: *contextual dialectics* that address "the place of friend-ship in the prevailing social order of American culture" (Rawlins, 1992, p. 9) and *interactional dialectics* that focus on tensions within a relationship.

The contextual dialectics include the tensions between public and private, and between ideal and the real. The actual friendship is a private affair, yet there are cultural forces that can inform that friendship. Culture is often a source of ideals, and these ideals must be negotiated into the "real" friendship.[3]

Valerie Freysinger (1995) applied the concept of dialectics to the uses of leisure among midlife men and women. In her interpretive study of leisure motives and practices, she found that leisure was an agency of affiliation with friends and family, an opportunity for self-expression, for learning and develop-ment, for challenge and accomplishment, and for recognition and credibility. In addition, three central dialectics emerged from her analysis: familiarity and nov-elty, engagement and disengagement, and agency and affiliation. With this last dialectical pair, Freysinger attempted to capture the tension between the self and the other in one's use of leisure.

The dialectical perspective informs this study in two important ways. First, all relationships are inherently dialectical. This includes our relationships with wilderness and environment. While these entities do not actively negotiate with us (although we do encounter consequences for land development, excessive hunting, and other activiites which could be interpreted as the earth "speaking

back to us"), we often engage in an internal dialogue when clarifying our relationship with the environment or other "inanimate" objects.[4] This analysis will
demonstrate how some of the established dialectical tensions are represented in
the SUV advertisements. Some tensions unique to the human/environment dyad
are also identified. Second, for both Rawlins and Baxter, culture informs and
frames the relationships being enacted within that culture. This insight is important because this study examines how the cultural or popular portrayal of the
SUV encourages a particular relationship with the environment at the individual
level.

Mark Meister's (1997) essay that connects the United Nations (U.N.) discussion on sustainable development and the Jeep Cherokee foreshadows the
dialectic perspective at the heart of this chapter. Meister argues that the Jeep
advertisements offer a "consumer vision of sustainable development by associating technology with nature" (p. 228). His analysis illuminates not only the
function of the Jeep as a metaphor for technology that provides protection and
comfort during the wilderness experience, but also the shortcomings of the U.N.
conception of sustainable development which focuses "almost exclusively on
human needs, without any attention paid to the non-human needs of nature" (p.
232). His analysis addresses one of the tensions embedded in the Cherokee
advertisements—technology and nature—as the basis for insightful critique of
the U.N. discourse. This analysis makes such tensions the central focus and
expands beyond the Jeep Cherokee to SUVs in general.

Liminality

In his insightful studies on ritual (1974, 1979), Victor Turner articulated a
unique "in between" state that many ritual participants experience. He calls this
state *liminal* and summarizes it as follows: "The ritual subjects pass through a
period of ambiguity, a sort of social limbo which has a few (though sometimes
these are most crucial) of the attributes of either the preceding or subsequent pro-
fane social statuses or cultural states" (1982, p. 24). Important to our analysis of
SUV advertisements is Turner's assertion that "passage from one social status to
another is often accompanied by a parallel passage in space, a geographic movement from one place to another" (p. 25). The attraction of television is in some
ways liminal. We are transported "there" while staying "here." We need not be
in a formal ritual for liminality to occur. Many of the SUV ads position the SUV
as the agency of liminality. That is, it is quite literally the vehicle that transports
us from one geographic *and social status* to another. We not only move from
suburbia to wilderness, but we also undergo a similar change in identity. Such a
change might be from "city worker" to "nature woman."

ANALYSIS OF SUV ADVERTISEMENTS

Even a cursory examination of recent SUV ads reveals a diversity of themes
and appeals. There are appeals to adventure, to security, to roominess, to maneu-
verability, and the list goes on. However, despite this diversity, many of the ads

possess an underlying drama. This analysis begins by describing the typical fantasy theme that is dramatized in SUV ads and then introduces four dialectics that the advertisements suggest the SUV will resolve.

The SUV Fantasy

"Damn the tuxedos, full speed ahead" is the caption on a Ford Expedition ad. The vehicle is traveling up and away from the town below. The driver cannot be distinguished. The vehicle is simultaneously presented as agent and agency—horse and rider. We know there must be a driver, but this is also somehow more than a machine. It seems to instinctively head for higher ground—SUVs almost always either travel upward or comfortably rest at the top. George Lakoff and Mark Johnson (1980) note that "up" is universally viewed as positive.

When SUVs are in the wilderness, or at the top of a mountain, they are presented without spot or blemish. The machines are apparently so at one with nature that they are not scarred by their encounter, nor, by implication, do they scar. There are, of course, exceptions to this description. Some companies do show their SUVs getting dirty. For example, Range Rover often shows their vehicles down in the jungle rather than up on hilltops, and Subaru often shows their SUV in snow. Jeep has had a Grand Cherokee shake off the mud like a dog shakes off water after a swim. Other ads depict the vehicle in an urban setting, but often these urban settings are reframed as "wild," a clear extension of the urban jungle motif. The underlying fantasy is that we can purchase something that will effortlessly take us from the banal suburban home front or urban jungle into pristine wilderness. Typically, the sun is rising or setting in the ad. We are there to either greet the dawn or, like many other creatures of nature, move under the safety of dusk. SUVs and their human companions like water, too. If we cross a stream, the vehicle remains perfectly clean and the stream remains crystal clear. The typical SUV drama takes full advantage of the journey metaphor and the archetypal uses of water, mountains, and deserts to suggest purification, renewal, and enlightenment. In this way the liminal dimensions of the SUV's appeal emerge. We are seekers, not drivers; initiates, not suburbanites. The time in the SUV is a liminal experience and we emerged from it with a changed identity, according to the advertisements.

Even the names of the vehicles suggest that we are transported to another place, action or new identity (for example, Durango, Montero, Escalade, Excursion, Expedition, Amigo, Blazer, Cherokee, Forester, Pathfinder, Trailblazer, and Trooper, among others). Within dramatic terms, the vehicle names imply scenes, plots, and characters. A GMC Yukon ad demonstrates that these names are critical to the trans formative dream of SUV ownership. For example, a Yukon ad claims "We redesigned the GMC Suburban so completely, everything worked but the name: The all new Yukon XL." Once the suburbs became the normal mundane mode of existence instead of embodying the dream to escape the city, the name Suburban lost its function as a catalyst for a cultural fantasy. The ideal SUV name must help us take the ordinary activity of driving and reframe it as a transformative action. This can be seen in a Toyota 4Runner slogan: "Adventure. Every Day." In the ad from which this slogan was taken, the vehicle is on the top of a mountain above the tree line at dusk. There is still, clear water in front of the vehicle reflecting the vehicle, which is spotless despite the implied recent ascent (the headlights are still on and the wheels are blurry indicating motion). The caption is, "Wouldn't you rather blend in with nature instead of traffic?"

An overlooked contradiction in the ad is the sentence that appears just below the showroom-clean 4Runner: "Mud makes the perfect camouflage." Apparently so, since it is invisible on the vehicle. This ad, among many, raises an important point about fantasy themes. Their "truth" is often irrelevant to their success as a convergence-inducing message. Fantasy themes need not be logically sound or factually accurate to be taken as truthful for a given group or culture. However, fantasy themes do need to reflect the ideals of the culture. This characteristic makes the fantasy theme a particularly appropriate tool for analyzing advertisements.

Dialectics in the Man/Nature Relationship

Each pole of dialectic can be seen as positive in certain circumstances. It is not a win/lose or good/bad continuum but rather a good/good (and in some ways, bad/bad) continuum that is constantly negotiated or managed. The ads themselves present a potentially infinite number of dialectics. BMW describes its X5 as "highly exhilarating yet extraordinarily safe. It's rugged yet thoroughly refined. It's playful yet ingeniously practical. In a word, perfection." This copy serves to position the X5 as the ultimate resolution to any troubling automotive dialectics.[5]

Many of the established dialectics listed in the footnote above can be found in the SUV ads as well. As an example, Rawlins' dialectic of judgment and acceptance in friendships is seen in ads that unconditionally accept the wilderness on its own terms and those that explicitly or implicitly judge it to be hostile or something that an SUV can and should conquer. In one Chevy Tahoe ad we are comforted by the "Autotrac advanced four-wheel drive system that instantly adjusts to changing terrain all over the world." The characteristics of the wilderness are accepted and the SUV does the adjusting. In a Cadillac Escapade advertisement the theme is very different: "Their mountains? Your speed bumps. . . . It's the power you need to cut any circumstance down to size, making obstacles obsolete." Here it is very clear that the vehicle doesn't adjust, but overpowers the wilderness. While many of Baxter's and Rawlins' dialectics can offer insight into the SUV ads, this section offers four broad dialectics (domain-harmony, tame-wild, familiarity-novelty, and material-spiritual), drawn from a distillation of existing dialectics and those unique to the civilization/wilderness tension typical of most SUV ads to guide the analysis.

Dominion/Harmony

A Ford Explorer ad begins with clever play on words: "Dominating the field." The field simultaneously refers to the competitive SUV market through design advancements and the field or landscape pictured in the ad. In the picture, the Explorer is apparently co-existing peacefully with a Bison. The bison symbol of the American plains, and the vehicle (no human is pictured) are almost nose-to-nose—neither is aggressive or subordinate to the other. The ad concludes that the Explorer is "The most evolved species out there." The effort to reframe a machine as animal and placing it in a field with the generally passive bison suggests a harmony with nature. The caption in boldface type, however, suggests dominion. A central distinction of much of Western civilization has been the assumption that man should conquer or subdue all that is wild. The bison was almost a complete victim of such a worldview. Misinterpretation of the biblical call to dominion (actually a call to stewardship or care-taking) and the rise of scientism (explanation, prediction and *control*) led to a historically antagonistic relationship between Western man and the wild. For example, nature is often depicted as the adversary in literature or the news, and natural disaster movies have had much commercial, if not critical, success. An assumption by those aligning exclusively with this polar position is that we must dominate nature or it will dominate us. This is a dysfunctional extreme. Even in a healthy management of this dialectic, however, there is a sense in which any species, including man, must assert itself somewhat if it is to survive.

On the other side of dominion is complete harmony with nature. This approach is often advocated by Eastern and Native American worldviews. From this perspective man is not outside nature or against nature, but in and of nature. The goal is to embrace the rhythms of the universe and the limitations that nature places on man's existence in it. The harmony concept also finds a place in the Judeo-Christian Garden of Eden. In the Garden, man is in direct communication with both the natural and the supernatural world. Adam and Eve experience the bounty of nature without having to toil in it or subdue it. Falling exclusively on the harmony end of the dialectic can cause trouble, just as falling exclusively at the dominion end can. Advocates may suggest nature or animal life is more important than human life. They may seek to lose themselves in nature, rather than find their place in it. In such cases there is an attempt at unison or enmeshment, rather than engagement or interdependence.

Owning an SUV is portrayed as an experience that will reconcile one's desire to be simultaneously "one with nature" and in a position of dominance. The purchase of an SUV integrates harmony and dominion into perfect resolution. In an SUV, we are above it all in the driver's seat and above it all on the mountaintop.

A Chevy Tahoe campaign illustrates the harmony/dominion dialectic and also how image and text interact to form the fantasy theme. The images in the ads place the Tahoe in a variety of pristine settings: desert mountains, uncivilized coastlines, and the like. There are no humans visible in the ads, though the vehicle is typically in motion. The font is suggestive of Eastern or Native American writing. All visual cues point to harmony with nature, but the text focuses on dominion. One ad discusses the power of the engine and concludes that, "fault lines aren't the only source of rumbling on the planet." This statement serves not only to integrate the mechanical with the natural but also to assert the potential for dominion even as the image implies harmony. The text in another Tahoe ad claims that "it's equally comfortable racing across the plains, exploring the back-woods or just being parked next to a placid fishing hole. It's big, powerful and willing to go just about anywhere you want to take it." The text treats the Tahoe as a central character in the drama: it is comfortable and it races and explores too. The text of this ad makes clear the potential for dominion while the picture of the Tahoe negotiating a pathway through some lower foothills accented by a stand of cedars suggests all is in harmony.

A significant characteristic of the dominion/harmony dialectic is expressed through Rawlins' affection/instrumentality dialectic. When one views the wilder-ness as a means to an end (dominion), it becomes an instrument. When one appreciates the wilderness without trying to derive anything from it—more indicative of harmony—one demonstrates Rawlins' notion of affection. Many of the ads are very explicit about getting out and doing things in the wilderness. A Subaru Outback ad shows the vehicle on the rocky shore of a riverbed. There is a kayak on the hood of the car. To the left of the kayak is the sentence, "Or you can spend the weekend surfing the Net." Later in the ad we are told, "you'll need the week to recover," further suggesting that weekends in the wilderness should be filled with activity. A Ford Explorer ad offers similar appeals: "Tom and Sally worked hard to get where they are. But now that they've 'arrived' all they want to do is get the heck out. So, last week they traded business talk for a babbling brook and conference calls for conifer pines."

Alliteration aside, these ads treat the wilderness as a tool, a means of escape, a way to recharge, a key to future success—what is in it for Tom and Sally. At the same time the overwhelmingly positive portrayal of the outdoors, combined with driving a vehicle designed for this natural environment, is depicted as a demonstration of appreciation for the wild.

Tame/Wild

The cover fold of an elaborate pullout brochure for the 2000 model year Ford line of SUVs features a key ring with about thirty keys that completely fill the ring. It is lying on top of an aggregate sidewalk surface. There are also two smaller pictures of a somewhat smoggy city skyline in the upper and lower cor-ners of the page. The caption reads, "They get you into your office, into your file cabinet, into your safe-deposit box, into locked up, locked-in places. But is there one that can get you out?" As the reader unfolds the insert the "out" places are further defined by natural images and text that includes the following: "Out where a trip to the bank involves waders and swirling waters. Out where hard drive describes a rutted half-road." The argument put forth is that the reader's current life is tame to the point of captivity: A forced tameness. There is enclosure and inclusion to the point of implosion. What is needed is an exit, and most Ford SUV names use the prefix "ex." What is needed is seclusion to release the wild aspects of the SUV owner.

The tame/wild dialectic is almost archetypal in its centrality to Western culture. Historically, the wild side of the continuum was seen as something to be overcome. However, the environmental movement, extreme sports, the men's movement and other cultural forces have made wild at least as appealing as tame. Fiske (1989) has offered similar dynamics through the inside/outside and nature/culture dialectics.

In his interpretation of a beach vacation, Fiske asserted, "A tanned body is a sign to be read by others, particularly others in the city. It signifies that the wearer, a city dweller, has been into nature and is bringing back both the physical health of the animal and the mental health that contact with nature brings into the artificiality of city life" (p. 46). In the same way, driving an SUV suggests, "I may be stuck in traffic now, but I'm part animal and can go off-road if my instincts compel me." Living in civilization requires some conformity and adherence to rules, whereas being in the wilderness, as defined by SUV ads, is a free, individual experience.[6]

The SUV promises resolution of this dialectic because it separates us from the mundane, urban, and tame while offering connection with the hallowed, natural, and wild. Yet, within this promise is an important qualifier: SUVs simultaneously promise comfort and power, as well as an uncontrolled encounter with the wild. For instance, a Pathfinder ad reads, "We're as macho as the next guy. But on a cold morning it sure is nice to fire up the heated leather seats." The reader is to identify with a wild character that is willing to be tame when convenient. The ad continues:

Even the most hardened mountain man knows enough to come in out of the cold. And that the next best thing to a warm fire in a snug, out-of-the-way cabin is a pair of warm, power-adjustable heated front leather seats in a snug, out-of-the-way Nissan Pathfinder, with the automatic temperature control set at, say, a balmy 78 degrees.

In this example, the wild/tame dialectic is addressed and managed through the features found in the Pathfinder. What might be construed as luxury, heated seats (tame), is reframed as fire (wild), rhetorically managing the tension of the wild/tame dialectic. A separate Pathfinder campaign features a Jane Goodall type character studying nomadic males in their natural habitat. The "wild men" in this ad are seen eating potato chips and watching a sporting event on a portable television. In this enactment of the fantasy, culture and nature are blended seamlessly to resolve the dialectic.

Familiarity/Novelty

Many of the ads discussed thus far emphasize the less desirable routines of cultural life, such as long commutes and high-stress jobs. The SUV is positioned as uniquely qualified to rescue its purchaser from the literal and figurative ruts we may encounter on life's journey. A slogan for the Nissan Xterra cautions one to "Choose your sick days wisely." A Jeep ad reminds us that we spend an average of 95 percent of our life indoors. Jeep is therefore "Designed to get you out— way out—into wide-open spaces." In these two ads we see appeals to break with the familiar in terms of both time and space. The familiarity/novelty dialectic is sometimes called the certainty/uncertainty dialectic. It recognizes that while people generally like to solve problems and know the answer, there is also excitement in mystery, spontaneity, and the unpredictable.

The wonderful thing about an SUV, according to the fantasy implied in the ads, is that one can have both the novel and the familiar simultaneously. A Toyota ad places a black 4Runner on a mountain ridge above the tree line and complements this image with the following text: "Air conditioning doesn't grow on trees. Neither does power windows and power door locks, aluminum alloy wheels, keyless remote, sport seats or premium 3-in-1 6-speaker stereo systems." The location is novel: it is remote, harsh, uncivilized, and potentially dangerous. The listing of design elements in the 4Runner offsets this novelty. The SUV is a portable enclosure of familiarity, of civilization, that people take with them to the uncivilized setting they are told they desire.

The familiarity/novelty dialectic exhibited in the ads might also be understood as a tension between security and adventure. A 1999 Blazer campaign focused around a slogan that read, "A little security in an insecure world." In one Blazer ad there is a white spotless lighthouse perched on a forbidding coastline. On top of the lighthouse is not a beacon, but a Blazer—with its headlights piercing the incoming fog. The lighthouse is a dialectically rich setting. It is at once a dangerous setting (harsh coastline) and a safe setting (secure tower).

In many SUV ads, wilderness is presented as both a haven and a place of danger. A Jeep ad with a red Cherokee in the desert suggests that we are viewing it "as seen by the poisonous Sahara scorpion." Within this dangerous setting the Jeep provides "an oasis of capability and confidence" that "even a toxic three-inch arachnid can see." In another example, a Pathfinder ad invokes early American history in a way that addresses this dialectic: "Lewis and Clark would have been appalled. Green with envy but appalled." One section of the text reminds the reader that "Exploration is supposed to be hard work," while another describes the Pathfinder's cabin as "blessedly serene, spacious and luxurious." The historical allusions to danger and discomfort associated with adventure and discovery are met with the balancing forces of serenity, spaciousness, and luxury found *within* the cabin of the Pathfinder. This combination of text and image fulfills both the wild/tame dialectic and the security/adventure dialectic.

Yet in many of the SUV ads, the wilderness, not the cabin, is defined as a place of rest. Tom and Sally escaped *to* the wilderness to find comfort. This vision of the wilderness is often contrasted with the urban or suburban setting as the source of danger or undesirable adventure. Isuzu alludes to this with an ad that reads, "The shortest distance between two points is always under construction." The text is accompanied by a picture of a Trooper out on the Western plains but surrounded by traffic cones and construction signs, much like a driver's education range. Visually we are told that even urban driving can be an adventure for which we must prepare through the purchase of an SUV. Also implied in the juxtaposition of wilderness and traffic cones is the idea that freedom and safety await outside the city limits where the Trooper is equally at home.

SUV ads offer two ways of managing the familiarity/novelty dialectic. First, the SUV owner can be in a familiar and safe cabin while surrounded by the unfamiliar and potentially dangerous environment. Second, the SUV owner can reframe the familiar, and even mundane, driving experience as an adventure, ripe with the possibility of a novel encounter. According to the ads, the potential for adventure and novelty lies within the unique characteristics of the SUV, as much as security and safety do.

Material/Spiritual

We come full circle in our exploration of the major dialectics embedded in SUV ads as they frame man's relationship with the environment with the material/spiritual tension. Man has often used machine (material) to enforce dominion over the environment. Yet there has also been a mystical attraction to become "one with nature." Machine has typically been masculine, while Mother Earth and nature generally are considered feminine. Wisdom has also been personified in the feminine. Spiritual journeys are typically defined as turning away from the material culture and heading out into nature where true wisdom can be found. The goal is moving from a position of dominion through materialism, to harmony through spirituality. Even on this hallowed ground, the SUV has left its customary tread mark.

The material aspects of the SUV include their technology and comfort. Virtually every SUV seems to be the "most advanced" at something. Infiniti highlights its MonoFrame that is "actually one solid structure, united by 4,200 precision welds." Suzuki markets the Vitara's power: "The secret to engineering the first V6 powered mini sport utility vehicle is in the details." This is an appeal to the material because engineering focuses on maximizing the potential of the material world. An ad from Jeep is particularly adept at integrating the two poles of the dialectic: "We added a new overhead console with a trip computer and compass, making it even easier to get lost." This ad clearly reminds the reader that the material advances made by Jeep will not interfere with the nonmaterial advantages of the SUV as it assists you in escaping the material world.

The desert is a frequent setting in SUV ads. This taps into long-standing connections between the desert and purification or spirituality. Abraham and Jesus were called to the desert, as were many other spiritual figures. It is stark and isolated and devoid of material comforts. It is an ideal setting for self-denial that may lead to spiritual epiphanies. Mountains also figure significantly in the ads. The connections here are also rich. Spiritually rich moments are often called "mountain top" experiences. Moses was given the keys to righteous living while on a mountain. Monasteries of many world religions are very often built upon mountains. Even when these settings are examined within a New Age perspective, where the journey itself is the goal, both settings remain spiritually charged. A Mercedes SUV ad shows eight different pictures of roads along with the caption "Go where other 4 X 4s fear to tread." The line "fear to tread" is borrowed from the more common phrase "where angels fear to tread" and the emphasis is placed on the act of journeying. The use of eight options in roads, not one, suggests that any road is valid. The key is to journey *somewhere*. Turning left or right or disappearing behind a hill, each road extends to an unknown destination. Just as important, seven of the eight roads head upward. The only exception is a long straight road that disappears into the shadows of the mountains.

Setting out on a spiritual quest is heady stuff. If embraced fully, such a journey takes one far outside of mainstream, consumer culture. Consequently, a balance between spiritual and material is sought within the SUV ads by presenting the SUV as the integral part of that journey. It is this *material* purchase that can equip its owner for the *spiritual* journey. A Jeep Wrangler ad pictures a Wrangler in the American desert next to a huge oblong rock that looks like an exclamation point. Awareness of Native American spirituality reminds us that such a location would likely be seen as spiritual ground. The proximity of the Jeep to such a symbol forms a spiritual/material cluster that seemingly resolves this dialectic. Mike Featherstone (1991) has argued that we live in a consumer culture and that such a culture traditionally emphasizes hedonism. Though he clearly points out that this pleasure orientation is not at the expense of the sacred (pp. 113 ff.), pleasure does shape how we define and pursue what is sacred. In this same Jeep ad readers are encouraged to define themselves by "Your passion for discovery. Your quest for fun." In a consumer culture, a challenging journey can be made pleasurable through the right purchase. "Quest" is a term typically reserved for meaningful journeys—here it is paired with "fun" suggesting that the pursuit of fun is a significant and fulfilling goal worthy of the term "quest." Nissan claims that if life is a journey we should "Enjoy the ride." The United States culture is also individualistic, so it is not surprising that the journey offered in the SUV ads is as individual as each consumer makes it. That same Nissan ad asks "Road maps? Who the heck needs road maps" *[sic]*. Roads are collective and cooperative and Nissan frees its drivers from such convention, allowing them to pursue their own journey.

Traveling in an SUV puts us in a transcendent position where there are no boundaries. SUV drivers are above boundaries for three reasons. First, the literal elevation of the driver's seat puts the driver above other drivers and above the earth. Second, these vehicles are frequently depicted as taking drivers to mountaintops and other revered locations. Third, the ads frame the driving of the SUV itself as a transcendent experience. The Lexus LX470 promises to "Go places mere mortals will never see" and the Lexus RX300 is "like no other vehicle on earth." Sitting in the cabin is itself a "mountain top experience" even if we never literally take to the hills.

Ford's "Outfitters/No Boundaries" campaign also offers insight into how the SUVs manage this material/spiritual dialectic. This $50 million television and print campaign was created, in part, from findings in focus group studies about another Ford SUV, the Sport Trac (Robinson, 1999). This was a particularly comprehensive campaign that positions all of Ford's SUVs, and much of their truck line, as vehicles through which to explore a wilderness knowing "No Boundaries." Your Ford "outfitter" (dealer) will recommend a vehicle that matches the quest you are planning to undertake.

The idea of no boundaries is, in many ways, a contemporary spiritual ideal. The notion of liminality discussed above is about being between boundaries. Yet if we are in a place (the cabin of a Ford SUV) where no boundaries exist, that liminality becomes tied to the unique status of the SUV since it alone is able to provide such a unique state of being. When we step out of the SUV we are back in a world of boundaries. Only when we are in the SUV are we caught up in a perpetually liminal state. The localized, relativistic nature of the postmodern attitude is also commensurate with a no boundaries philosophy. No boundaries can apply geographically, but also can be projected out to psychological and moral dimensions of our lives as well. Psychologically it resonates with the "if you can dream it, you can achieve it" doctrine. Morally it supports the hedonism articulated by Featherstone and symbolically it suggests that the dialectical tensions outlined in this chapter need not even exist. If they don't exist, they need not be negotiated. The "No Boundaries" campaign attempts to permanently resolve inherent dialectics by denying their existence.

Two Other Important Dialectics

Once one adopts a dialectic perspective, it is difficult to see any list as complete. At the risk of cluttering up the "big four," this chapter concludes with two less central but still important dialectics. The first is the ideal/real dialectic identified by Rawlins. In the world of advertising, idealized representations far outnumber realistic portrayals. The idealized version is frequently a spotless vehicle on the pinnacle of some remote vista, enjoying the view with or without an obvious driver present. It has arrived there seemingly on its own, untouched and apparently having touched nothing. There are some exceptions to this portrayal. Nissan and Land Rover ads often dipict muddy vehicles. Though, in truth, this too is an ideal: The mud is the right mud in just the right places. It is more like makeup than dirt—and it never leads to scratches or even minor dents.

The second minor dialectic that captures elements of each of the dialectics discussed above is that of inside/outside. Inside life is good, but outside life is, too. In the inside life, humans have dominion. Inside life is tame and domesticated. "Not in the house!" is a parent's cry to remove wild behavior from the inside and take it outside where wild behavior belongs. We are familiar with the interior—it is our creation. We are less familiar with the outside—it is not our creation. The inside life is dominated by the material. It is tangible and close. The spiritual life is found outside in the seeking journey and is often ephemeral and diffuse. The SUV promises that we can be inside and outside at the same time. An interesting extension of Ford's "Outfitters" campaign has some showrooms transformed into outdoor settings complete with streams (Green, 2000, p. 9). That is really the SUV fantasy in reverse. A version of outside life brought inside. The SUV promises to take an idealized version of inside life (air conditioning, comfortable seating and a great sound system) outside.

DISCUSSION

The SUV is presented as a way of managing several cultural dialectics embedded in man's relationship with the environment. The consistent use of elevation (physical, natural, socioeconomic) and other images in these ads suggests that we no longer need to manage these dialectical tensions because we can transcend them. This transcendence ushers in a state of liminality. We are at a place of no boundaries and infinite possibilities about where we will go, what we will do, and who we will be.

But just as true liminality is temporary, so is any resolution of a relational dialectic. The harmful myth in the ad is that the purchase of an SUV *permanently* resolves the man/environment relationship and positions the owner as somehow in harmony with nature and perhaps even its advocate. It is a static fantasy that belies the process nature of dialectics, the process nature of organic systems, and the literal impact of SUVs on the environment.

A contributor to this problem is identified in Featherstone's (1991) concept of consumer culture. In this culture there is a "dominance of the commodity as sign" (p. 85). That allows the symbolism discussed above to work powerfully in shaping not only one's decision to own an SUV, but also the set of meanings that inform such a choice and the perceived impact of such a choice on cultural and natural systems. Barry Brummett (1991) elaborates on how this works. He suggests that a message works on three types of meaning that exist along a continuum from left to right: exigent, quotidian, and implicative. By exigent he is suggesting that a message addresses an immediate concern. Within the SUV ads we see explicit claims to establish a particular SUV as the one the reader should purchase now. There are appeals and sets of meanings that relate specifically to that decision at that time.

At the quotidian level there is no immediate decisional crisis. Rather these messages serve to inform the basic set of public and personal meanings that inform everyday decisions. At some point the SUV becomes the preferred vehicle ideal or a widely recognized status symbol. This is now an accepted cultural meaning we may bring to other areas of our life. For example, family members in a movie are shown to be successful because they drive SUVs. While we are generally explicitly aware of appeals made at the exigent level, we are less aware of those operating at the quotidian level: "We are almost on automatic pilot as we manage the meanings of everyday life" (p. 43). The movie example would be "decoded" without much—if any—conscious effort. In addition, quotidian levels of meaning are established indirectly through a variety of texts.

Three examples illustrate the themes apparent at this level. First, the rationalizing of luxury as necessity is central to these ads. Heated seats are compared with fire in their centrality to our survival. Six-speaker audio is the least we can do for our psychological well-being and serenity. This is the natural extension of a set of meanings born of a consumer culture being applied to a symbolically rich commodity. Second, bigger is better. This is a general assumption of the consumer culture as well. The framing of the Excursion, Navigator, and Escalade (among others) as "advancements" only works if the "bigger is better" set of meanings is in place. Third, many SUVs are now actually two-wheel-drive models. While they still possess sturdy frames and powerful engines, the two-wheel drive and various other hybrid models have become signs of signs.

Finally, the messages examined in this chapter also operate at Brummett's implicative level. "This area includes the management of meanings that are unproblematic and taken for granted; the farther to the right on the continuum we go, the more sedimented and unquestioned are the meanings" (p. 44). For instance, some of the dialectics used in this analysis, particularly wild/tame, are so fundamental to various cultural productions; literature, film, scientific documents, and others that one would hardly think to question them as "real" categories.

At the implicative level, the messages within SUV ads are much further reaching than the individual appeals made at the exigent level. Those appeals might also merit analysis, but they do not frame humanity's place in the world as directly as the themes outlined above.

The most damaging assumption in the ads is that nature is infinite. "No Boundaries" suggests an unending quality to nature. This slogan is reinforced visually because virtually every image of nature proceeds beyond the frame provided by the ad. Images of nature in SUV ads are generally devoid of any other signs of civilization. No humans, houses, fences, silos, domestic animals, vehicles, or the like are included. The implicit conclusion here is that pristine nature is commonplace out there, and ours for the consuming at the individual level. In the SUV universe, one might assume that no one actually owns the land or does anything else with it. The land is our playground and squatter's rights are still the norm. Environmentalists have spent decades trying to inform legislatures, captains of industry, and the general citizenry that nature is indeed finite. The fantasy of the SUV drives in direct opposition to that message.

The final message analyzed in this chapter, which lies at the heart of the consumer culture, is that materialism is good and consumption is great. Even though there is evidence that the SUV is framed as a way to manage the material/spiritual dialectic, it is important to remember that the SUV is ultimately a rather expensive piece of material. The SUV is popular because it has been defined as a solution to a set of problems that are fundamental to man's relationship with his environment. Brummett uses the term *commodification* to suggest our culture's preoccupation with things purchasable and consumable. This orientation is taken for granted and thus lies at the implicative level. It is particularly important to be aware of those times when we attempt to commodify things that defy commodification. Harmony with nature and serenity are obvious examples discussed above, but so are balanced lifestyle and contentment. These things cannot be purchased. Certainly an automobile, regardless of specific characteristics, does not play a central role in the achievement of such abstractions. Yet within a consumer culture where commodification is a central assumption, such logic is powerful, and it is in full operation in the SUV advertisements.

CONCLUSION

This chapter presents the argument that the SUV's popularity is fundamentally symbolic, not pragmatic. The SUV's popularity is based not on what it actually does for its purchasers as a machine, but on a fantasy it helps create for the user and the larger culture. This fantasy is clearly revealed in the SUV advertisements. The fantasy theme offered in the ads suggests that purchasing an SUV will resolve the ongoing and inherent dialectical tensions of man's relationship with his environment. This relationship can be expressed in terms of four central dialectics: (1) dominion/harmony, (2) tame/wild, (3) familiarity/novelty, and (4) material/spiritual. This fantasy is dysfunctional on a number of levels. First, resolving such dialectical tensions is not possible. Dialectics must be managed, not resolved. Second, the power of the fantasy draws from fundamental assumptions operating at the implicative level of the consumer culture. These assumptions reinforce a view of the natural environment and our place and role within that environment that is harmful. It is harmful to the individual lives of each person subscribing to such beliefs, to the larger culture, and to the environment. Kenneth Burke defines man as being separated from nature by instruments of our own making (in Foss, Foss, & Trapp, 1991). The SUV is erroneously portrayed as an instrument of our own making that can breach this separation.

NOTES

1. As of the writing of this chapter, there is a web campaign urging listeners of the popular NPR show *Car Talk* to help get the Ford Excursion nominated as the worst car of the millennium.

2. Human nature and culture are inherently complex and are best explained by multicausal models. While the symbolic dimensions are important should be explored and offer significant explanatory value, other factors likely contribute to the SUV's current popularity, which include: (1) a strong economy providing a high percentage of discretionary income, (2) a general shift from outdoor jobs to indoor jobs which allows outdoor vehicles to become signs of leisure rather than signs of work, and (3) conspicuous consumption which is a habit of our culture generally.

3. Within friendship, four dialectical tensions emerge for Rawlins. The first is the freedom to be independent and the freedom to be dependent, which are similar to Baxter's dialectic of autonomy and intimacy. The second dialectic is affection and instrumentality. This dialectic manages the friendship being an end in itself, and the friendship as a means

to an end. The third dialectic is judgment and acceptance. A friendship must negotiate the tension between unconditional acceptance and the advice and criticism of a "true friend." Finally, the dialectic between expressiveness and protectiveness addresses the degree of spontaneity and strategy in self-disclosure. Baxter's set of dialectics is similar to Rawlins' as each has a manifestation within the relationship, as well as between the dyad and the larger community. A dialectic not addressed by Rawlins, however, is that of certainty and uncertainty. Friendship is characterized by a certain degree of stability and predictability but also must avoid becoming a lifeless routine.

4. Anthropomorphizing might be seen as anecdotal illustration of this tendency. When the thing we want to enter into relationship with is unable to fully participate in the dialectic, then we do that work for that entity by endowing it with human qualities and speaking to it and for it.

5. Many of the high-end entries into this market are naming their SUVs in the same way that sports cars are named. BMW offers the X5, though we never did see X 1-4. Lexus/Infiniti offers the QX4 and the RX300. Mercedes offers the ML430.

6. In stark contrast to the Ford campaign is the 2002 Mercury Mountaineer pitch that begins with the caption "Beauty lives here." A Mountaineer is said to be built *for* the city, "to handle the rigors of where you drive most." Other captions in the multipage ad also stress the attractiveness of the city setting: "Strength lives here," "Grace lives here," and "Safety lives here." Each caption is accompanied by a monochromatic picture of urban structures. Although the variety of messages may increase, I believe the central messages will remain those expressed in this chapter. With so many SUVs on the market, the search for a niche will increase significantly.

REFERENCES

Baxter, L. A. (1988). A dialectical perspective on communication strategies in relationship development. In S. Duck (Ed.)., *Handbook of personal relationships* (pp. 257-273). New York: John Wiley & Sons.

Bormann, E. G. (1972/1995). Fantasy and rhetorical vision: The rhetorical criticism of social reality. *Quarterly Journal of Speech, 58,* 396-407. Rpt. in C. A. Burgchardt (Ed.) *Readings in Rhetorical Criticism* (pp. 242-253). State College, PA: Strata.

Bormann, E. G., Knutson, L. R., & Musolf, K. (1997). Why do people share fantasies? An empirical investigation of a basic tenet of the symbolic convergence communication theory. *Communication Studies, 48,* 254-276.

Bradsher, K. (2000, January 16). No wonder SUVs are called light trucks. *The New York Times,* 44.

Brummett, B. (1991). *Rhetorical dimensions of popular culture.* Tuscaloosa: University of Alabama.

Cox News Service. (2000, February 16). Gas prices won't force owners to give up SUVs. *Wilmington Morning Star,* 6C.

Darsey, J. (1994). Must we all be rhetorical theorists?: An anti-democratic inquiry. *Western Journal of Communication, 58,* 164-181.

Featherstone, M. (1991). *Consumer culture and postmodernism.* Thousand Oaks, CA: Sage.

Fiske, J. (1989). *Reading the popular.* London: Routledge.

Foss, S. K. (1990). Constituted by agency: The discourse and practice of rhetorical criticism. In G. M. Phillips, & J. T. Wood (Eds.)., *Speech communication: Essays to commemorate the 75th anniversary of the Speech Communication Association* (pp. 33-

51). Carbondale, IL: Southern Illinois University.

Foss, S. K. (1996). *Rhetorical criticism: Exploration and practice.* (2nd ed.). Prospect Heights, IL: Waveland.

Foss, S. K., Foss, K. A., & Trapp, R. (1991). *Contemporary perspectives on rhetoric.* (2nd ed.)., Prospect Heights, IL: Waveland.

Freysinger, V. J. (1995). The dialectics of leisure and development for women and men in mid-life: An interpretive study. *Journal of Leisure Research, 27,* 61-84.

Gaudette, K. (2000, December 27). 'Mad taggers' have say with stickers. *Wilmington Morning Star,* 4A.

Green, J. (2000, January 3). Ford dealers take "Outfitters" to next level, via sponsorships and freebies. *Brandweek, 41,* 9. Retrieved February 10, 2000 from EBSCOhost (Academic Search Elite, 2702964).

Halliday, J. (1999, November 15). Bravada sets sights on women buyers. *Automotive News, 74,* 18. Retrieved February 10, 2000 from EBSCOhost (MasterFILE Premier, 2556235).

Kluger, J. (1999, December 31). Light trucks and dirty air. *Time, 154, 22.* Retrieved February 10, 2000 from EBSCOhost (Academic Search Elite, 2629064).

Lakoff, G. & Johnson, M. (1980). *Metaphors we live by.* Chicago: University of Chicago.

Leff, M. (1980). Interpretation and the art of the rhetorical critic. *Western Journal of Speech Communication, 44,* 337-349.

Leff, M. (1986). Textual criticism: The legacy of G. P. Mohrmann. *Quarterly Journal of Speech, 72,* 377-389.

Littlejohn, S. W. (1992). *Theories of human communication.* (4th ed.). Belmont, CA: Wadsworth.

Mateja, J. (2000, December 17). Toyota gets into SUVs in a big way. *Chicago Tribune.* Retrieved December 21, 2000 from EBSCOHost (Newspaper Source, 2W60017649363).

Mead, G. H. (1934). *Mind, self and society.* Chicago: University of Chicago.

Medhurst, M. J. & Benson, T. W. (1991). Introduction: Rhetorical studies in a media age. In M. J. Medhurst & T. W. Benson (Eds.)., *Rhetorical dimensions of media: A critical casebook* (2nd ed.) (pp. ix-xxii). Dubuque, IA: Kendall/Hunt.

Meister, M. (1997). 'Sustainable development' in visual imagery: Rhetorical function in the Jeep Cherokee. *Communication Quarterly, 45,* 223-234.

Memo to Steve Ford. (2000, Winter). *Earth Island Journal, 14,* 3.

Needham, D. (1996, October). The new ute culture. *Ski, 61,* 165. Retrieved February 10, 2000 from EBSCOhost (MasterFILE Premier, 9609224573).

Neil, D. (2000, February 13). Camping with the incredible hulk. *New York Times,* 44.

Rauber, P. (Nov/Dec. 1999). Arms race on the highway. *Sierra, 84, 20-22.* Retrieved February 10, 2000 from EBSCOhost (MasterFILE Premier, 2416602)

Rawlins, W. K. (1992). *Friendship matters: Communication, dialectics and the life course.* New York: Aldine de Gruyter.

Robinson, A. (1999, December 20). Ford plots hefty light truck campaign. *Automotive News, 74,* 16. Retrieved February 10, 2000 from EBSCOhost (Business Source Elite, 2632191).

Turner, V. W. (1974). *Dramas, fields, and metaphors: Symbolic action in human society.* Ithaca, NY: Cornell University.

Turner, V. W. (1979). *The ritual process: Structure and anti-structure.* Ithaca, NY: Cornell University.

Turner, V. W. (1982). *From ritual to theatre: The human seriousness of play.* New York:

Performing Arts Journal Publications.

Welch, D. (2000, January 17). Downsizing those monster machines. *Business Week, 3664*, 40. Retrieved December 21, 2000 from EBSCOHost (MasterFile Premiere, 2656878).

Welch, D. (2000, May 29). It isn't easy going green alone. *Business Week, 3683*, 54. Retrieved December 21, 2000 from EBSCOHost (MasterFile Premiere, 3129005).

Index

About the Editors and Contributors

MICHAEL S. BRUNER is an Associate Professor in the Department of Communication at Humboldt State University. He received his Ph.D. in communication from the University of Pittsburgh. Dr. Bruner is interested in applied rhetoric, rhetoric and values, and environmental rhetoric. His essays have appeared in *Argument and Advocacy, Communication Quarterly, Environmental Ethics, International Social Science Journal,* and *Landmark Essays in Environmental Rhetoric.*

JULIA B. CORBETT is an associate professor in the Department of Communication at the University of Utah where she teaches and researches environmental communication and media coverage of science, health, and environment. She received her M.A. and Ph.D. from the University of Minnesota. Current projects include a book *Green Messages: Communication and the Natural World,* and a collection of personal essays about human relationships with the environment. A former environmental reporter, park ranger, and environmental policy wonk, Corbett makes her home in the Salt Lake valley and visits the Wasatch Mountains frequently.

MARK DeLOACH is former Debate Coach and Associate Professor in the Department of Communication Studies at the University of North Texas, and currently is an associate with a communication consulting firm based in Connecticut. Dr. DeLoach is the author of several essays on argumentation and debate, including contributions to the *Proceedings of the International Conference on Argumentation.* He received his Ph.D. in communication from the University of Southern California.

JOHN S. GOSSETT received his Ph.D. from the University of Southern California. He serves as Chair and Associate Professor in the Department of Communication Studies at the University of North Texas. Dr. Gossett's research interests include First Amendment/free speech issues and rhetorical analysis of public argument. He is published in *Free Speech Journal*, the *Journal of the Association for Communication Administration*, and the *Kansas Speech Journal*.

DIANE S. HOPE is currently serving as the William A. Kern Professor in Communications in the Department of Communication, Rochester Institute of Technology, where she teaches visual communication, persuasion and social change, and critical research methods. Her most recent publication "Earthwork: Women and Environments," *Women's Studies Quarterly,* (Guest Editor), *29*, nos. 1 and 2 (spring/summer 2001). Presently, she is the Editor of *Women's Studies Quarterly.* Dr. Hope received her Ph.D. from the State University of New York at Buffalo.

DEBRA K. JAPP is a Professor of Communication Studies at St. Cloud State University (Minnesota), and the Academic Affairs Coordinator for the Inter Faculty Organization, the faculty union for the Minnesota state universities. She received her Ph.D. in communication studies from the University of Nebraska. Her scholarly interests include the rhetoric of the socialist women of the Great Plains and the rhetorical and ethical dimensions of popular culture.

PHYLLIS M. JAPP is an Associate Professor in the Department of Communication Studies at the University of Nebraska at Lincoln. She received her Ph.D. in communication studies from the University of Nebraska. In addition to environmental communication, her research interests include rhetoric and popular culture, communication ethics and popular culture, and gender issues in communication.

MARK MEISTER is an assistant professor in the Department of Communication at North Dakota State University. He received his Ph.D. from the University of Nebraska. His primary area of scholarly interest is how politics, popular culture, religion, and international development symbolically manifest nature. He has published articles in such venues as the *Quarterly Journal of Speech, Environmental History, Communication Studies, Communication Research, Mass Communication and Society, Communication Quarterly, Communication Studies, Environmental History,* and *Critical Studies in Media Communication.*

RICHARD K. OLSEN, JR. earned his Ph.D. in rhetorical studies at Regent University and is currently an assistant professor at the University of North Carolina at Wilmington in the department of Communication Studies. He teaches in the areas of rhetorical theory, research methods, and popular culture. His program of research involves using contemporary and classical rhetorical theory to understand popular culture. Other projects have included analysis of the NBA draft and the American Dream, Martha Stewart and the Broadway "musical" STOMP.

ANDY OPEL received his Ph.D. from the School of Journalism and Mass Communication at the University of North Carolina at Chapel Hill. His work has also appeared in the *Journal of American Culture*. His research interests include the intersection of consumer culture and the environment as well as the emerging media and democracy movement. Andy currently teaches documentary video production and media studies in the College of Communication at Florida State University.

DONNALYN POMPPER is an associate professor in the Department of Communication at Florida State University. Prior to earning a Ph.D. in Mass Media and Communication at Temple University, she worked in print journalism covering environmental issues in the Philadelphia area, as well as in corporate and agency marketing communications. Her research has focused on health and environmental risk policy, as well as gender and diversity issues.

DIANA L. REHLING received her Ph.D. in Communication Studies from the University of Nebraska at Lincoln in 1998. She is presently an Assistant Professor in Speech Communication at St. Cloud State University in St. Cloud, MN. Her primary research interest is the intersection of interpersonal and family communication and public discourse.

JEAN P. RETZINGER is a lecturer and the assistant director of the Group Major in Mass Communications at the University of California, Berkeley. She received her Ph.D. in communication studies from the University of Iowa. Her 1992 dissertation, *"Still, All Day Long, Nebraska": Reading Landscape as a Cultural Text*, launched her research interest in investigating the links between culture and agriculture in the media.

ANNE MARIE TODD is a Ph.D. Candidate at the University of Southern California's Annenberg School for Communication. She is writing her dissertation entitled: "The Globalization of Mobilization: Protest Strategy of Global Justice Movements, 1999-2001." Her research interests include the discourse of environmental activism and environmental globalization, and the environmental rhetoric of tourism.

Printed in the USA
CPSIA information can be obtained
at www.ICGtesting.com
LVHW011304290124
770218LV00003B/159